THE FEAR THESAURUS:

A Writer's Guide to What Holds Characters Back

ANGELA ACKERMAN
& BECCA PUGLISI

THE FEAR THESAURUS: A WRITER'S GUIDE TO WHAT HOLDS CHARACTERS BACK

ISBN: 978-1-7361523-5-5

Visit the authors at their Writers Helping Writers® site.

Edited by Lisa Poisso and Michael Dunne
Book cover design by JD Smith Design
Book formatting by JD Smith Design

THE BEST-SELLING WRITERS HELPING WRITERS® DESCRIPTION THESAURUS SERIES

Over 1.4 Million Copies Sold Worldwide

Available in ten languages, sourced by universities, and recommended by editors and agents across the globe, this series is a writer's favorite for brainstorming fresh descriptions and powering up stories.

The Emotion Thesaurus: A Writer's Guide to Character Expression (Second Edition)

The Positive Trait Thesaurus: A Writer's Guide to Character Attributes

The Negative Trait Thesaurus: A Writer's Guide to Character Flaws

The Urban Setting Thesaurus: A Writer's Guide to City Spaces

The Rural Setting Thesaurus: A Writer's Guide to Personal and Natural Places

The Emotional Wound Thesaurus: A Writer's Guide to Psychological Trauma

The Occupation Thesaurus: A Writer's Guide to Jobs, Vocations, and Careers

The Conflict Thesaurus:
A Writer's Guide to Obstacles, Adversaries, and Inner Struggles (Vol. 1)

The Conflict Thesaurus:
A Writer's Guide to Obstacles, Adversaries, and Inner Struggles (Vol. 2)

The Emotion Amplifier Thesaurus: A Writer's Guide to Character Stress and Volatility

TABLE OF CONTENTS

FEAR: A PRIMAL FORCE IN FICTION AND LIFE

Have you ever woken in the dark, certain that something is amiss? Your heart jackhammers as you strain to hear some telltale creak or rustle that shouldn't be there—something to explain the unease pebbling your skin. Seconds tick past with your breath on hold. You pray it's nothing, just the remnant of a fading dream.

Fear is a powerful force, and it can hit anywhere, at any time. It's how our brains respond to real or perceived danger, a visceral flare sending up a warning.

Sometimes the threat is obvious: a thug brandishing a knife, a van in the rearview window approaching too fast. Other times, it's more subtle—an odd slant of light, a too-long pause between words, a twig snapping in the woods. Once fear is triggered, even if we don't yet realize why, our brains sound the alarm and our bodies react: fight, flight, or freeze.

The triggers for fear and the way it affects us differ from person to person, but fear's ability to unravel us—to override logic and seize control—is universal. That's what makes it a potent tool in stories. Readers recognize fear instantly. They know how it feels, and it unnerves them even as they understand that, in a fictional context, it can't personally touch them.

Readers intuitively grasp another truth about fear: It lingers. A touch on the back of the neck, an unseen presence in the room... Fear whispers to us: *The world isn't safe. People can't be trusted. Stick to what you know, because if you try something new, you'll fail.*

Readers know this voice. They've heard it before.

Fear can protect, but it also sabotages, warping how characters perceive the world, relate to others, and respond to change. It feasts on their insecurities and sends them into a spiral of avoidance that keeps them from chasing meaningful goals.

When we bring our audience close to a character's fear, we hold up a mirror, and the character's psychological struggle becomes their own. And with higher stakes come worry. Readers are emotionally invested in a character who is, in some ways, just like them. They need to know the character will be safe and will break free from whatever's holding them back. So what do they do?

They turn the page, of course.

Fear is more than an emotion; it is an underlying force that runs through every story element, including character development, plot, arc, conflict, and theme. It's what draws readers in, holds their attention, and makes your story feel human and true.

THE PROM QUEEN OF DARK EMOTIONS

While all emotions are important, some pack more of an oomph than others. If there were a homecoming dance for feelings, most people would expect love or hope to secure the coveted crown. But our vote's on fear—and for good reason: *Fear keeps us alive.*

THE EFFECTS OF FEAR

Survival is our most primal human instinct, and fear is the self-preservation mechanism that alerts us to potential danger. It keeps us vigilant. It helps us manage risk and avoid people and situations that threaten our physical or emotional well-being.

But fear has a dark side too. Yes, it keeps us safe, but it can also trap us, darken our worldview, and change us in unfortunate ways. Unchecked, it limits our ability to apply reason and logic, hijacking our decision-making processes so we miss out on opportunities that would make us happier and more fulfilled.

Yikes.

And if fear can do all this to us, it can shape our characters as well, causing long-term harm as it tightens its grip. Let's look at what happens when fear's cold fingers dig in.

Distorted Perception

When fear takes hold, it distorts a character's perception. They become hyperaware of their surroundings, and possible threats seem magnified. Shadows appear menacing, angles are sharper, and other people become potential sources of conflict. Anything in their environment that reminds them of a negative experience or awakens personal anxiety makes them believe they're in danger.

Imagine your character feels uneasy around dogs because they were attacked by one as a child. Out for a walk, they spot a stray ahead, and their brain immediately zooms in on certain details: the animal's lips pulled back to expose its teeth, muscles quivering in a precursor to an attack. But it turns out the dog is merely panting from the heat. Their paths cross without issue, and the character's unease fades.

Fear works well as an early warning system, but it doesn't frame every situation accurately. As it erodes the character's objectivity, they see threats everywhere, robbing them of the ability to identify potential opportunities.

Consider Hamil, traveling abroad for the first time. He encounters a woman struggling with heavy shopping bags, so he offers to help. She brushes against him while transferring the load to her car, and only after she's driven off does he realize his wallet is missing. The experience generates a fear that sours him on the locals, and now he meets their smiles with scowls, believing they're all looking to take advantage of him. This suspicion becomes part of Hamil's viewpoint, and whenever he travels to a new place, he now keeps to himself instead of interacting with people and learning to appreciate other cultures.

Once a fear has been planted, it can cause your character to see shadows or villains where there are none, ultimately holding them back.

Disrupted Logic and Irrational Thinking

When fear is triggered, the fight, flight, or freeze response short-circuits logic and rational thought. In a truly dangerous situation, this can save someone, because rapid reactions help them evade harm. But when someone overestimates potential danger, they overreact and make rash decisions. They don't stop to think, or if they do, their thoughts are skewed by personal biases or hurtful past experiences.

This spells trouble for a character like Adam, who spots a stranger speaking to his nine-year-old daughter in the ice cream line. He rushes in, shoves the man, and demands to know what he's doing. Only then does he learn that the two were just chatting because she has the same fuzzy backpack as the man's daughter.

Flawed Choices

Fear often drives characters toward choices based on safety and comfort instead of their true wants or needs. A character who's afraid of losing their job might endure abuse from a coworker rather than report them to management. Someone secretly in love with their best friend might stay silent about their feelings if they're afraid of being rejected. A character who fears disappointing their family might decide not to change their major and continue pursuing a career they'll come to hate.

Over time, choices based on what's perceived as safer or easier lead to dissatisfaction. Worse, these decisions create unmet needs. The character begins to resent the very people they've sacrificed for, and they grow angry or depressed at the direction their life has taken. To better understand the role of missing needs in a character's arc, see the section entitled **The Connection Between Fear and Human Needs**.

Procrastination and Avoidance

Fear of future events is uncomfortable, whether it's over an awkward but inevitable conversation, a hard decision, or a promise that's difficult to keep. Procrastination and avoidance are attractive alternatives because they defer discomfort—emotional get-out-of-jail cards. This is why someone puts off seeing a doctor after discovering an odd-looking mole on their back or pretends they're not home when their clingy brother-in-law rings the doorbell.

The problem with avoidance and procrastination is that while they do provide immediate relief, they increase pressure over time and make small problems bigger. When an issue isn't dealt with, it becomes more urgent, and a character who hasn't planned or prepared must eventually rush to respond.

Unhealthy Coping Mechanisms

Fear and anxiety send people seeking comfort in all the wrong places. For example, to avoid being hurt in romantic relationships, a character might choose married partners who don't want commitment. While this achieves the end of sexual gratification without strings, it deepens self-worth issues and creates relationship friction with friends who don't approve.

Self-medication, shopping, escaping through work, gambling... Characters embrace the same self-soothing behaviors as we do in the real world. These behaviors aren't random; they're attempts to guard against emotional harm. Problems arise when they're used repeatedly to avoid the root issue, but even then they serve the story, making excellent show-don't-tell opportunities. When readers see these responses to life's stressors, they'll know the character is struggling and recognize what's triggering them.

Damaged Relationships

Emotional pain frequently comes from other people, so it's natural for fear to leach into relationships.

A coworker sabotaging the character by bad-mouthing them to the boss could lead the character to carry new feelings of mistrust and betrayal home with them. A trivial situation could trigger their fear of betrayal and make them doubt even their spouse's loyalty. Pretty soon, they're searching their partner's phone, hacking their email, or following them during the day. Their quest to prove an imagined betrayal could manifest the very thing they feared when their spouse gets fed up and seeks comfort elsewhere or leaves the marriage.

Another way fear enters relationships is through emotional baggage from the past. Someone who grew up with hypercritical parents may overreact when family or friends ask questions, offer feedback, or try to help with decisions. Their constant fear of falling short of expectations causes them to see disapproval and judgment where they don't exist, and their most valued relationships suffer from it.

Negative Self-Image

Decisions based on fear feed the inner critic who likes to crow about every mistake—chances the character didn't take, options they avoided, dreams they didn't pursue. This leads them to believe they're fundamentally flawed, lack courage, don't deserve happiness, or are unworthy of what others have.

Risk Aversion

Because the fear response exists to protect us, it tends to magnify risk. Characters worrying about what might happen or what could go wrong may sacrifice opportunity just to be on the safe side. For someone who's risk-averse, possible undesirable outcomes carry more weight than potential rewards, and this steers their decisions. They say no to the camping trip because bears live in the woods. They don't submit their novel to an agent because it could be rejected. They avoid taking a stand on political or social topics because they're worried about offending others.

When someone shuns risk due to an unhealthy relationship with fear, their world grows smaller, and two outcomes occur. First, they become dissatisfied and turn that unhappiness either inward (blaming themselves) or outward (blaming others or the world for treating them badly). Second, they become less capable of handling real conflict when it arrives. Rather than responding to trouble in a measured way, their lack of resilience paralyzes them or leaves them uncertain of what to do.

Limited Potential

Fear-induced risk aversion limits characters because they'd rather stay in the comfort zone than stretch themselves and reach for big goals. It seems safer to settle—going to school locally rather than applying to their dream university or working for the family business instead of striking out on their own.

The problem is that settling for less is never a happy long-term solution. People are meant to grow, strive, and reach their potential. A character who, out of fear, chooses the status quo over personal betterment will eventually regret it. Low self-esteem will erode their faith in themselves and their abilities, making them even less likely to challenge their fears or overcome them.

THE CONNECTION BETWEEN FEAR AND HUMAN NEEDS

It's impossible to understand the psychology of fear without discussing basic human needs, because the two are intertwined.

In case you've forgotten that psychology class you took back in the day, Abraham Maslow was the psychologist who determined that five primary human needs drive all behavior:

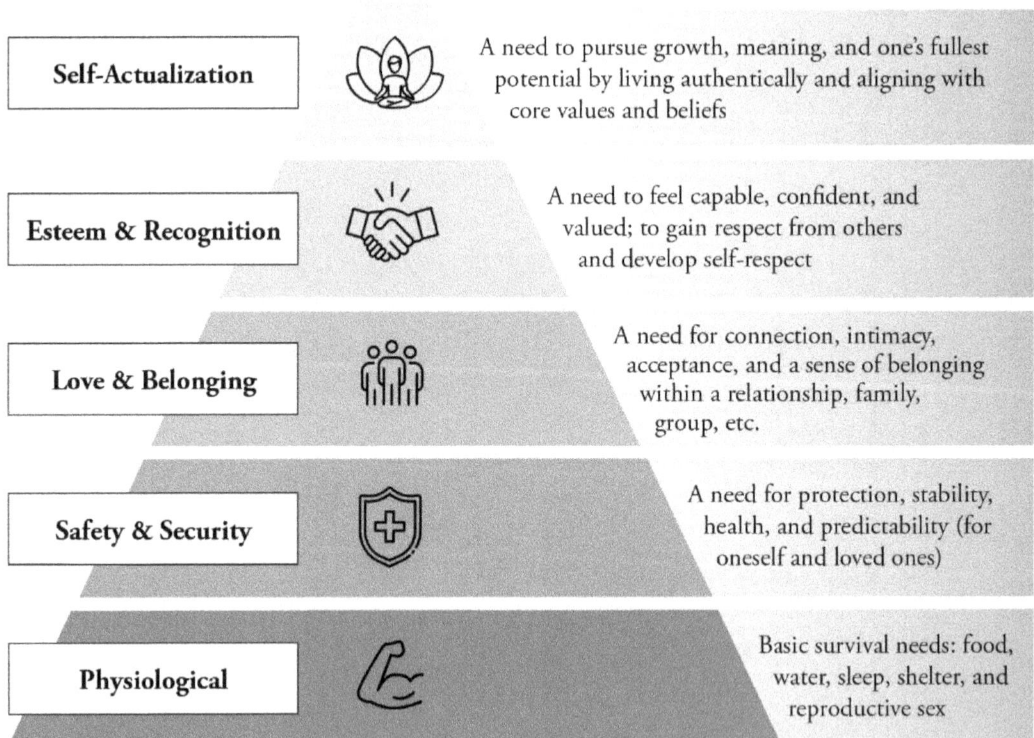

Physiological Needs: These are necessary for survival—food, water, shelter, air, sleep, and reproductive sex (to ensure the continuation of the species).

Safety and Security: These needs center on stability, ensuring a person and those they love are safe, financially secure, in good health, and protected from threats.

Love and Belonging: Humans are social beings, hardwired to seek connections with others. These needs are all about acceptance, love, intimacy, and belonging.

Esteem and Recognition: Humans need to feel respected, appreciated, and valued, which fosters self-esteem, worthiness, and identity.

Self-Actualization: To feel whole, individuals must make room for self-discovery and personal fulfillment. This need is about living with authenticity and purpose, truth, creativity, spiritual or existential connectedness, and meaningful goals.

Because writers strive to reflect reality in fiction, these human needs represent the non-negotiables for a character to feel complete. If one of them is absent, their life will feel imbalanced, as we see in the life of Tim.

> Tim is happy, with all the resources he needs to live a good life (physiological needs). He has a house in a safe neighborhood (safety and security), a caring family (love and belonging), and a passion for restoring old canoes (self-actualization). He works at a local golf course as a groundskeeper and feels pride in maintaining its beauty (esteem and recognition).
>
> Life is wonderful until the head groundskeeper retires. Instead of promoting someone from within, the owner's kid, Liam, is given the job. For some reason, Liam takes an instant dislike to Tim. He calls Tim out in front of everyone and invents ways he's dropped the ball. He even foists his managerial responsibilities onto Tim to cover up his own inadequacies. Everyone sees that this treatment isn't warranted, but they're afraid to complain to the owner about his idiot kid's behavior.
>
> Tim feels betrayed by his coworkers, especially considering all the times he's gone to bat for them. But what really gets under his skin is the disrespect and abuse from someone half his age with no experience, especially when he himself should've been promoted to the position. He's the best groundskeeper at the course—and until recently, it's been a great career. But now Tim finds himself looking into job openings at other courses, wondering if he'd be happier somewhere else.

What's really happening is Tim's hierarchy of human needs has a hole in it where esteem and recognition should be. Mistreatment and disrespect have created an **unmet need**, and the worse the situation gets, the more likely he is to take action to fill that void.

As you can imagine, unmet needs are powerful tools for figuring out what drives your characters toward specific goals and understanding why they behave in certain ways.

> Tim's situation has shown him a sad truth: Not everyone values or respects him the way he deserves. To make matters worse, the guys at work don't have his back. Clearly their friendship isn't as solid as he thought.
>
> When Liam finally goes too far, Tim quits. He secures another job at a new golf course, but in the back of his mind, he fears the same mistreatment could happen again. He protects himself by being aloof with new coworkers so they can't disappoint him later. And rather than go above and beyond to show his work ethic, he sticks to his duties, believing any extra effort won't be recognized and he'll only be taken advantage of again.

Fear is a funny thing, because while Tim's protective measures seem to make sense, they're going to create problems for him. He won't build healthy relationships with his new colleagues (goodbye, love and belonging) and a lackluster performance at work will make promotions unlikely (meaning his esteem and recognition will continue to suffer). Ironically, holding back out of fear will result in less fulfillment for Tim.

This is the problem with giving fear too much power: It causes people to perceive threats that don't exist and take actions that limit them. That's rough for our characters, but it's great for our stories—because readers are also hindered by personal fears, so they can relate. And the journey to breaking free of fear makes for compelling fiction.

FIVE FEAR CATEGORIES THAT THREATEN MASLOW'S HIERARCHY

Fear comes in all forms, and when someone's personal world is threatened—their safety, relationships, identity, etc.—it hits like a gut punch. Choosing a fear that targets an area of need is a powerful way to expose the cracks in their life. It reveals where they're the most vulnerable while reminding readers how fragile their own stability can be.

Because each fear naturally undermines certain needs, we've grouped the fears in this book into five categories: Survival, Security and Control, Relationship, Identity, and Moral and Existential. Each category relates to a specific human need, guiding you to fears that can stress-test the foundations of your character's inner world.

BASIC HUMAN NEEDS		RELATED FEARS
SELF-ACTUALIZATION A need for growth, fulfillment, deeper understanding, and to live authentically		**MORAL & EXISTENTIAL** Regret, Being Unable to Achieve a Dream, Having No Purpose
ESTEEM & RECOGNITION A need to be respected, valued, and have self-belief and self-worth		**IDENTITY** Losing the Respect of Others, Failure, Inadequacy, Humiliation, Being Viewed as Weak, Criticism
LOVE & BELONGING A need for love, belonging, intimacy, and meaningful relationships		**RELATIONSHIP** Abandonment, Rejection, Betrayal, Never Finding Love, Isolation, Loneliness, Infidelity, Heartbreak
SAFETY & SECURITY A need for stability, health, financial security, control, etc.		**SECURITY & CONTROL** Being Unsafe, Not Being in Control, Change, Losing Financial Security, Being Powerless, Being Returned to an Abusive Environment
PHYSIOLOGICAL A need for survival: procreation, food, water, air, sleep, etc.		**SURVIVAL** Death, Physical Pain, Being Hunted or Pursued, Being Physically Attacked

Survival Fears

When life is free of conflict, it can be easy to forget that we depend on many things for our survival (physiological needs). Yet when true danger emerges, this realization rushes in and shakes us to our core. Characters are no different. The fear of imminent death, pain, or the loss of a key resource makes for potent storytelling.

Real and perceived threats to a character's survival raise the stakes and generate tension. Urgency goads characters into immediate action, which drives both plot and pacing. Perhaps most important of all, life-and-death situations that give characters little or no time to think reveal who they are—their strengths and weaknesses—through how they respond.

Let's say a cougar appears on a trail where the character is hiking with his girlfriend. Will he freeze in place, run away, or step between her and the animal, waving his arms and raising his voice? If the cougar moves to attack, will the character maintain eye contact and continue his show of strength, or will fear send him fleeing?

In a crisis, emotions go into overdrive, often crowding out common sense—but the opposite can also be true. Without the luxury of time, a person's values and priorities come through, revealing their true character.

Survival fears are unsettling to readers too. As characters are put through the wringer, readers can't help but contemplate what it would be like to be in that situation. This naturally leads to an uncomfortable question: What would they do—and sacrifice—if they were faced with such a threat?

Stability and Control Fears

Stability is something we plan our lives around. We buy homes in safe neighborhoods, research the best health insurance, and protect our personal information (safety and security), all to control outcomes and minimize risk. Characters do the same, working hard to create order so life goes smoothly.

But here's the problem: control is an illusion. No matter how carefully a character plans, life is unpredictable. And when the unexpected happens—a family secret comes out, a car accident drains their savings, or the doctor delivers bad news—it can spark deep fear of losing their carefully acquired stability.

Consider Daniella, a newly promoted advertising manager whose latest campaign contained an embarrassing typo and went viral for all the wrong reasons. Now her job is at stake. Determined to keep this from happening again, she clamps down on her department, involving herself in every decision and demanding to see each ad before it goes out.

Danella's fear of losing her job has turned her into a control freak. She's now hurting productivity and may drive away her best talent. Overreactions are understandable when fear is triggered by a control or security lapse, but they typically create new problems that decrease safety rather than bolstering it.

Stability and control fears are universal, so when they show up in a story, readers instinctively empathize. They've been there and know the desperation of wanting life to remain steady. As a character struggles to regain balance, readers root even harder for them to succeed. This makes these fears a great option to weave into character arc.

Relationship Fears

Social needs (love and belonging) are central to being human, which is why we seek connection with others. Positive interactions, love, and acceptance are important to us. But the more valuable we perceive something to be, the greater our fear that it might be stripped away.

This is why the idea of losing a cherished relationship is so distressing. Our brains process social pain much like physical pain, so we feel heartbreak, rejection, and exclusion not only in our minds but also in our bodies.

If your character is true to life, they've been hurt by someone before. Probably a few times. Wound-based fears around abandonment, betrayal, and separation are powerful because they involve people closest to the character. They cut deep. Even the idea that these painful events could recur causes the character to preemptively try to protect themselves by pushing others away, resisting opening up to people, or steering clear of certain relationships altogether.

Identity Fears

One of the biggest tasks a person faces in life is figuring out who they are. This isn't easy because the expectations of family, peers, and society pull us in many directions. Characters, like people, struggle to balance acceptance (esteem and recognition) with being true to themselves. These desires commonly clash—and when they do, fear steps in.

> Fatima is a second-generation immigrant who fears she'll never be enough. Her relatives criticize her for abandoning her roots when she changes certain aspects of her appearance to fit in. At night school, she can't help but see how some teachers and students treat her differently because of her ethnicity.
>
> Caught in the middle, Fatima starts to hide pieces of herself depending on who she's with. This works in the short term, but compromising herself to have friends and make others feel comfortable is eating away at her self-worth.

While identity fears are most often tied to esteem and recognition, they can also stem from other needs, such as not living authentically because it isn't safe to do so (safety and security) or believing that certain aspects of who they are don't align with their purpose (self-actualization). Take this into account if your character is struggling with an identity fear.

Moral and Existential Fears

Life is more than a series of choices designed to maintain safety, stability, connection, and reputation. People also value the need to live meaningfully, understand their purpose, and explore spirituality or their connection to the universe (self-actualization).

It takes a lot of internal work to find answers to life's biggest questions. And of course, the more important the question—*Am I a good person? Am I living the life I should? Do I even matter?*—the greater our fear of getting it wrong.

Existential fears remind us of truths we'd rather avoid—that we'll die someday or won't leave a legacy behind. Moral fears run alongside, tied to what we believe is right and what that says about us as people.

Imagine a character who fears mediocrity, so they become a world-class surgeon—not out of a noble mission to heal but for the prestige. They sacrifice everything in pursuit of the goal: friendships, family, and other passions. But when they finally reach the pinnacle of their profession, they feel empty. They've traded what mattered most for something that doesn't fulfill them at all.

At this point, the character has a choice. They can find a big new goal to chase and hope to regain their emotional rush from that. Or they can examine where their fear of mediocrity came from and how to get free of it to live a more purposeful life.

Narratively, this is where moral and existential fears shine. Wrestling with them helps characters break old patterns, change priorities, and seek true fulfillment. These fears drive characters to explore who they are at their core.

The Versatility of Fears

Categorizing fears in this way can guide you toward unmet needs for your character that will support the big picture of the story and help you discover their greatest fear. But it's important to remember that these psychic knives don't always stay in one drawer. While each fear fits neatly into its assigned category, a bit of bladesmithing can align it with others too.

Consider the fear of failure. This best fits into the identity category, since failure erodes a character's sense of self-worth and changes how others view them. We might see this if our protagonist is a writer who's afraid their novel will flop, proving they aren't talented.

A fear of failure could also work with other categories:

- A doctor forced to operate at gunpoint, knowing that if the patient dies, she's next (survival)
- A parent trying to secure a good therapist to treat her child's mental health condition (stability and control)
- A teenaged robotics programmer terrified of screwing up during a competition, disappointing their friends, and getting booted off the team (relationship)
- A scientist agonizing over testing data that will either pave the way to a cure or prove they've wasted their life chasing phantoms (existential and moral)

As you explore the fears in this guide, remember that their placements aren't absolute; we've just put each one in the category it's most obviously connected to.

UNIVERSAL FEARS

No matter what genre you write or who your audience is, one thing is certain: Everyone experiences fear. This makes it a great tool for reader engagement, especially when we choose one that's woven deep into the fabric of humanity. To pull readers in, go with a universal fear.

Change

Any list of universal fears must begin with one that touches every story: the fear of change.

Change means leaving the familiar for something new. *New* often feels unpredictable and uncomfortable, at least initially, so avoiding it can be as natural as breathing. Change also involves risk, and the brain responds with a built-in defense mechanism to it: resistance.

How much resistance a character feels depends on the situation and their ability to handle uncertainty. Adaptable characters may recognize when something needs to shift. But even when change is a good thing, characters typically react with caution. They pause. Weigh their options. This hesitation is an instinctive pushback, an ordinary and even expected response to the unknown.

Characters who have been hurt or blindsided by change in the past will display higher levels of resistance. Their fear insists it's safer to cling to what they already have or know rather than risk losing it.

Whether the character welcomes change or dreads it, we can add realism in the moment by showing their initial resistance. Here are some subtle (low-resistance) and fear-reactive (high-resistance) responses to draw inspiration from.

Low Resistance	High Resistance
Pausing to assess the situation Reflecting on what the change means for themselves and others Asking questions to better understand the proposed change Calculating any risks Considering alternatives, in case a different solution might be better	Denying that change is necessary Rationalizing: *Things aren't so bad.* Blaming others for existing problems Refusing to listen Arguing with or gaslighting others Attacking the reputation or motives of those proposing change Walking out

Keep in mind that resistance is situational. Some changes are no-brainers for the character, while others feel complicated and unpredictable or trigger deep fears or phobias. In the latter situations, the very idea of change can send characters reeling. Regardless, whether they accept change willingly or are forced into it, their behavioral responses should reflect which camp they're in.

Healthy Responses	Unhealthy Responses
Staying open-minded Seeking to be part of the solution Sharing ideas and asking questions Being a good listener Offering to help Stepping up to lead Creating a plan Being proactive to minimize risk Gathering information or resources Asking for help Soliciting advice Optimism Encouraging others to share concerns or fears Adapting when it makes sense	Sulking Procrastinating or delaying tasks Making excuses Refusing to be held responsible Trying to take over Judging and criticizing Micromanaging the process Overplanning and not executing Pushing a personal agenda Manipulating others Complaining Sabotaging the efforts of those spear-heading change Disengaging and withdrawing Falling into depression

At some level, every story is about change, which generates conflict and friction and forces characters to make decisions about their future. How they respond to those challenges is story gold.

For more ideas on how your character might behave in response to this fear, check out the **Change** entry.

Death

Facts are facts: The final stop on the bus route of life is coming. Even for readers who believe death is the beginning of something else, it still marks the end of what is tangibly known, making mortality a touchy subject. It awakens uncomfortable feelings and existential worry about what was or wasn't accomplished in life, final assessments of personal value, and the meaning of it all.

So when a character is facing their own end or a loved one's demise, readers can't help but feel for them. This is why death stakes—the death of someone or something significant like a career, relationship, or dream—are often used to increase tension and motivate characters to avoid this tragic outcome at all costs.

Rejection, Abandonment, and Betrayal

Having someone in your corner is the best feeling. When people are taken from us, leave of their own volition, or aren't who we thought they were, we feel abandoned or betrayed, and we often unfairly blame ourselves. This torment is especially sharp when it's delivered by someone we trusted.

Rejection, abandonment, and betrayal are so universal that readers can't help but ache for your tortured character. They understand how the need for protection creates chains of fear that bind the character's heart in their relationships, and they'll cheer when characters eventually find someone who sees and appreciates them for who they are—someone worthy of trust who'll stick with them no matter what.

Loneliness

The need for connection is built into our DNA. We all want people in our lives who celebrate our wins and support us during difficulties because navigating these experiences alone is hard. Nothing tugs at a reader's heartstrings like a character facing tough times alone or not being able to build relationships and make profound connections.

Humiliation

People can be cruel. At some point, every reader has been ridiculed or diminished in the eyes of others, or they've seen it happen to someone else. They understand the emotional pain of humiliation and identify with characters who seek to protect themselves. But they also want to witness the character growing past that fear, because they know that hiding and never putting themselves out there leads to issues like regret and a lack of purpose.

Because fear is part of being human, there's a very good chance readers will know the ones you bring into your story, either through first-hand experience or as an observer. Your characters will encounter a range of fears, from small discomforts to those that leave them feeling cracked open and hollowed out. Use your own experiences with fear to inform your characters' responses and reactions so their behavior and choices ring true.

UNDERSTANDING FEAR INTENSITY LEVELS

Fear may be universal but it's also personal, affecting each character in a unique way. And different fears operate at varying intensity levels. This can guide you in deciding how emotionally volatile a character will become and how fear will influence their immediate and long-term actions and choices.

Imagine fears as tenants in the world's worst apartment building who become more unsettling and dangerous the farther down the elevator goes.

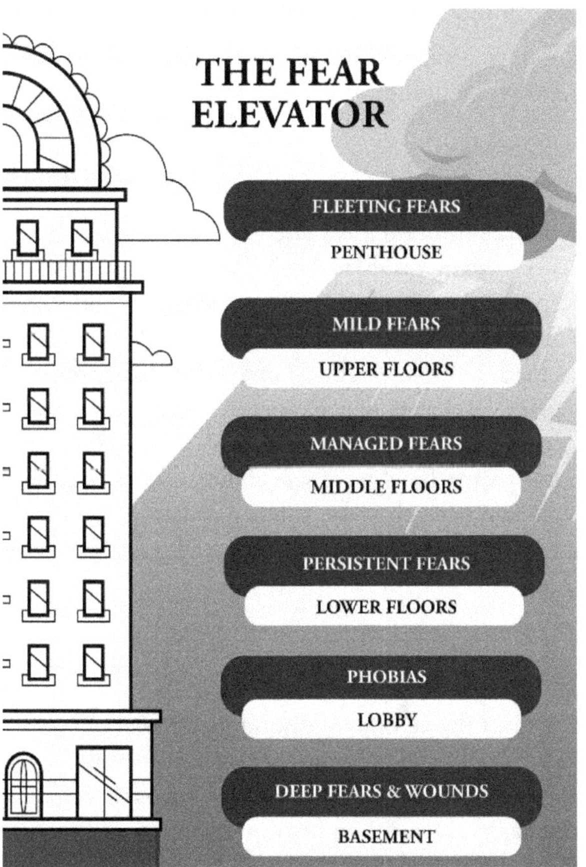

The Penthouse

The elevator starts at the top of the building, where the fears are mild, all things considered. This floor is reserved for small frights—life's little jump scares: the sudden crash in another room that turns out to be the cat, flickering lights as a storm rages, or the bulbous spider clinging to the character's sleeve that they fling away with a shriek.

Fleeting fears are part of everyday life, creating a spike of adrenaline that quickly fades. They can add realism, tension, or even levity to a scene, but once the moment passes, they're forgotten.

The Upper Floors

These floors house low-level fears that cause discomfort or delays but don't paralyze characters or stop them from doing what must be done. Mild fears are usually connected to anxiety over what might happen rather than direct experience (what did happen). Examples might be having to walk home at night alone, getting pulled over by police, or wanting to ask someone out on a date. The fear is real and requires willpower to overcome, but it doesn't derail anyone's life.

The Middle Floors

In this part of the building, fears make for unpleasant neighbors. Mostly, they stay behind their doors, but every so often the character meets one in the hall. Passing them by requires nerve—especially when the character remembers past run-ins—but they manage it. The encounter is unsettling, yet they're able to move on.

Managed fears are created by negative memories that resurface in certain situations, but because the event that caused them was addressed, the character can move forward. For example, it may take time to get behind the wheel again after a car accident, but they do. Or they may have zero hopes for dating after a divorce, but sitting at home because they're afraid of meeting another Mr. Wrong isn't the answer, so they get back out there. Managed fears are still present, discouraging rash decisions, but they don't control or limit the character.

The Lower Floors

These floors are shabbier than the ones above, featuring old carpets, peeling wallpaper, and scurrying rats. Here, fears shape behavior in a lasting way based on *avoidance*. Characters avoid confrontation because of the ridicule it brings. Scarred by failure, they sidestep responsibility. No more romantic relationships, either—they're not worth the risk of another betrayal.

Persistent fears cling with hooks that are hard to shake. The outlook of characters with these fears is more jaded. Instead of chasing opportunities and being open to new experiences, they shrink their world to minimize risks. Life may be unfulfilling in the comfort zone, but at least it feels safe.

The Lobby

The air in the lobby is thick and oppressive, and the front desk is staffed by an attendant cloaked in shadow. Everything smells sour. This is where **phobias** dwell. Rather than responding with fear to a genuine threat (or the perception of one), phobias trigger irrational terror and panic even when no danger exists.

Phobias can apply to anything—spiders, blood, crowds, heights—and go beyond a simple dislike or aversion. They provoke an intense panic-level response that doesn't match the threat.

Because this reaction is so overwhelming, characters with phobias often reorganize their lives to steer clear of anything that might trigger them. They make safe choices, adopt routines that avoid risk, and are careful of where they go and what they do. While phobias can be limiting in that they steer behavior, they don't necessarily alter a character's sense of self the way deep fears do.

The Basement

Here, the elevator door opens to darkness. Somewhere in the void, fear cackles and a gut-churning stench lurks. Characters cower against the elevator walls, frantically stabbing buttons to close the doors and escape. The basement contains **deep fears,** ones fused to a person's most painful wounding experiences. These fears put the character in a chokehold while also causing insidious shifts in their personality, identity, and worldview. They influence how the character interacts with others, protects themselves, and which goals they pursue (and avoid).

As you can see, fear's emotional impact spans a range from fleeting doubts to deeply rooted agony. Just as real people do, your character must contend with many fears. The most damaging ones lurk in the basement, tied to the wounds of the past. This explains why facing trauma and overcoming the fear attached to it is the centerpiece of a character's arc. We'll discuss this in depth in the chapter entitled **The Role of Fear in Fiction**.

PHOBIAS

When we think about phobias, extreme fear comes to mind. But phobias are actually considered a class of anxiety disorder, and they hijack the body's alarm system. Understanding how this happens is important to ensure we don't inadvertently perpetuate mental health stereotypes in our writing.

Fear is an instinctual reaction to a real or perceived danger, triggering a chain of physiological responses: senses heighten, awareness sharpens, and the body prepares to fight, freeze, or flee. A **phobia**, on the other hand, bypasses the brain's ability to assess danger. Panic overrides logic, resulting in an overwhelming feeling of terror disproportionate to the object, situation, or activity that triggers it.

Imagine a mother with a phobia of enclosed spaces who needs to take her chronically ill son to a specialist. She approaches the building and sees a revolving door that allows one person through at a time. Her son runs ahead; he loves these spinning doors. But her? Suddenly the ground is uneven, and the glass doors warp before her eyes. She can't breathe. Nausea hits, and her knees buckle. She sinks to the pavement and grips her chest, sure by the rapid bashing of her heart that she's about to die.

This is a panic attack, an extreme response to a phobia. Most characters, like people, will do anything to avoid experiencing such intense panic and terror. The severity of a response depends on the character's phobia and how frequently they're exposed to its triggers, but even low-level phobias can hinder a character's happiness and freedom.

The Origin of Phobias

Everyone has an irrational fear or three, but when these minor issues become so severe they prevent someone from living a full life, it's considered a phobia. How do these serpents sink their fangs into us in the first place? The most common reason is trauma.

No logic leap is needed to see how surviving a plane crash could cause a paralyzing phobia of flying, or how being repeatedly locked in a closet as a child might spark panic at the sound of a door clicking shut. Emotional trauma forges links between painful feelings and a specific object or situation—a trigger.

Phobias can also be learned. For example, a character might develop a germ-related phobia from growing up with parents who followed strict cleaning protocols and constantly preached the dangers of bacteria and viruses. Genetics play a role, too, making some people more susceptible than others.

Whatever your character's phobia, explore its backstory so you can foreshadow appropriately and plan suitable responses. Even if you don't show the exact reason it develops, readers need to feel that it has a place in the story and you're writing it with authority, not winging it.

Differentiating Phobias from Fear
The key difference between phobias and fears lies not in how intense they feel but in how they came about and what happens after each is triggered. These factors can help you determine whether the character is dealing with a fear or a phobia.

Is there a credible reason to believe a threat exists? People rely on experience, instinct, and survival knowledge to determine danger. For example, a grease fire erupting on a kitchen stove will naturally cause your character to experience fear and even a measure of panic. Phobias are triggered even when someone is obviously safe, meaning a character with a fire phobia would likely react the same way when encountering a lit candle.

Is there a specific trigger? Danger and threats come in many forms. A phobia is generated by a specific trigger (or type of trigger), and the character will avoid it at all costs.

How intense and immediate is the reaction? Characters who experience extreme fear may not jump to terror immediately (or at all). Because the brain can adequately analyze the danger level of a threat, a character's fear may escalate gradually. But a phobia triggers an anxiety response that bypasses the brain's assessment process, resulting in a profound leap to panic.

Is your character able to calm down? This is the big one. Once a crisis is over, someone in a state of fear can regain control quickly. But panic lingers for those gripped by a phobia, even after the trigger is removed.

Should My Character Have a Fear or Phobia?
Choosing your character's main challenge comes down to which serves the story best. Since phobias are intense, personalized, and less common than fears, a struggle with phobia would likely be more memorable to readers. But simply wanting more attention for a character isn't reason enough to give them a phobia. A more compelling reason is to show the character learning to manage (rather than overcome) their difficulty—because a phobia isn't likely to be completely conquered.

Phobias limit a character's life, often shutting down their ability to function. Therapy, gradual exposure, support, and medication can help but won't typically abolish them. Instead, these measures allow the character to manage their phobia. This journey is a powerful one, because learning to live with any permanent struggle is an experience many readers can identify with. If this is the kind of story you want to write, a phobia is a good choice.

Fear, on the other hand, requires a different battle: the fight to subdue and overcome it so the character can move forward with life. This is a common path for change arc stories, so if this is your goal, work with fears that target basic human needs.

If the goal is a simple one—to give the character an interesting, human layer—consider using mild or even irrational fears. Readers will have their own dislikes and illogical triggers, so they'll relate to a character who fears something as inane as clowns (Columbus in *Zombieland*) or sock puppets (Homer in *The Simpsons*). They'll understand the character's reactions and desire to gain distance from the objects of their discomfort.

THE ROLE OF FEAR IN FICTION

It's hard to overstate the importance fear plays in characters' lives. As a key motivator for human beings, it informs decision-making, spawns new habits and tendencies, and pushes them to pursue certain goals.

Not all fears are equal, though. The intensity or severity of a character's fear will determine how much of a driver it becomes at the scene level and across the wider story. Minor fears have their place, but it's the debilitating ones that can really limit characters, spawn conflict, and create dysfunction.

At the top of the food chain is your character's greatest fear, the one that hinders them most in the story. It's something they'll have to face and subdue if they want to achieve their goal. Their degree of success (or failure) determines their character arc and the kind of story you end up writing. As such, this fear plays a major role in both character arc and story structure.

CHARACTER ARC

This is the character's inner journey: how they grow and change, devolve and retreat, or remain internally steady over the course of the story. Many unique elements factor into a character's arc, and some of them belong to the past. To understand them, you'll need to delve into their backstory.

Backstory Elements

Emotional wounds. Somewhere in your character's rearview mirror lies at least one formative event that played a part in determining who they are today. It might be traumatic—abuse, heartbreak, or death. It might be something less tragic but no less defining, such as cracking under pressure at a critical moment or growing up in a dangerous neighborhood. It could be a series of moments—the criticism of a parent or facing a mental health challenge—rather than an indelible one.

Whatever form it takes, an emotional wound is a negative experience that causes pain on a deep psychological level, generating uncomfortable feelings and distressing memories that the character never wants to endure again. And just like that, a deep fear is born.

Greatest fear. In the aftermath of an emotional wound, the character fears a repeat performance. This terrible thing took place, and they never saw it coming—which is terrifying, because if it happened once, it could happen again. The character becomes deeply afraid that something similar will recur if they don't take measures to prevent it.

False beliefs. Trauma generates intense emotional pain that causes the character's psychological defense mechanisms to kick in and seize control. To stop the hurt and prevent it from happening again, the mind must identify the threat. It turns inward, seeking answers: *Why did this awful thing happen to me? Why didn't I see it coming?*

This self-assessment isn't compassionate or gentle. It isn't balanced. It's a critical examination driven by fear, and because the mind knows it can't control other people or change the past, it scrutinizes what it *can* control: the character. It's searching for a weak spot, a personal failing responsible for their situation.

- A tendency to see the best in people? *That's why you were taken advantage of.*
- Being an honest person? *Great job. Look at how that exposed you.*
- Stepping in to lead? *This mess wouldn't be yours if you'd let someone else take charge.*

During this internal audit, a character's esteem is stretched thin because all they can see is how they screwed up, even when they didn't. This is why, at their lowest point, they come to believe a falsehood that explains how they were hurt:

- *I couldn't stop what happened because I'm weak.*
- *He left because I'm not interesting enough to keep his attention.*
- *This was my fault; I was selfish for putting myself first.*
- *Once a failure, always a failure.*

The character may also come to believe untrue things about others and the world that are shaded by their newfound distrust and disillusionment:

- *People only want to use me.*
- *If you let someone get close enough to hurt you, they will.*
- *Everyone in authority will abuse their power.*

False beliefs like these are drenched in fear-based thinking. They reinforce the idea that the character is incapable or broken or the world is a dangerous place. They stoke the fear that emotional pain will follow unless they make changes.

Once a false belief takes root, it supplants positive self-thoughts (*I can do this*) with negative ones (*I'm stupid*) and installs biases.

Emotional shielding. This harsh analysis twists how the character views themselves, and they start viewing some of their best qualities through a warped lens, seeing former strengths as traits that make them weak, exposed, or easy to exploit. To protect themselves, they swap these perceived vulnerabilities for traits, attitudes, and behaviors that will make them stronger: Friendliness is replaced by standoffishness. Openness is replaced by suspicion. If a certain feeling is identified as a gateway to weakness, shields go up.

These unhealthy changes (along with biases born from false beliefs) become armor that keeps people and situations at a distance so they can't inflict harm. And while emotional shielding does keep those potential threats at bay, it comes at a cost: it brings dysfunction and friction into their life and eventually creates a void that must be filled at all costs.

Unmet needs. The character's new flawed behavior and biased ideas generate friction with others, impairing their ability to connect with them. Addictive behaviors and dysfunctional relationships erode their sense of safety and security. Limiting beliefs and fears keep them from becoming the fullest, best version of themselves.

As discussed earlier, when any of the basic needs go missing, deep dissatisfaction and unrest arise. Self-shielding may stave off another wounding experience, but it also opens an emotional sinkhole that must be dealt with.

Can you see how these events work together, eventually creating an unmet need for the character? For clarity, here's a visual representation of how this works.

EMOTIONAL WOUND (Unresolved)	An emotionally painful event that causes lasting psychological hurt. It shapes how the character perceives danger moving forward.
FEAR	A specific fear (based on the meaning a character attaches to the emotionally wounding event) emerges, fueling anxiety that a similar painful event could happen again.
FALSE BELIEF	An internal lie that helps the character make sense of their hurt and why it happened. It warps how they view themselves, others, and the world, reshaping their expectations for the future.
EMOTIONAL SHIELDING	Protective strategies and methods the character relies on to avoid emotional hurt and prevent the original wound from recurring. These may include: **Personality flaws | Defensive behaviors & avoidance | Maladaptive coping mechanisms | Dysfunctional habits & behaviors | Biases | Negative outlook or attitude | Fatal flaws**
UNMET NEED	Over time, these protective yet dysfunctional shielding patterns prevent the character from feeling whole by voiding an **unmet need** in one or more of these areas: **Self-Actualization | Esteem | Love & Belonging | Safety & Security | Physiological**

At the start of the process is a wounding event, which spawns a specific fear that becomes the character's primary motivator. When it takes over, it sets in motion a chain of events that drastically changes the character's ability to thrive.

> Jetta had it all: top marks, a starting volleyball spot, and friends everyone would kill for. Not that they were the best fit—all they talked about was clothes and videos, and when Jetta mentioned the graphic novel she was working on, you'd have thought she'd said she was playing with dolls. So her sketchbook went in the closet, and she started thinking more about her outfits.
>
> And then there was Cara. Jetta's friends picked on her nonstop about her unicorn backpack and teddy bear t-shirts and how childish she was. She usually ate lunch by herself, earbuds in, pretending not to hear. Jetta tried to stay out of it, but her friends made it clear that loyalty meant joining in, not standing by. When they pressured her to "put her drawing skills to good use," Jetta drew a picture of Cara with pigtails, a bib, and a pacifier, and posted it to her social feed. Her friends piled on, and the post went viral.
>
> Cara didn't show up to school for a few days. When she came back, something had changed. Her shoulders were hunched. She had a plain blue backpack. She wouldn't meet anyone's eye. Jetta shared one class with her, but even after Cara returned, her seat stayed empty. In the locker room, Jetta overheard whispers that she'd transferred classes and asked the counselor if she could eat lunch in the office.
>
> When they crossed paths in the hallway, Jetta couldn't look at her. She could barely look at herself. Cara had liked kid things. Bright, joyful things. And Jetta had taken that from her. Cara never had much to begin with, and now this too was gone.
>
> How had she become this person? She used to be kind. Brave. Someone who thought for herself and made her own choices. When had she turned into such a doormat?
>
> Well, not anymore. Jetta quit volleyball, the clubs, and her friends. She distanced herself by trading her trendy clothes and lip gloss for black hoodies and eyeliner. Her easygoing reputation at school got a makeover too. Teachers wanted to program everyone to think the same way, so why bother sharing what you really thought? Sometimes she argued on principle, just to prove she was nobody's puppet.

In this example, we see how fear takes over Jetta's life. When she caves to peer pressure and does something shameful, her greatest fear becomes being influenced by others. So she slaps emotional shielding in place. Once social, she now keeps to herself and seeks to stand out rather than conform, changing her look, giving up clubs, rejecting inclusion. She replaces compliance and agreeability with belligerence and obstinance, and her biased view of the world—that people just want to mold you into a version of themselves—creates trust issues.

These protective measures make Jetta virtually invulnerable to peer pressure, but they also change her identity. Her withdrawal, oppositional behavior, and attempts to become unknowable make her unrecognizable even to herself. This creates a crisis: Who is she now? Her zeal to not identify as a weak-minded popular girl clone has created an esteem and self-actualization hole. Her unmet need will continue to make her miserable if she doesn't address it.

Note that this is a picture of Jetta *at the start of the story*. Who she was before, and what made her this way, are part of her backstory. But once her current story begins, more pieces emerge stemming directly from these formative elements from her past. Let's have a look at those character arc pieces—the ones that set up the framework of Jetta's current story—and how her greatest fear fits in.

Current Story Elements

Outer motivation. Simply put, this is the character's big goal—the objective they'll pursue over the course of the story. Examples of outer motivations include surviving a disaster, winning a competition, being accepted by others, and finding true love.

Inner motivation. But why has the character chosen that goal?

The beginning of their story starts one of two ways. In the most common scenario (and in Jetta's case), they begin from a place of deficiency. Their fear changes them, and they're no longer fulfilled or satisfied. Even if they can't verbalize it, they feel stuck and unhappy because something is missing. In other stories, everything starts off great and the character is living their best life—and then the bottom drops out. Something occurs that changes things and creates a void.

This void is the character's unmet need. Filling it is their inner motivation, because replacing what's missing will return them to a state of completeness. On a subconscious level, they know they're missing esteem or love or a sense of safety, and they can't be complete without it, so they make a conscious choice to pursue a goal they believe will fill that hole.

Outer conflict. Good fiction requires conflict—and lots of it. This means the character should experience significant adversity over the course of a story. But there should be one main external adversary blocking them from achieving their goal. This could come in the form of an enemy, an environmental factor, a supernatural force, or a prevailing cultural or social norm. This outer conflict arises repeatedly. It triggers the character's fear and threatens their success, and they'll have to eventually conquer it to get what they want.

Inner conflict. Along with external forces, characters are plagued by internal conflicts that put them at odds with themselves. Opposing wants and needs, confusion, self-doubt, and uncertainty keep them in turmoil, unable to approach their goals from a position of strength. Just as the outer motivation has a primary outer conflict, the character also faces a primary inner conflict—their greatest fear, the biggest thing that stands in the way of fulfilling their missing need. This fear mocks, intimidates, threatens, and terrorizes them throughout the story, and until they face it, they're doomed to failure.

To see how these current story elements fit together, let's check in on Jetta.

> The school year ends in a fiery cataclysm of F's and summer school. To get out of sophomore purgatory, Jetta must complete a project and get a passing grade from

> Mr. Reed, the new English teacher. Short on time, she goes with what's quickest, digging her sketchbook out of the closet to finish her graphic novel.
>
> She'd forgotten how much she loves this—writing, drawing, losing herself in the story. How *easy* it feels. But now she has to share it with Mr. Reed, who keeps checking in with totally unwanted feedback. He makes her join a teen writer's group, and everyone there has an opinion too. They all want to change her story, but no one knows this book like Jetta. She'll spend the rest of her *life* in tenth grade before she lets anyone ruin it.

The story begins with a protagonist who has no identity of her own and keeps others at arm's length. This leads her to a goal of finishing her graphic novel. Why, of all the options, does Jetta decide to do that? Because even if she's confused about who she is, deep down, she's a writer and an artist. She knows this at her core, and if she can embrace that again, she'll have regained her identity.

But when Jetta encounters outer conflict in the form of Mr. Reed and the other writers, her fear takes over. Terrified of being manipulated again and pushed into doing something against her will, she refuses their feedback, virtually ensuring that she'll never finish her book and causing her to wonder if she's meant to be an author after all.

Jetta's fear and everything that stems from it comprise her inner conflict, keeping her from getting the very identity she so desperately seeks. Until she faces her fear and overcomes it, she'll never embrace who she is and be true to herself.

Jetta's story shows how fear is interwoven through the entirety of a character's arc. Rooted in the wounds of the past, it changes them, molding them into who they are in the here and now. It shapes their personality traits, goals, desires, belief system, and decision-making. As they move toward their objective, their fear becomes an obstacle to their success, and they must neutralize it before they can become happy and fulfilled.

This is the role a character's greatest fear plays in their arc. Initially meant to protect them, their fear ends up binding them so completely that they're unable to escape their circumstances. As authors, it's our job to lead characters to a crucial choice. Will they break fear's bonds to embrace new habits and thought patterns that bring about fulfillment? Or will they give in to their fear, allowing it to keep them from the future they've envisioned?

Fatal flaw. In fiction, a character's fatal flaw is the dysfunctional shield they use to protect themselves from their greatest fear. It has two parts—a behavioral component (the traits, actions, habits, or patterns they rely on), and a cognitive component (a false belief that drives those behaviors in the wake of a wounding event). For Jetta, the fatal flaw is the idea that everyone wants to impose their will on her, along with the stubbornness and defiance she embraces to keep that from happening.

In your story, the fatal flaw is where the false belief, emotional shielding, and story goal collide. Up until now, this shielding has helped the character feel safe, capable, or in control. But within the pressure cooker of your plot, that old method stops working. Their protective behavior becomes the very thing that blocks progress. If the character can't let go of the flawed behavior *and* the false belief fueling it, they won't achieve their goal. Their journey hinges on realizing that the shield they've depended on is now the obstacle they must overcome.

How do we get our characters to this point? That's where story structure comes in.

STORY STRUCTURE: THE THREE-ACT FORM

Let's start by addressing the elephant in the room: Not everyone loves the idea of writing by structure. Some feel it's confining and stifles their creative spirit. Others who think and operate intuitively struggle with following a model.

We understand these concerns and recognize that every writer needs their own process. And if structure were solely a tool to make life easier, we'd be happy to recommend chucking it if it doesn't work for you. But here's the thing: Structure is important because it helps the story work for readers.

Certain stories resonate deeply with the human psyche, and a big reason for this lies in how they're structured. Readers' brains are wired to respond to narratives that follow a blueprint, with pivotal events happening at certain points in the story. Structure provides that framework with a clear beginning, middle, and end.

There are many story models out there, making it easy for an author to find one that matches their writing style, personal preferences, and creative purposes. Choose the model that works best for you and incorporate it into your process when it's most helpful, either during planning or revision.

Fear's role within plot and structure is sometimes hard to tease out because it's so deeply tied to characters and their arcs. But even at a high level, fear helps power a story's framework. Consider where it shows up in three-act structure.

Act 1: The Beginning

In Act 1, fear sets the stage:

- It introduces a danger, threat, disruption, or challenge targeting the protagonist.
- It creates consequences (stakes) if the threat isn't addressed.
- It makes characters look ahead with trepidation about what might happen next.
- It uses tension to prime readers to worry about the characters they're invested in.
- It hints at how things can and will get worse, setting up the main conflict.

Act 2: The Middle

During Act 2, fear burrows deeper into the plot and characters:

- It escalates tension as the cost of failure increases and stakes get more personal.
- It intensifies a character's distress as they discover they're up against something bigger and more difficult than they originally believed.
- It forces characters into situations they're not ready for, often leading to mistakes and unintended consequences.
- It increases as new threats or dangers are introduced.
- It raises the level of urgency with every setback or failure.
- It creates increased vulnerability to threats and opposition, pushing characters to the brink of giving up.

Act 3: The End

In Act 3, fear escalates everything:

- It drives characters to prepare for a climactic clash.
- It amplifies the stakes to their highest point.
- It forces the character into a face-off with their threat.
- It brings tension to a peak.
- It introduces uncertainty about the protagonist's fate.
- It's instrumental to the story's resolution as the protagonist overcomes fear to succeed or succumbs and fails.

These examples only scratch the surface of how fear supports narrative development. Its true superpower emerges as story structure and character arc come together to create the question readers most need to know: Will the character surrender to their fear—or master it?

STORY STRUCTURE: THE TURNING POINTS

Turning points—pivotal events or complications that force characters to make a choice—are essential to story structure. They're called turning points because the story *turns* based on the character's decision, either toward the goal and success or backward in fear, away from their objective.

The best thing about turning points? If you're writing a story with a change arc, you can use them to shape both the outer and inner story in one fell swoop. At each turning point, the protagonist is tempted to challenge their fear or give into it and stick with the status quo. They don't always make the right choice, so the story must give them multiple chances, and turning points can provide these critical opportunities.

While many structure models share similarities, they often use their own terminology or include a different number of turning points. This is why it's important to explore a variety of structures to figure out which works best for you.

For clarity, we'll use Michael Hauge's Six-Stage Plot Structure model to examine an Academy-award winning movie and see how fear fits into the turning points.

Turning Point 1

Often called the *inciting incident* or the *catalyst*, the first turning point creates a crisis, opportunity, or challenge that shakes up the hero's world and reveals a new path forward. The character is largely unaware or in active denial of their greatest fear, so while it subconsciously influences them, it may be downplayed or not overtly stated to readers.

> In *Rocky*, Rocky Balboa wants to become a successful boxer. He's chased this goal for ten years, but he's failing—at this, and pretty much everything else. When he discovers the gym owner, Mickey, has given away his locker, Rocky decides to confront him. Mickey calls him a bum and says he should retire. This plays directly into Rocky's unmet need for esteem and reinforces his fear that he'll never be respected or be able to respect himself.

Turning Point 2
At the end of Act 1, the second turning point brings a new complication, development, or problem that clarifies things for the character about reaching their goal. Very often, it provides a glimpse of who they could be if they abandoned fear and embraced their true self. This turning point adds a heaping dose of motivation, stirring strong emotions that lay the groundwork for change and facing down their fear.

> The opponent of heavyweight champion Apollo Creed drops out of their upcoming match, and Creed must find a replacement. Rocky is offered a shot at the title. He initially declines, afraid that he's no match for the champ. But he accepts when he hears that Creed hand-picked him as a worthy opponent. Even at long odds to win, Rocky can't bypass the opportunity to make something of himself.

Turning Point 3
The third turning point, aptly named the *midpoint*, falls dead center in the story. Here, the character's circumstances become more difficult than they could have anticipated, making the goal harder to achieve and tempting them to cut their losses, quit the quest, and retreat to their old life and way of operating.

> Mickey unexpectedly offers to be Rocky's manager and train him for the fight—the same Mickey who disrespected and dismissed him in the past. He represents Rocky's ineptitude and lack of respect and highlights his fear that he'll never find the esteem he craves. Rocky says no but soon recognizes he can't win on his own, so he begrudgingly accepts Mickey's offer.

Turning Point 4
As Act 2 winds down at the fourth turning point, the forces against the hero orchestrate a devastating setback or failure. It appears that all is lost, with no way to recover from defeat. The opposition has all but won. In the darkness of this moment, the protagonist's fear and a brush with some form of death or loss wars with determination to obtain the goal and satisfy their unmet need.

> On the eve of the fight, Rocky has a devastating epiphany: Despite his best efforts, he simply can't beat Creed. Not only is he going to lose, but his loss will be broadcast worldwide, proving to everyone that he's no good and ensuring the death of his boxing career. But then Rocky realizes that maybe he doesn't have to win to gain respect. No one's ever gone fifteen rounds with the champ, and if Rocky can do it, he'll prove he's not just another bum.

Turning Point 5
In the *climax*, the hero faces the final and biggest challenge or obstacle to their goal. With a Herculean effort, they renounce their fear and faulty coping mechanisms, instead applying all their new knowledge, skills, and will toward winning. Success often requires a sacrifice, and the hero willingly makes it for the greater good.

> Rocky fights Creed. It's a brutal, seemingly endless battle, but he gives it everything he's got. At the ring of the final bell, he's still standing when Apollo is announced as the winner. But Rocky has also won, because his performance and heart make him a contender with a long and promising boxing career ahead. Finally, he's earned his self-respect and the respect of his peers.

Rocky is a near-perfect example of how structure can be used to further the protagonist's arc. The inner and outer journeys are seamlessly woven together. Rocky's greatest fear of never being respected is threatened with each turning point, when he's prompted with a choice to either give in to it and continue living in obscurity or push through it and make something of himself.

There's an appealing synchronicity here in that the same fear crops up at each turning point. This creates a satisfying story because the storyline is tight. No meandering subplots, one clear need and theme—it's all connected, making it easy for viewers to see what Rocky needs to do and what's at stake if he fails.

When you're planning a story around turning points, look for events that jab at the character's greatest fear. The result is a streamlined story where the fear ruling your character on page one is the same fear they must battle at the end.

Defining Elements of Each Turning Point

To utilize fear to its full effect, ensure the following is true for each turning point.

The outcome of the turning point drives the story. The event itself may not be monumental, but the character's response to it determines where the story goes—whether it moves toward hope and change (growth) or slips backward into discontent and a limited existence (fear).

Each turning point is bigger than the last. Turning points escalate as the story progresses. Each one should be more challenging and have higher stakes than the preceding one, triggering more fear. This pattern ensures that tension and emotion steadily rise and keep the pace moving so the story doesn't flatline.

Turning points generate a choice for the character. Will they step out on a new path or continue as they've always done? Will they use their new knowledge and habits to resolve their issues, or will they fall back into their ineffective fear-based ways of operating? Will they continue toward the goal at the risk of loss or death, or will they throw in the towel? Will they commit everything to the fight or continue with half-measures?

These are some of the many questions a turning point could raise, but they're similar in one important way: Fear is a prominent player in each. The protagonist's choices, while different on the surface, boil down to the same options: Give in to fear and stay stuck in the old life, or defeat the fear, take control of the future, and move forward in health and wholeness.

BLENDING FEAR WITH CHARACTER ARC AND STORY STRUCTURE

As you can see, protagonists navigate two stories at once. The outer story (plot) includes everything external: the pursuit of an identifiable goal, scene-level interactions, confrontations with adversaries, and events that push the character toward or away from their objective. The inner story (character arc) is where characters grapple with their beliefs, desires, emotions, motivations—and especially their fears.

In a character's journey to conquer their fear, these two stories typically happen in tandem, with progress or regression in one reflecting progress or regression in the other. Here's how they work together for a character navigating a successful change arc.

Act 1—The Beginning. Readers are introduced to the protagonist: their everyday world, their emotional shielding, and at least a hint of what's missing for them. Fairly quickly, something happens that upends their life, putting them on a new path. As they move forward, mistakes are made, but they don't yet realize that their fear and flaws are to blame. Then they encounter a new complication or development that gets their attention, and suddenly they know what they want. They lay claim to their outer motivation and begin working toward it.

Act 2—The Middle. The protagonist makes small successes, overcoming minor conflicts and becoming more self-aware, but they still rely on the same old faulty methods and fear-driven responses. Then they experience a brush with death that causes them to look within and see the fatal flaw that's holding them back. Recognizing the need for change, they commit to personal evolution and move forward with new ideas, coping mechanisms, and confidence. This ushers in a period of increased conflict that allows them to practice their resolve and do things differently—until they experience a devastating setback or defeat, when all seems lost. In this moment, they must choose to retreat into fear and return to their old behaviors or push forward, shattering their inner lies and discarding their dysfunctional flaws for good. They fully embrace their internal change and are no longer bound by their fear or false beliefs.

Act 3—The End. The protagonist puts everything on the line in pursuit of the goal. Fueled by their new mindset and positive habits, they face the biggest challenge of all. Win or lose, the situation is resolved. The aftermath shows that their life is different now: balanced, complete, and no longer ruled by fear.

This summary illustrates how a character's outer journey toward the story goal and the inner journey of betterment are intertwined. Story events build up to the major turning points, which provide the character with a choice: Give in to fear and revert to old habits, or deny fear and do the hard work of changing how they respond to conflict and relate to others.

Turning Points in Static Arcs

What if your character doesn't have a defining fear at all? This often happens in stories with a **static or flat arc**.

Stories that feature high action or are intensely plot-driven put less emphasis on internal growth and more on achieving a specific goal. Their protagonists are more mission-driven than fear-driven, and while wounding events may frame the root cause of certain behaviors and tendencies, they don't necessarily need to be unpacked and addressed in the story. The characters may have insecurities or secrets to safeguard, but these won't keep them from success.

Instead, these characters' development is centered on dynamics—honing a skill, gaining knowledge, acquiring the right allies—that help them overcome enemies or hostile environments. With no big fear or backstory trauma to deal with, the turning points primarily serve the plot by managing pacing, escalating conflict, and propelling the character toward the final showdown. At the climax, the protagonist doesn't face a deep fear or employ healthier habits and attitudes; rather, they win by applying what they've learned during the story.

Turning Points in Failed Arcs

Another type of character arc is found in stories that end tragically, with the hero not reaching their goal: **the failed arc**. Here, the character was working toward internal growth, but their fear was too great and they were either unable to change or unable to change enough to attain the desired outcome. Failed arcs often leave the protagonist in a worse position than they started from because salvation was within reach, but they lacked the courage to shed their emotional shielding (and most notably, their fatal flaw) and overcome fear. In the end, though they may still talk tough, their needs remain unmet and they continue to cling to unhealthy coping methods, viewpoints, and habits.

The failed arc is the path taken by many antiheroes and villains. Its structure is the same as that of the change arc, with each turning point providing characters with a choice to evolve or retreat to what's comfortable. Rather than using these moments to discover, acknowledge, and eventually subdue their fear, characters in failed arcs regress. They may start out making progress but eventually become overwhelmed by fear, give in to their base desires, and fall back into old ways of dealing with problems. Unable or unwilling to break fear's stranglehold, their fatal flaw proves to be lethal, and they're doomed to continue to live in brokenness.

A good example of this is Arthur Fleck, the main character of the movie *Joker*. Arthur has grown up in poverty, never knowing his father and struggling with a mental health condition that sets him apart from others. Desperate to be seen and accepted (inner motivation) and driven by the fear of never fitting in, he decides to become a comedian (outer motivation).

The story starts with Arthur at work, putting on his makeup as he prepares for a gig as a professional clown:

> **Turning Point 1:** After Arthur is assaulted, coworker and father figure Randall offers him a gun for protection. At first, Arthur refuses because taking it is against the law and he's never been a violent person. But daddy issues and his need for acceptance prompt him to accept it. When he accidentally drops it at a work event, he is fired, and Randall denies giving him the gun.
>
> **Turning Point 2:** On his way home, still wearing his clown makeup, Arthur's condition causes him to laugh uncontrollably when a group of men harass someone on the subway train. His laughter draws their attention, and they attack him. The incident reinforces Arthur's fear that he'll never fit in, and the men—employees of Wayne Enterprises—represent the very system he's been unsuccessfully trying to work within to find acceptance. In self-defense, he shoots and kills two of the men—a reasonable response. But when a third offender tries to escape, Arthur chases him down and shoots him in the back. For the first time, he ventures outside society's norms, and the result brings him a sense of peace and relief.

Turning Point 3: Arthur's recent stand-up gig is highlighted on his favorite TV show. At first, he's excited to be acknowledged and seen, especially by host Murray Franklin, who he has always admired. But his happiness turns to anger when he realizes Murray is making fun of him. Arthur's dream of becoming a comedian and being accepted by others suffers a huge blow from the public mocking, and he marks Murray as another representative of the establishment and therefore an enemy. Soon after, protestors in clown masks—an homage to Arthur's anonymous killing on the train—revolt against the wealthy elite and their apathy for the poor in Gotham City.

Turning Point 4: After the death of Arthur's mother, Randall pays him a visit—ostensibly to offer condolences, but really to find out what Arthur told the police about the subway murders and make sure Arthur hasn't implicated him. This second betrayal prompts Arthur to kill Randall, creating a mirror moment of Turning Point 2. He's killing again, but not in self-defense. It's cold-blooded murder, without hesitation, and he feels better and more fulfilled. The protestors' acceptance of his subway killings reinforces the idea that being violent and sowing chaos brings him the attention he craves.

Turning Point 5: In new clown garb and going by the name "Joker," Arthur confronts Murray Franklin live on his show, admits to committing the subway murders, and kills Murray. Fully embracing his new identity, he has nothing left to lose. Nothing can hurt him anymore. He has killed Arthur Fleck and found notoriety and acceptance among the people of the city who are as violent and chaos-loving as he is. Finally, he feels seen.

For practical help connecting a character's fear to the key moments in their story, use the turning point maps for change and failed arcs found in Appendix B.

UNCOVERING A CHARACTER'S GREATEST FEAR

Your character's greatest fear touches everything in the story, fueling plot and arc and directing their behavior and motivation. Once you know what it is, choosing the conflict scenarios and challenges becomes easier as you'll want ones that provide the richest opportunities for growth. The last thing we want to do is pluck a fear randomly from the dark and slap it on a character to see what they do with it.

Whether you're a plotter or pantser, being strategic about this decision can keep you from heading down the wrong path and save you time and frustration during revision. Let's look at some ways to unearth a fear worth building your story around.

Dig into the Character's Backstory

Because the most devastating fears arise from wounding events, an easy way to find a character's greatest fear is to look at their trauma. Like most people, your character has endured many experiences that left a mark. Zero in on the one that could generate a fear that will eventually become their biggest internal obstacle in the story.

To identify a character's emotional wound, think about their history. How did they grow up, and what difficulties did they suffer through? Who hurt, betrayed, or tried to manipulate or control them? If there's anyone they avoid or wish they could get away from but can't, look for the *why*.

Another area to probe is their childhood, when they lacked the life experience and physical and emotional strength to protect themselves from harm. Childhood wounds, such as a sibling's betrayal, growing up in foster care, or being raised in poverty, fester for years. These long-standing wounds can do a lot of damage, and the fears attached to them are often harder to cast off.

For another connective thread between your character and their trauma, examine their current behavior and attitudes. If they're subservient or overly submissive, what caused them to be that way? Were they stuck in an abusive relationship or raised by controlling parents?

There will always be a *why* behind your character's behavior, worldview, and attitudes. Dig deep enough and you'll likely find a terrible experience, the fear it left behind, and a need to protect themselves from being hurt again.

Ask Uncle Maslow

Don't know your character's emotional wound? No worries. If you know their unmet need, use that to figure out their wounding event and follow the breadcrumbs from there to the greatest fear.

We shared previously how certain fears are often tied to unmet needs. Relationship fears, for example, revolve around scenarios that impact a character's love and belonging. If this is your protagonist's missing need, look at the entries in the relationship section of this book to find fears that connect to a wounding event they're afraid of experiencing again. And, voilà, you've found their greatest fear.

Plunder the Character's Secrets

For a fun route into your character's greatest fear, think about their deepest secrets. What do they not want others to know? What causes them regret, shame, guilt, or some other painful emotion? Secrets are often tied to an emotionally wounding event that could be hiding your character's biggest fear.

Follow Your Own Imagination

Writers are insatiably curious—imagining impossible situations and hopelessly addicted to what-if scenarios. Fear naturally threads through these, making them a goldmine of potential options. And, of course, we can always explore our own fears. This makes a story exceptionally personal and gives us (and readers) a safe way to probe what hurts.

Not every character in your story needs a deep fear holding them back, but the important ones do. Once you identify your character's greatest fear, find out how deep those roots go. Entwine them in the character's relationships, show them through the situations they avoid, and let their insecurities act like a neon sign. Fears don't work alone, either, so give them some toxic friends to hang out with. Show the impact of fear throughout your character's life so readers feel its weight.

HOW TO WRITE AUTHENTIC FEAR RESPONSES

By this point, you've seen that fear isn't just any old emotion; it's a thread running through the entire fabric of a story. It connects character arc and plot, heightens the stakes, anchors tension, and exposes a character's deepest wounds. Fear shows up in countless forms and intensities, influencing everything from quiet moments of doubt to life-altering decisions.

Now it's time to explore the most effective ways to show it.

Cause and effect go hand in hand with fear; something triggers it, and your character reacts to it. Writing their response authentically puts readers smack in the middle of the experience. They know fear—they've felt it, tasted it, been driven by it. Even when the character's fear is illogical or new to readers, their own encounters awaken empathy, putting them on the character's side.

Writing realistic responses and reactions does require careful handling because fear sets off a chain reaction inside your character. A basic understanding of how it manifests in the body and mind can be super helpful, so let's tackle that before getting into the nitty-gritty tips for writing a character's fear.

THE BRAIN-BODY CONNECTION TO FEAR

Found deep within the brain, the amygdala plays a central role in processing emotion and tying those feelings to the experiences that caused them. It's also responsible for attaching emotion to memories, which explains why some feelings stick with us, especially the painful ones.

Imagine kindergartener Jasmine, busily painting an elephant when the teacher scolds her in front of the class for not following instructions. Seeking to erase her mistake, Jasmine sweeps her arm across the paper.

This cause and effect happened thanks to Jasmine's limbic system. It processed stimuli, detected whether something might be a threat, then triggered an emotional response and activated the body to react.

While you don't need to understand the nuts and bolts of it all, you do want to show emotional responses in the correct order, as follows:

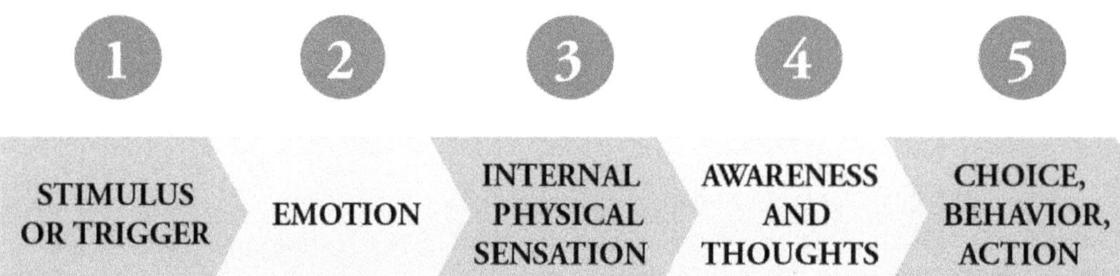

To see what this looks like, let's rewind Jasmine's unhappy experience to when she was happily painting with the rest of the class. She's wearing one of those oversized, paint-splotched shirts, tongue jutting out the corner of her mouth as she concentrates. The teacher's voice drones instructions, and Jasmine outlines and colors the elephant's head, ears, trunk, front legs...

> **Stimulus:** The teacher appears at Jasmine's shoulder, pointing at the elephant's legs. Her tone is sharp and angry. "You're not listening! You're supposed to wait, not jump ahead!"
>
> **Emotions:** Jasmine is flooded with fear and shame, aware that everyone is watching her.
>
> **Physical Sensations:** Her heart races, her face flushes, and her temperature rises as her brain kicks off the stress response.
>
> **Awareness/Thoughts:** *I made a mistake—I have to fix it!*
>
> **Action:** She swipes her sleeve across the painted legs so she won't be ahead of the rest of the class, turning her picture into a ruined smear.

Charged with intense emotion, this moment gets encoded in Jasmine's memory. As she grows, situations that feel even vaguely similar—being criticized, evaluated, or given instructions—trigger these feelings of discomfort. Jasmine's brain flags these situations as risky, and over time, she adapts her behavior to reduce the threat by following directions meticulously. However, she suffers low-level anxiety until each task is finished—all because of one negative moment and her brain's attempt to protect her from feeling that discomfort again.

When it comes to your character's own fear response, while you need to observe the order, you don't need to describe every sensation, thought, and behavior. That would be tedious to read, and it's unnecessary most of the time. Choose which parts of the response to show, in order. Consider the intensity of the situation and level of the threat. For example, a character fighting for their life on the battlefield likely won't have room for self-awareness or deep thoughts; they're only concerned with swinging their sword and blocking the enemy's blade. Delving into internal responses and thoughts is best saved for less immediately threatening situations or when a character's fear is just getting established.

SHOW THE TRIGGER

Showing the trigger for a character's fear seems like a no-brainer. People don't feel fear without cause; something happens that makes them afraid. As the puppeteer pulling the strings, the author knows the triggering event because they orchestrated it, but problems emerge when it's not communicated clearly to readers.

Imagine a scene where the character goes from smiling and placidly humming to wide-eyed and shaking in their stilettos. Readers can see that fear is in play, but confusion arises when they don't know the cause. The character seemed fine, so why are they freaking out now? Rather than being pulled into the story, readers are left scratching their heads and flipping pages to find what they missed.

Threats must be conveyed clearly if we want readers to stay immersed in the character's experience. Sometimes this means being obvious: someone being stalked receives another letter in a manila envelope that smells like gardenias. Readers have seen that kind of envelope before and they know it was sent by an unhinged person, so when the character drops the envelope and locks themselves in the bathroom to call for help, readers are right there with them, hoping for the best.

At other times, a subtle clue is enough. For a character who fears growing old, catching sight of their face in a mirror may be all that's needed to set them off. This is especially true when you've laid the foundation for the fear early on, because readers already have the necessary context.

KNOW YOUR CHARACTER'S FIGHT, FLIGHT, OR FREEZE RESPONSE

We know fear is a universal emotion that hits everyone the same way physiologically. Rational or irrational, whether the threat is real or perceived, fear triggers a chemical process in the brain that shoots throughout the body. But once the biological process has kicked in—quickening breath, prickling hairs, jittery nerves—individual makeup dictates someone's fight, flight, or freeze response.

Humans are hardwired to react a certain way to real or perceived danger: They either go on the offensive, retreat, or freeze up. The intensity of the response depends on the severity of the threat, but which way a character reacts is usually consistent. Here's what it might look like for a character with each tendency:

Fight Responses

- Making themselves look bigger (standing up straight, squaring the shoulders, turning to face the threat, etc.)
- Shifting the conversation to something that makes the other party uncomfortable
- Invading the other person's personal space
- Calling the offending party out
- Getting physical (nudging, pushing, or hitting)

Flight Responses

- Subtly changing the subject
- Taking a step back or turning slightly away
- Avoiding people, places, or topics that induce fear
- Procrastination
- Literal fleeing—leaving the room, running away, ending a conversation

Freeze Responses

- Not answering direct questions
- Stumbling to a halt
- Feeling paralyzed, as if they're physically unable to move
- Squeezing the eyes shut and going still
- Dissociating

Another reaction worth noting is the fawn response, which involves a character's attempts to defuse the threat through appeasement. What does this look like? Apologies. A soft tone, careful movements. Conveying understanding and empathy. Characters who fawn are agreeable and offer help and flattery as a way to deescalate potentially threatening situations.

Fawning often develops in people who have experienced mistreatment, abuse, or volatile relationships because they've learned that placating is safer and more effective than other responses to fear. While not a hardwired response like fight, flight, or freeze, fawning can become ingrained through repeated use, making it common enough to consider for your character.

Each character's default response to fear is built into their psyche and physiology, and knowing how they operate is crucial in conveying their fear to readers. This information provides a framework of reasonable reactions you can pull from to provide consistency and authenticity for your characters. For a helpful visual of fight, flight, freeze, and fawn responses, see Appendix A.

KNOW THEIR EMOTIONAL RANGE

Along with knowing a character's default response pattern to fear, it's helpful to get an idea of their emotional range in general—behavioral tendencies unique to them. This ensures you don't end up with overblown or understated reactions that make no sense. To get a feel for what their baseline looks like, explore the following factors for your character:

Demonstrative or Reserved? Demonstrative characters have bigger reactions, both verbal and physical, while reserved characters play it closer to the vest. They feel the same emotions but exhibit them less dramatically.

Defining Traits. Personality plays a significant role in how a character processes and expresses fear. Someone who is cautious has a lower threshold for this emotion than an adventurous or reckless character. A paranoid person sees threats where there are none and feels more fearful in general. Someone who's needy or timid will cling to others when they're afraid. Personality is nuanced and complicated, so identifying your character's core traits narrows the field in terms of their responses and gives you a clearer idea how they'll react when fear hits.

Discomfort with Fear. Although fear isn't something anyone enjoys, some characters are less comfortable with it than others. For instance, someone who believes fear is a weakness—because they're macho, highly independent, or were forbidden to show fear as a child—will express it differently than someone who has no need to hide or deny it.

Discomfort with Certain People: Some characters are comfortable expressing fear—just not around certain individuals. A critical older brother, a rival, the boss they want to impress... When these people are in the room, the character's fear response changes. If this is the case, use their baseline to show their reactions in generally frightening situations, but switch to their alternative pattern when those people are around.

SHOWING A CHARACTER'S FEAR

By now, you should have a general idea of who your character is emotionally and how they're likely to react when they're afraid. Next, as with any aspect of storytelling, you need to convey that information consistently in a way that draws readers into the character's journey and allows them to share the experience. The best way to accomplish that is by showing the character's fear, rather than stating it outright.

As you might know, we've been yammering for over a decade about the benefits of showing and how to do it well—so you're in luck, because we've got a laundry list of tried-and-true vehicles for conveying fear in those nail-biting scenes.

Physical Changes and Visceral Reactions

Fear is a primal emotion that jump-starts a series of internal reactions. Adrenaline surges, redirected blood flow, glucose spikes, and increased cortisol production are just a few of the body's biological responses to fear. These reactions generate external physical changes that others can perceive, such as the following:

- The face going pale
- Pupils dilating and eyes widening
- Goosebumps rising on the skin
- Increased sweating
- Trembling extremities
- Knees giving out
- Accelerated breathing
- Swallowing convulsively
- Blinking rapidly
- Tendons standing out in the neck or forearms

Body Language and Expressions

Body language and expressions are the power couple that give you the most bang for your showing buck; because readers are hardwired to pay attention to these cues in the real world, they'll quickly pick up on them in fiction. Even better, you can use them to describe the fear response of any character—not just the one telling the story.

But while they're common to everyone, we shouldn't write them generically. Be sure to personalize gestures, movements, posture, and other cues to each character. Their personality and default fight-flight-freeze response will determine the right fit. Here are a few examples.

- Growing utterly still
- The head jerking backward or a full-body flinch
- Retreating a step
- Bringing the arms up quickly to protect the chest
- The mouth popping open
- A darting gaze as they try to see everything at once
- Hands tightening into fists
- Squaring up against the threat

There are so many ways the body reveals what's happening emotionally. This is why it's important to know your character well, so you can determine what responses make sense when they're afraid.

Thoughts

When fear strikes, the mind kicks into overdrive to identify the threat, assess its severity, and analyze possible options. And as mentioned earlier, it can warp perception and disable logic.

Thoughts can also provide context around the trigger because, in the moment, they'll focus on the threatening element in the environment. Letting readers into the character's mind allows them to access this information in an organic way. No infodumps, telling, or author intrusion needed.

But it's not just the thoughts themselves that prove useful; the character's mental process can be incredibly revealing. When we pull back the curtain, readers see the character's inner conflict impairing their thinking. And, of course, clues like a racing mind, scattered thoughts, or an inability to focus can be indicators of their emotional state following a triggering event.

Granted, the point of view you're writing from will determine whose internal thoughts you can share. So keep that in mind.

Dialogue and Speech Patterns

One of the most obvious ways fear manifests is in the voice. Increased muscle tension in the neck and vocal cords influence timbre and make the voice sound tight, husky, or brittle. Rapid, shallow breathing can impair breath control so the character's words sound shaky and weak. Fear also commonly causes the voice to pitch higher.

Changes in the brain itself can also cause dialogue shifts, mostly in the character's speech patterns. Distraction leads to stammering and stuttering. High anxiety might make it hard for the character to find words at all. A talkative person might slip into flight mode and resort to one-word answers, or a reserved person could begin babbling nonstop.

When fear comes to visit, it impacts the whole body and settles into the voice itself. Marking these vocal and speech changes is a great way to show that a new emotion has taken over.

What's Said vs. What Isn't Said

While we're focused on the voice, let's consider the impact fear has on a character's actual words. Most people choose their words carefully when threatened. They may fawn to defuse the danger or avoid saying things that could make the situation worse. They'll hold information back or lie to protect themselves.

This is another instance where providing access to the character's thoughts clarifies what they're feeling. When a threatened character hides certain truths, changes their stance, or lies, their thoughts show not only their level of their fear but also what's most important to them. A lot can be said by what *isn't* said when someone is afraid, so be sure to make allowances for those omissions in their dialogue.

Spare Descriptions

When fear is on the rise, the unimportant stuff fades to the background as the character focuses on how to neutralize the threat. Their world narrows down to the immediate danger and how to deal with it.

For instance, a character fleeing a killer in the streets of Amsterdam isn't going to observe the gabled facades or catch bits of conversation from people around them. Their senses are fine-tuned to the details pertaining to the danger and how close it is: stumbling over uneven cobblestones and straining to determine if that sound is the lap of water in the canal or the assassin's footsteps catching up from behind.

In scenes of high emotion, details matter—but our descriptions shouldn't kill the pace. Focus on strong language choices that set the mood and clarify the threat without slowing things down. Draw readers into the scene, then keep them focused on the intensity of the danger and what might eliminate it, because that's what the character is dialed into.

Avoidance and Denial

Given a choice, no character wants to face a serious threat. Avoidance is the easiest and often the first response. If we show a character going to great lengths to dodge someone or something, readers will pay closer attention to unravel the thread leading to what's causing that fear.

And then we have denial, which is avoidance taken to the next level. Early in a story, readers may not pick up on a character's attempts to ignore or deny reality because they don't know yet what the reality is. But as time goes on, they'll begin to see that the character is living in a dream world meant to insulate them from something connected to their fear.

The best way to convey avoidance and denial is to show them in real time as the story unfolds. Let the character's actions reveal their fear realistically and naturally.

Responses that Match the Situation

The tips we've shared so far can be applied to any frightening situation, but they should be tailored to the intensity of the character's fear. In other words, strong responses should be reserved for strong scenarios.

Dizziness, the knees giving out, rapid breathing to the point of hyperventilation—these are extreme reactions. If this is what happens when, say, a car backfires outside, readers will wonder why the character's panicking. Their action reads as melodramatic because the response shouldn't be that acute. But if there are extenuating circumstances like a phobia, mental health diagnosis, or traumatic wounding event tied to that sound, the reaction might make sense. Just be sure the reader is aware ahead of time so they'll understand the response.

The other thing to keep in mind is that a character's fear response varies according to whether they're reacting freely or hiding their feelings. Many people try to ignore, downplay, or fully repress fear, so let's talk about what that could look like.

SHOWING REPRESSED FEAR

Most characters are willing to express this emotion. When a friend grabs them in the dark, they startle or swear, but they're okay. As long as they generally feel safe, they can admit to being afraid or bothered by a lack of control. This level of comfort with fear is standard.

But it's also normal for people to hide it in some situations. This kind of situational fear will inevitably present itself at some point in your character's journey. Here are a few scenarios when your character might hold back on their feelings:

- They're with someone they want to impress.
- They're with someone who views fear as a weakness.

- They don't want people to know they're afraid of a particular thing.
- They need to be strong for someone else.
- Hiding or denying the fear is necessary for survival.
- They need to maintain a power dynamic or the status quo in a tense situation.
- They want to avoid facing a past trauma.

If any of these situations cause your character to suppress fear, their response will be more subtle, possibly not even discernible to others. But readers need to see what they're hiding. This means you'll have to show the character's muted response while indicating to readers that it's a front and fear is in play. Here's how.

Body Language

Characters who want to mask fear will downplay their physical cues. Basically, they act normal.

> "I'm afraid it's not good news," Ms. Bozeman said. "The judge has determined that for your mom to get better, she needs to be in a place that can best service her mental health challenges. But don't worry—while she's staying at Ravencrest, your dad's agreed to take you in."
>
> Melody took a deep breath. "Okay."

Here, readers see no outward sign that this news has rocked the character's world. Her response seems reasonable. Good thing Melody has a father to take care of her, right?

Visceral Responses

But this isn't Melody's situation, and inside, she's fighting panic. We need readers to see that, so we show it through what's happening internally.

> "But don't worry—while she's staying at Ravencrest, your dad's agreed to take you in."
>
> Melody's stomach tightened. The air fled her lungs, and she had to remind herself to inhale. This couldn't be happening. All the moving, starting over at new schools, avoiding social media—Mom had explained it all when she was still lucid.
>
> They'd left him when Melody was little, and her few memories of that time were hazy and fear-tinged. But she did have a clear vision of him looming over her and relaying in terrifying detail what he'd do if she told anyone the truth about him.
>
> She dragged her gaze up to Ms. Bozeman, who was watching her intently. It was too dangerous to say anything now that her father knew where she was. She'd have to try to get away before he came.
>
> Melody took a deep breath and forced her fingers to loosen their death grip on her armrests. "Okay."

If readers see only Melody's physical cues, nothing seems amiss; her deep breath is an expected response for someone dealing pretty well with a hard reality. But her thoughts tell another story, and her internal visceral reactions (the tightening stomach, difficulty breathing) underscore the truth: Melody is terrified. Thanks to her mental process, we know she has good reason; we now have context for her fear. The outward physical cues, thoughts, and inward visceral reactions work together to show readers Melody's true emotional state, what caused it, and why she must hide it.

One note of warning for this technique: Include thoughts strategically so they don't slow the pace. Show only as much as is needed, then move on to action.

Tells

Most people aren't totally comfortable lying, and their tics and tells give them away in moments of dishonesty. Melody might fiddle with an earring, pop her knuckles, or slouch to appear unconcerned. Maybe her voice betrays her as it rises in pitch or breaks, making her clear her throat. If your character often lies when they're afraid, use their tell as a clue for readers. Just don't overdo it.

Cracks in the Mask

One final thought about hiding fear: A character shouldn't be one hundred percent successful in masking it. Remember the physiological changes that happen when fear sets in? The trembling limbs, increased breathing, eyes going wide, vocal changes ... It's hard to disguise all that. (Just look at the death grip Melody has on those armrests.)

Unless the character is a deception expert, authenticity requires the mask to slip—and readers need to see it.

CRAFTING THE FEAR-DRIVEN SCENE

We know the importance of effectively conveying a character's fear so readers can connect with it. In danger-filled scenes, tension should loom like a disconcerting shadow. But this can only happen if scenes are properly constructed; pacing plays a key part in pulling readers to the edge of their seats. There are two pacing strategies you can use to keep fear-filled scenes dynamic, and each produces a different reading experience.

THE "SCREAM" APPROACH

If you've seen the original *Scream* movie, you already know what we're talking about.

In the opening scene, Casey Becker is home alone when the phone rings. She doesn't know the caller, but she's bored, so they chat. In a few minutes, the conversation takes a dark turn, and Casey realizes she's dealing with a sicko. She hangs up, but he keeps calling. Things escalate until she learns he's in the house with her. She panics, and a quick game of cat-and-mouse ensues that ends with Casey disemboweled and hanging from a tree in the yard. For both Casey and viewers, it's a breakneck escalation from contentment to full-on terror.

This model is a staple for horror scenes when fear blows up in a hurry without giving readers time to catch their breath. It's an effective way to show and elicit fear, particularly in a genre where consumers *want* to be afraid. They relish the process.

The key is to not mince words. In *Scream*, there's a very short setup sequence where readers get a feel for the character and her environment. But once the mood shifts from amusement to concern, it's nonstop acceleration to the inevitable. The pace never lets up. Had the writers tried to downshift at any point and then rebuild the lost tension, the scene would feel very different. When you're structuring a scene with this approach, once fear makes an appearance, don't slow down. Keep the fear coming until the scene ends.

The beauty of this approach is that it's not just for horror stories. It can be used in any scene where you want to sweep readers rapidly into extreme fear.

THE SLOW-BURN APPROACH

The alternative and more popular approach to fear-based scenes is a slower build. With this technique, events move characters along the same emotional progression with more time and mental processing between shifts. Let's see how this could work.

> Mira and her boyfriend are cooking dinner at his apartment—easily navigating the space, chatting about work. Louis asks about her day, and she tells him. Then, while chopping zucchini, he mentions that when he called her office today, she wasn't there.

> Her tension immediately intensifies—she knows what will happen if he finds out she's even thinking of leaving him—but she continues to casually stir the pasta. She tells him she went for coffee and worked for a while at the shop, knowing that would match up with the tracking app he's installed on her phone.
>
> His voice rises and his questions come faster. She answers, outwardly calm, while her mind races to stay a step ahead. After all, there's no way he could know she was meeting someone from the Women's Resource Center, could he?
>
> Then Louis is yelling, calling her a liar. Her hands aren't quite steady as she circles the island with the pasta—seemingly to drain it in the sink, but really to get closer to her phone. She knows she can't hide her fear from him, that he's already zeroed in on it like a predator smelling blood, so she tells him that he's scaring her, that she's not lying.
>
> And when he lunges for her, knife in hand, Mira grabs her phone and runs.

This scene propels Mira along the fear continuum at a steady, reasonable rate. Contentment reigns in the first stage, with no indicators of any threats. A leading question from the abusive boyfriend moves her to nervousness, but she's been in this situation before, so she's able to hide her emotion and try to soothe him. When he insults her and starts yelling—signs that his control is slipping—she slides full-on into fear. He's beyond placating, so she physically retreats, putting space between them while she considers escape routes. His progression to physical threats sends her into terror mode, and she runs—literally—for her life.

The slow-burn approach works for this scene because the protagonist needs processing time. The reading experience is enhanced by watching Mira slowly unravel internally while playing it cool on the outside. Along the way, tension builds in the best way possible, keeping readers glued to the pages.

This tantalizing unfolding is why the slow-burn approach is so popular. It also explains why these scenes tend to run longer. Imagine a rubber band slowly being stretched out. The more it's stretched, the tighter it becomes and the more tension and uncertainty are created—in the band, yes, but also in the person holding it. How far can it stretch without breaking? When you're trying to decide how long your scene should be, aim for just shy of that breaking point.

Obvious triggers like the ones in Mira's example (a leading question, yelling, verbal and physical attacks) are threats that can organically spark or intensify a character's fear, imbuing the scene with tension. But sometimes other characters aren't around, or you need more subtle ways to kick things up a notch. In that case, consider one of the following techniques for drawing out an intense scene.

Foreshadowing

Simply put, foreshadowing is an indication of things to come. When what's coming is bad, foreshadowing creates tension that primes readers and the character to jump to fear more quickly.

A fantastic example of this is in the movie *A Quiet Place*. In this post-apocalyptic story, the world is inhabited by alien creatures who hunt by sound, forcing the few survivors to be absolutely silent. Early on, protagonist Evelyn is dragging a bag of wet laundry up the stairway when it snags on a nail and pulls it loose, leaving it standing straight up on the tread. Evelyn is oblivious, but viewers are not. They know that nail is going to cause serious problems later.

(Spoiler: They're not wrong.) As frightening as the alien "death angels" are, an exposed nail, in that moment, is even scarier.

This is the magic of foreshadowing. It lays the foundation for a future escalation so when the anticipated event arrives, readers know what's coming. Foreshadowing also starts the tension train rolling sooner and keeps readers wondering with every passing scene when the dreaded event will unfold.

Purposeful Sensory Details

When it comes to writing scenes, details matter. But too many details can bog down the pace, diminishing the experience for readers having to slog through endless minutiae. At strategic moments, though, a touch more description can work in your favor.

When potential danger looms, part of our survival instinct is to pay attention and look for threats. This is why fearful characters often experience a sensation of slowing time. Their senses are heightened. Their eyes widen as they take in everything around them. Their mind races to process what they're seeing and decide how they should respond.

These mental and physiological responses to fear make it possible to take in details the character would normally miss—sounds, movement, odors, etc. This hypervigilance is a natural response to both real and perceived fear, and capturing this state in your story brings authenticity to fear-laden scenes.

Your character's heightened watchfulness will also alert readers to perk up and take notice. If you've been spare with the details but suddenly the protagonist's observations are laser-focused, it's a sign that something has shifted. When readers spot physical and mental reactions to fear, they recognize that the character's emotional state has changed and they'll be on the lookout to identify the threat themselves and gauge just how much danger the character is in.

Hidden Threats

Very often, the biggest threat is the one the character can't see. Hiding it from readers elevates the tension, so when you're introducing a new danger, consider concealing it at first. For example, maybe the protagonist senses something in another room, or on the roof, or right outside the window. Put light and shadow to use, keeping the danger just out of sight.

For threats that are more existential, think of ways to show something's wrong without revealing it. Maybe a single dad's payment to the utility company fails, and when he checks his bank account, it's wiped out. Where did the money go? Who's responsible? Or the lacrosse jock learns that he's got competition on the team and his starting position is no longer guaranteed. Which teammate is the threat?

Symbolism

A well-placed symbol can do some seriously heavy lifting, escalating a character's fear without it being spelled out.

In Stephen King's *It*, a red balloon always precedes Pennywise, the terrifying clown. When the children in the story see it, they (and readers) know something horrible is just around the corner. This symbol is particularly poignant because balloons are associated with childhood and frequently used to represent joy and innocence. Subverting them as a symbol of terror is a genius turn by the master of horror. (And who better to learn from when writing about fear?)

For maximum effect, choose a single symbol that elicits fear in the protagonist, then sow it early. Readers will know what it represents, and their own fear will rise when they spot it throughout the story.

Weather

Weather is a natural vehicle for manipulating a character's emotions and priming them for fear. As a commonly used technique, however, it can come across as heavy-handed, creating writing that's clunky and obvious rather than smooth and subtle. One example is that storm on the horizon signifying impending doom, a device that's been overdone to the point of cliché.

But this doesn't mean we should shy away from using weather phenomena to symbolize or elicit fear. Animals can perceive changes that signal dangerous weather patterns, and they respond with unease and anxiety. Anyone riding out a thunderstorm with a dog has seen this in action.

Humans are animals, too, so consider which weather elements might impact your character's emotional state and signify incoming danger: A fog bank rolling in at dawn obscures a threat when the morning sun should illuminate it. The full moon breaking through clouds lights the landscape when the character needs darkness to remain safe. The onset of spring, typically associated with rebirth and renewal, melts the ice and exposes something the character desperately needs to remain hidden.

Weather is also effective when it's combined with other mood-setting tension builders. A new driver expressing nervousness about their car trip provides a decent dose of foreshadowing, but add sleet and the resulting black ice and you've built a tension dream team. Take your character's situation into account to tailor weather that works specifically for you and against them, creating meaningful options that prime readers for fear.

Contrast

Contrast is a brilliant technique when used to bolster the ones we've already discussed. It involves the unorthodox comparison of two elements, and it's effective because it's almost always unexpected. Contrast is the sunlight heightening danger, rather than diminishing it. It's the buoyant, brightly colored balloon that terrifies children. Combine contrast with symbolism, foreshadowing, weather, or other dynamics to supercharge a character's fear in a heavy scene.

False Flags

Remember the rubber band metaphor in the slow-burn approach? One way to extend a fear-driven scene and wring every ounce of emotion from your readers is to plant a few false flags. Let them think the situation is resolving, then *bam*! It goes sideways. This resets the tension but at a higher level, because readers haven't fully recovered from earlier events. And it lengthens the scene itself because the initial resolution was a false one, and the character must keep working to sort things out.

Here are a few tools you can use at the scene or story level to mislead readers and keep tension rising:

Misplaced trust. In this scenario, the character is in trouble with no clear way out when a savior arrives—a stranger rescuing them when their car breaks down, or a trusted friend comforting them in a moment of grief. The character relaxes and begins thinking about next steps, but then they realize their savior is a snake. The Good Samaritan is a serial killer with impeccable timing. The comforting friend is a master manipulator hoping to take advantage during a vulnerable moment.

It's devastating to learn that a trusted someone wasn't a true friend or ally. The character's out of the frying pan and back in the fire, often in a worse situation than before. Only this time, they're blaming themselves, thinking they should've known better.

Lost assets. Whatever your character's facing, they should possess at least some of the assets they'll need to succeed—supportive friends, strategic allies, a special talent or skill, or financial means. They've likely been using these resources to overcome difficulties already, and they're doing well, so how do we keep fear on the front burner and prevent the character from growing complacent?

We take something away.

What happens when an ally goes missing at a critical moment or the character can no longer count on a skill they used to have? Sheer terror. Despair or anger may come later, but initially, fear rules. Add a ticking clock offering very little time to concoct a Plan B, and emotions stay high until matters resolve.

Unreliable information. Many times, characters seeking intel find it just in time to make a vital decision or fling it in the adversary's face.

But alas, sometimes the intelligence is wrong. Or the enemy got the information first and countered it. Unable to regroup in the moment, the character is embarrassed and fearful because defeat seems certain. Readers, too, are disconcerted and unsure of the hero's fate.

Wrong decisions. Because scenes are finite, your character will have a set period to make choices—important decisions with long-lasting and potentially devastating results. They'll have to think quickly in the moment.

One way to keep scenes feeling dynamic is to allow the character to make a decision that seems right. Tension drops, adversaries are unsettled, and the character's fear turns to elation. But then they realize they've made the wrong choice. The reasons for this lapse in judgment are myriad: being blinded by bias, underestimating an enemy, missing a potential threat, placing faith in the wrong person, or being driven by fear and insecurity. Even the most careful and methodical characters come to the wrong conclusions sometimes.

A crucial error at a critical time thrusts the character back into fear, but now it's heavier because they feel responsible. If their confidence is shot, they might hesitate when quick thinking is needed again—and you'll be sure it is.

Unresolved fear. Ever since the character realized what's holding them back, they worked to master it. It hasn't been easy, but they've done well and eventually reached the point of conquering it. Then they face a scenario that proves they aren't as far down the track as they thought they were.

Consider a character with a long-standing mental health condition who's always feared losing their sanity. They've worked hard to master that fear, and they think they've done it. But in the climactic scene, they're told that they're living in an alternate universe and reality is not what they believed. Now the character must decide if this information is true or a figment of their psychosis.

TWISTING THE KNIFE

To adequately challenge characters, their circumstances must escalate and become more arduous over time. Fear is a frequent companion, and they shouldn't always handle it well. Let's look at some ingredients to add to an already frightening situation that will make it harder for characters to master their fear.

An Audience

Working from a place of fear is always hard, but it's more difficult when others are watching. To make a situation more challenging, play it out in public: Put the character in a group, record them, or place them with someone they admire and desperately want to impress. An audience creates nervousness for the character, increasing the likelihood of screwing up and making it harder to hide weaknesses. And witnesses ensure that any failure will be remembered and possibly shared with others.

Vulnerabilities

To escalate a situation, one of the most potent things you can add is a vulnerability.

> In *The Nightingale*, Vianne Rossignol is living in Nazi-occupied France, raising her daughter alone while her husband is a prisoner of war in Germany. The situation is difficult but manageable until Vianne is forced to house a German soldier in her home. She must cook for him, share her space, and act like she's fine with everything—all under the watchful eye of an enemy who holds the power.
>
> Vulnerabilities like these encourage reader empathy while upping the stakes and enhancing the character's fear. If you need some ideas, consider **emotion amplifiers**, states and conditions that cause emotional instability capable of sending your character down the path of poor judgment and mistakes.

Increased Stakes

As the story progresses and you need increasingly impactful scenarios to test the character, try upping the stakes.

> Vianne is already in the tricky position of having to share her home with Officer Beck. It becomes more precarious when someone else moves in: her sister, an underground resistance fighter. Isabelle is headstrong and reckless and has difficulty hiding her disdain for Beck. Despite their close proximity, she continues distributing illegal correspondence for the resistance, helping Allied soldiers escape from France, and even hiding an injured airman in their barn.
>
> With these new complications come higher stakes. Because Isabelle struggles with subserviency and hiding her feelings, her presence alone makes Vianne's already tenuous situation downright deadly.

Escalating stakes like these create ever more alarming scenarios that stir up a character's fear, making it harder to master.

Unpreparedness

Suppressing or mastering fear is always difficult, but it's even harder when the character feels unprepared. Maybe they've only recently become aware of their fear, or they're still learning to manage it and aren't always successful. To up the ante, present the character with a battle against their fear when they feel ill-prepared and don't think they can win. You'll probably prove them right.

HOW VILLAINS AND ANTAGONISTS USE FEAR

Fear is the stranger's face at the window, the shadowy gap of a half-closed door. But what it represents, how it's perceived, and how it can be used depend on the type of person your character is. That's right, kids, gather round. It's time to talk about antagonists and villains.

One thing most story baddies are great at is proclaiming how they're impervious to fear. If you know what to look for, however, it's obvious this isn't the case. Everyone feels fear. Characters who deny feeling it are just wearing a mask, projecting strength, power, and control. And as it turns out, their rigid refusal to remove that mask will ultimately lead to their undoing.

That being said, fear looks different on protagonists than it does on antagonists.

PROTAGONISTS

These characters are aware of their greatest fear because it's kept close via emotional shielding, like a thick cloak they pull around themselves. The material is heavy and restrictive but functions as a constant reminder that threats are always near and they must be wary.

At some point in the story, though, the protagonist's shoulders begin to ache. They feel encumbered and overheated. They're limited by the cloak's weight, forced to give up opportunities too difficult or risky to tackle in their state.

One day it hits them that they're unhappy, and if they didn't have this burden, they might feel lighter and find it easier to get around. It's not easy, but they make the choice to let the cloak fall, even though it exposes them. They understand that while life contains danger and emotional risk, letting go of fear leads to freedom, self-empowerment, and joy.

> **The pattern for protagonists:** Fear starts as protection, but the character soon learns it's also limiting. Deep unhappiness from unmet needs forces awareness. The character chooses to be vulnerable and cast aside fear so growth can occur.

ANTAGONISTS

For antagonists and villains, much is the same. The weight of their fear is equal, and they wear the cloak for the same reason. But when their unhappiness surfaces, they become resentful and angry that what they want is out of reach. Rather than remove their cloak, they cinch it tighter and continue to manipulate situations, control people, and steal power to get what they want.

What they truly need, though, remains out of reach. Their inability to let go of their fear and accept emotional risk as a part of life ultimately destroys them.

> **The pattern for antagonists:** Fear begins as protection, but it also limits. Unhappiness and unmet needs spark resentment. The character clings to fear for a sense of control, but it makes them weaker and imprisons them, resulting in failure.

This is how fear causes an antagonist or villain to perceive events and people differently than a protagonist, leading to vastly disparate actions and choices. A great comparison of these two character types is found in Andy Dufresne and Warden Samuel Norton from Stephen King's *Rita Hayworth and Shawshank Redemption* (spoilers ahead).

> In 1947, banker Andy Dufresne is framed for his wife's murder and lands in Shawshank State Prison. Everyone and everything there is controlled by Samuel Norton, a corrupt religious fanatic who believes harsh discipline is the way to inmate salvation. The irony is that the warden uses his position to commit a host of crimes. He takes a shine to Andy for his banking and accounting knowledge and uses him to embezzle money and commit tax fraud. As warden, he's the king, and his greatest fear is losing his power and control.
>
> Andy is determined to prove his innocence, but he's repeatedly victimized in the brutal prison system. He earns protection when the warden realizes what Andy can do for him, but this means trading one form of pain for another, since Andy's fate now depends on protecting the warden and hiding his criminal activities. Along the way, Andy's greatest fear develops: becoming institutionalized and losing all sense of himself and the will to fight for his innocence.

Andy and the warden handle their fear in different ways. Andy pushes against fear by holding onto hope that he will eventually be free. He finds small joys to sustain him—reading, carving, building a library for the inmates, encouraging higher education, and planning his escape. The warden feeds his own fear by using intimidation and violence to run the prison and force Andy to help hide his crimes. From his position of authority, he consolidates power and deploys cruelty, even murder, to neutralize threats.

> Andy is innocent, and the warden knows it. But once he declares that he'll never let Andy go, Andy knows it's time to "get busy living or get busy dying." If he doesn't escape, he'll never leave Shawshank, and his hope will die with him.
>
> Andy uses the tunnel he's been digging for over a decade to get away, but not before stealing the warden's ledger. Once free, he sends evidence of the warden's activities to the authorities, who come for the warden at Shawshank. Rather than face accountability for his crimes, the warden ends his life.

These two characters are bookends, one using the fear of hopelessness to push him to risk everything and gain freedom, and the other using a fear of exposure to push him to do anything to hoard power and control.

Another difference between protagonists and antagonists is that antagonists don't simply respond to their own fear with avoidance or harmful methods. They weaponize other people's fear. They're experts at sniffing out vulnerabilities, and they exploit them. This is precisely what happens in *Shawshank Redemption.*

COMMON MISTAKES WHEN WRITING FEAR

The natural evolution of a character is hard to write well, and fears are notoriously tricky because characters seek to ignore, diminish, or hide them. When it's time to examine your character's fear journey with a critical eye, look for the common stumbling blocks, and revise accordingly.

EMPHASIZING THE WRONG FEAR

Fears are complicated and well-protected; that's why we dedicated an entire chapter to discovering your character's greatest fear. Even armed with that knowledge, it's easy to get sidetracked by the following scenarios.

Too Many Fears

Characters, like people, aren't afraid of just one thing. Very often, their biggest fear spawns new ones, or they develop unrelated fears from other wounding events. Before you know it, you've got a Hydra situation, with so many tentacles that it's hard to identify which fear is the biggest threat.

Take Sabrina, whose fear of flying causes her to turn down opportunities that require long-distance travel. She also has a fear of conditional love, which makes her a people-pleaser continually seeking to meet the expectations of others. This has contributed to body image issues and a fear of gaining too much weight, which impacts her health.

If we included all these issues in the story, we'd have to address each one with separate turning point scenarios—basically, a separate character arc for each fear. It's too confusing to write and too convoluted for readers to follow.

Instead, recognize that minor fears (and some phobias) should play a peripheral role. They may present quirks, create inconveniences, or even provide comic relief (looking at you, Indiana Jones), but they shouldn't be the character's greatest fear. Whittle down the options to the fear at the character's core that makes their goal all but unreachable until they subdue it.

Secondary Fears

Sometimes the fear you've chosen for your character isn't the primary one causing their problems. Instead, you've focused on a secondary fear that sprouted from the first. This is a problem, because even if the character addresses it, it won't remedy the foundational fear that's causing the issues. To identify the primary one, you'll have to dig deeper.

First, list your character's fears and strike any that stem from a deeper one. For instance, Sabrina's fear of weight gain realistically grows out of her fear of conditional love. In this case, we can disregard the former and focus on the deeper fear.

Once you've drilled down to what you think is the core fear, make sure it ties into the character's backstory. Fears are born from certain distressing factors in life: emotional wounds, missing human needs, negative experiences, and major mistakes or failures. Does the fear tie into any of these for your character? It should. They don't appear randomly, so if you don't know what caused a fear to form, you have more backstory research to do.

The Fear Isn't Connected to the Goal
A character's greatest fear is part of their inner conflict. They've invested a lot of effort learning new ways of thinking and acting that keep fear at bay, but this blocks them from achieving their outer goal, which they desperately need to be whole and fulfilled. In this way, a character's greatest fear is connected to their story goal. If they're pursuing an objective that doesn't somehow touch their fear, there's a mistake somewhere in their character arc.

To fix the problem, review the main components of their arc (found in the Character Arc section). Spend some time filling in the blanks until the elements connect. When you find which pieces don't quite fit the rest of the puzzle, adjust as needed.

Random or Insignificant Fears
When we haven't clearly mapped out a character's arc, it's easy to lose sight of the primary fear at the heart of their dysfunction. We end up applying random or inconsequential fears strictly as a conflict device to add complications. These nuisances have no real bearing on the character arc or the overall storyline, resulting in a less cohesive plot, an unfocused character, and a less than satisfactory reading experience. This is closely related to the problems we've just described, so be sure to identify the character's core fear and connect it to their outer motivation.

Overstated Fear
Not every aspect of a character's fear must be prominently displayed on the page. It's a lot like backstory. As the author, you should know a lot about your character's past. But if you write it all into the manuscript, it will become bloated, overloading readers with things they don't need to know.

The same is true with fears. The story's turning points can be opportunities for the hero to respond to their fear, but readers don't need an in-depth narration of their self-awareness and decision-making process every time. Often the most poignant moments are understated. A choice arises, and after a brief internal battle, the character makes a decision. Consequences result. Readers know exactly what transpired, all with a much-appreciated economy of words.

It can be hard to find the balance between sharing too much and not enough. Begin by determining not to spell everything out at every pivotal moment. This is an area where critique partners can earn their dues. Ask them if the fear journey is too spare or heavy at those key points, then flesh out or prune them as needed.

A HERKY-JERKY RESOLUTION
We've all read stories with meandering, inconsistent subplots, where something's referenced at the beginning but then peters out, never to be seen again. Or it pops up sporadically, as if the author has just realized it hasn't made an appearance in a while and needs to be revived.

The same issue can happen when a character's fear shows up intermittently—often when a crucial conflict appears, because that's when they're most likely to be afraid. It's established in the beginning and overcome at the end, but we don't see the growth and setbacks along the way. Other times the journey is too easy, and the character always makes the right choice or overcomes the fear too quickly.

If you struggle to maintain a gradual, realistic progression in your character's fear journey, use the story's turning points to map it out. This ensures a good number of opportunities for the fear to escalate, ties it into the plotline, and spaces it out in a way that's satisfying for readers.

DESCRIPTION ISSUES

The micro-details of showing a character's fear are fundamental for writing authentic emotions that readers will connect with. Aim to avoid these mistakes that are easy to make when we're describing a character's fear.

Telling Instead of Showing

In real life—say, when you're giving directions or are short on time—it's often best to explain things as simply as possible. But writing fiction is different because you're creating an experience for readers and inviting them into the character's world.

"Telling" thwarts this effort because it's a form of talking down to readers. By spelling things out, the author is unintentionally saying *I'm not sure you'll get the point if I write it subtly, so I'll make it super simple.* It also says that you doubt your ability to make yourself understood without stating things outright.

Telling also fails to draw readers in because it doesn't create an experience for them to share. It merely relays information. Instead of joining the character on their journey, readers are kept out of it, forced to hear about events at a distance.

So don't tell readers the character is afraid. Use physical cues to show it. If you're in the character's point of view, share a thought or two that shows them struggling to process the triggering event. Add sensory details that engage the senses and make readers feel as though they're in the scene.

> A log shifted and crumbled in the fireplace, waking Julian from a doze. He blinked and closed the book in his lap. Past time for bed. He gathered breath to blow out the lamp when something thumped on the porch.
>
> His head whipped around. It had sounded like something heavy, but nothing seemed amiss. The door was barred, anyway. After a long moment of listening, he let go of his breath. Maybe a branch had fallen or a barrel had tipped over in the wind.
>
> Then a glaring light flashed, flooding the windows.
>
> Blinded, Julian stumbled to his feet. The door shook violently, and the bar rattled. A shrill keening rose on the porch, and he caught a whiff of sulfur. Heart pounding, he jammed his fists over his ears and scrambled back to the hearth, lips moving in a frantic prayer that was cut off as the door blew off its hinges.

A trick for identifying places where you've told the character's fear is to look for emotion being spelled out: *afraid, terrified, panicked, fearful,* etc. In most cases, these telling words can be replaced with stronger details that show the character's emotional state.

Too Much Description

Julian's example contains the right mix of sensory details, physical fear cues, and internal dialogue. Put together, they create a believable response. But it's not always easy to strike the right balance. Too much of any of these can turn a strong description into a tedious one.

To keep readers engaged, be judicious with physical cues. Choose only the ones your character would notice in their current state. As their fear grows, they'll continue to take in their surroundings but will register less of it while their focus is centered on the danger or threat. In a highly emotional scene, short, snappy details and sentences are your pacing friends.

Melodrama

Julian's example shows his fear so clearly that readers can see what he's feeling and maybe get a twinge of it themselves. This is possible because his emotions follow a natural progression. He begins at peace, becomes concerned at the unexpected sound outside, and surges to full-blown fear when the situation escalates.

Melodrama is created when we disregard the natural emotional progression and send characters immediately from a mild emotion to an intense one. This doesn't ring true for readers because they recognize that what they're reading isn't a realistic depiction of how fear escalates or feels.

To avoid this trap, plot the character's emotions to evolve naturally and sensibly. Be patient. Let the scene play out with enough escalations to move the character from one emotion to the next until they reach the level of fear you need.

Another cause of melodrama is overblown emotional reactions. A character who's always fainting, hyperventilating, or screaming in terror grates on readers' nerves because extreme responses like these aren't the norm. To prevent these problems, map out your character's emotional baseline so you're familiar with their emotional range and how they're likely to react. This gives you a blueprint for writing realistic, reasonable responses in those harrowing moments.

Lack of Sensory Details

Sensory details elevate descriptions, creating a multi-faceted world readers can see, hear, feel, smell, and taste. They pull readers into the scene, so we always want to include them.

Many writers get tripped up here because they're hyper-focused on maintaining a quick pace or relaying important information. But when we don't engage the senses—when we provide only visual details and dialogue—readers can't become fully immersed in the scene.

To see this in action, look back at Julian's example and read it without any sensory details: no shifting logs, no fiercely rattling door or unearthly shrieking, no stink of sulfur. Without those, the scene is reduced to a one-dimensional picture that readers must view from a distance.

Protect those sensory details, but write economically. Choose the ones that highlight important sounds, smells, and textures. With them, you'll provide contextual clues and keep readers engaged and attuned to the character's fear.

Repeated Fear Cues

We all struggle to some degree with conveying emotion well, so when we find fear cues that work, it's easy to fall back on them. But if a character's eyes are always going wide or their knees continually buckle, readers begin noticing the repetition and it pulls them out of the story. Vary your descriptions to give characters a wider range of reactions and avoid redundancy.

A similar problem arises when those cues transfer to other characters, and *everyone* is wide-eyed with knees on the verge of giving out. No two people are identical, so each person's response to fear (and what triggers it) should be different. Study your character and get a feel for how they each react. Many authors find character bibles helpful for recording and tracking emotional range, personality traits, nervous tics, and other factors that influence their character's reactions in moments of high emotion.

FINAL WORDS FROM THE AUTHORS

Whether they know it or not, your character's greatest fear is a major part of who they are. What frightens them the most, they'll avoid at all costs, making it a key motivator in the story you're writing. As such, it's imperative to take the time to ferret out your character's fear. Dig deep to unearth the wound that birthed it. Explore the fear's connection to their outer motivation and how it blocks them from achieving it. Map out and space turning points to provide opportunities for the character to face and overcome their fear or remain stuck in fear-based patterns.

This may not be easy, but that's okay, because authors are used to doing hard things. You do them every day when you build characters, plan stories, and sit down to write, and we hope this volume and its accompanying resources make your job a little easier.

A couple of closing notes about using *The Fear Thesaurus.*

First, remember that each entry is only a sampling of what's possible. There's not room or time to include every possible internal struggle, hindrance, and triggering scenario for each fear. This means the information we've gathered might only be a jumping-off point to find the perfect match for your character.

The good news is that *you* know what *is* perfect for them. Consider their temperament and tendencies, formative events from their past, and go-to habits and mannerisms. Apply those to the ideas we've shared, and adapt them to fit. We suggest making notes directly in your copy of the thesaurus, so your inventions can provide more inspiration for future characters.

Likewise, the list of fears covered in this book isn't exhaustive. There are so many events, scenarios, people, and objects a character might find frightening that it's simply not possible to fit them all between these covers. As we formulated our list, we focused on deep-seated fears that significantly limit characters and block them from achieving true happiness because we feel these are the most helpful to writers. If you can't find exactly what you're looking for, we've likely covered something similar, so check those fears for ideas.

We also wanted to make the fears as accessible as possible—hence, breaking them into needs-based categories. But as we mentioned, some fears are associated with multiple needs, meaning they could go into more than one group. If you're curious about all the ways a certain fear could affect your character, look at the **Human Needs That Could Be Impacted** field for that entry.

We learned a lot while writing this book, which led us to create more than the usual number of resources to help authors identify, explore, and convey their characters' fears. But space limitations are, well, limiting. So we've created a **Fear Thesaurus Companion Hub** (https://writershelpingwriters.net/fear-thesaurus-resource-companion-hub/) at Writers Helping Writers that's chock full of fear-related resources just for you, our dear reader:

Fear By Genre: Fear is present in every story, but genre shapes how its delivered and the forms it takes. This genre overview helps you identify fear categories that work best for each type of story and provides ideas for building tense moments and inner struggles that will pull readers in.

Character's Greatest Fear Worksheet: This printable helps you discover which fear is holding your character back so you can use it to plot the story and shape their character arc and behavior.

Fear Factor Workshop: Do you like presentation-style learning? We've baked up a special recorded workshop that pairs well with this book. Unlike the *Fear Factor* reality show, though, we won't make you eat anything horrific to access it!

We continue to be thrilled to offer craft resources that help writers do what they love most, and you humble us with your trust and support. As always, we're in your corner and wish you all the best in both your fictional worlds and the real one.

Happy writing!

THE FEAR THESAURUS

Survival Fears

BEING HUNTED OR PURSUED

NOTES: No matter how strong and resourceful a character is, someone or something will be higher up the food chain—a wild animal, person, alien lifeform, or supernatural creature. It may be hard to imagine being in someone's crosshairs, but for some characters, the risk to their survival is so intense, they live in fear of being caught.

WHAT IT LOOKS LIKE

Being on high alert all the time
Being very observant of their surroundings and those they encounter
Heightened safety protocols
Living in a place where the predator is unlikely to be (in a remote area off the grid, surrounded by people in a densely populated neighborhood, underground, etc.)
Moving frequently to avoid detection
Dressing and acting forgettable; doing nothing to call attention to themselves
Being as self-sufficient as possible
Carrying a weapon
Learning self-defense
Educating themselves about the person or creature who could be following them
Attempting to be undetectable (staying off social media, avoiding surveillance cameras, paying for everything in cash, etc.)
Avoiding relationships and connections
Varying their routines so it's harder for someone to track them
Working jobs that pay in cash
Being wary of strangers
Having an obscure, untraceable communication method to stay in touch with supporters
Banding together with others who are at risk
Sleeping lightly and restlessly
Keeping a go-bag (containing money, IDs, a change of clothes, etc.) at the ready

COMMON INTERNAL STRUGGLES

Never feeling safe
Being paranoid that someone is watching or following them
Constantly worrying about the safety of loved ones in their care
Being suspicious of everyone
Wanting to expand their support system but struggling to trust others
Needing to stay undetected but fearing the attempts are pointless
Being overwhelmed with thoughts of what will happen if the pursuer catches them
Struggling with the mental load of constant vigilance and a lack of sleep
Knowing the likelihood of someone hunting the character is miniscule but still needing to protect themselves and loved ones from the possibility

HINDRANCES AND DISRUPTIONS TO THE CHARACTER'S LIFE

Living their life always on the run and looking over their shoulder
Approaching others from a place of suspicion rather than one of openness

Always being in survival mode and unable to simply enjoy life
Suffering from exhaustion
Developing physical ailments from chronic stress (digestive issues, headaches, frequent illness, etc.)
Being short-tempered with trusted companions
Difficulty focusing on tasks
Relationship friction with children who don't appreciate the character's rules and restrictions
Viewing everything outside of escape and survival as frivolous and a waste of time
Being limited when traveling or accessing services that require credit cards or ID
Needing help but not seeking it out due to the danger of exposure
Struggling through life alone because it's easier to survive on their own

EMOTIONAL WOUNDS IT COULD STEM FROM: A Home Invasion, A Physical Assault, Battling a Mental Condition, Being Forced to Keep a Dark Secret, Being Forced to Leave One's Homeland, Being Held Captive, Being Stalked, Being Treated as Property, Living in a Dangerous Neighborhood, Living Through Civil Unrest

SCENARIOS THAT MIGHT TRIGGER THIS FEAR

Discovering that someone has been in the character's apartment
Being followed home from work
Someone new entering a loved one's life
Hearing sirens, gunshots, or other situational triggers associated with capture
Seeing what looks like someone being chased but turns out to be a dog running after its owner or children playing hide-and-seek
Being in a location that's being live-streamed or filmed by TV crews
Reading a news report of someone being attacked by a wild animal
Discovering that someone they know was caught and killed
Witnessing a crime and needing protection from a violent criminal
A child rebelling and stepping outside of the character's protection and control

HUMAN NEEDS THAT COULD BE IMPACTED

Self-Actualization: A character driven by a need to avoid detection or certain people will be limited in what they allow themselves to pursue or participate in.

Love and Belonging: A character who views others with suspicion or keeps people at a distance will have a lack of supportive, satisfying relationships.

Safety and Security: As long as the character fears being caught by someone or something they won't feel secure, no matter how many safeguards they put in place.

Physiological: If their fear is realized, they could be captured and executed.

HOW THE CHARACTER CAN MINIMIZE OR OVERCOME IT

Leaving behind an old identity and reinventing themselves completely
Recognizing that any past event that spawned this fear isn't likely to be repeated
Analyzing evidence and accepting that no one is after the character, that it's all in their head and there's nothing to fear
Finding a reasonable balance with living their life and safeguarding themselves
Making a habit of finding small joys and appreciating everyday life

BEING PHYSICALLY ATTACKED

NOTES: A fear of being attacked can arise for many reasons—from a past assault, witnessing a brutal beating, or even growing up being taught that the world is full of violent people. For your character, this could be a general fear or focus on a specific type of violence, such as a sexual assault, mugging, or hate crime. It could also be ever-present or only associated with a particular location or situation (in a parking lot at night, while jogging alone in the woods, etc.).

WHAT IT LOOKS LIKE
Refusing to travel alone
Not going certain places at night
Taking a martial arts or self-defense class
Carrying mace, pepper spray, a taser, or a firearm
Being suspicious of strangers
Always locking the doors and windows
Owning a watchdog
Being cautious about sharing information online
Sharing their location with people before leaving home
Not inviting new friends or dates to their home
Protecting their home with a security system
Saving emergency numbers on speed dial
The character being on high alert when they're in public
Being skilled at reading people
Avoiding certain types of places (downtown, busy streets, etc.)
Keeping both hands free when walking
When in public, choosing a seat against the wall so they aren't approached from behind
Flinching at noises and unexpected movements
Being nervous around certain kinds of people (if a past assault figures into this fear)
Rubbing or touching the site of an old injury when they're afraid
Adhering to a security routine (checking all windows and doors before bed, reviewing security footage frequently, using devices to secure hotel doors on vacation, etc.)
Having weapons stashed around the home
Insomnia
Having nightmares about being attacked

COMMON INTERNAL STRUGGLES
Being uncomfortable in new places
Not trusting people of a certain race or gender—even though they know most people are harmless
Reading into things and second-guessing the motivations of others
Wanting to achieve intimacy with a romantic partner but being unable to go there
Being unable to relax when they're in a crowd or a public space
Jumping to conclusions about people and situations

Worrying obsessively about the safety of their children
Constantly feeling like they're being watched or stalked
What-if scenarios playing on an endless mental loop

HINDRANCES AND DISRUPTIONS TO THE CHARACTER'S LIFE

Being unable to enjoy dates or outings with others
Their children growing up extremely sheltered and overprotected
Their activities being limited because they can't go anywhere alone
Consistently getting inadequate sleep
Being too afraid to leave their own house
Being unable to fully trust others

EMOTIONAL WOUNDS IT COULD STEM FROM: A Home Invasion, A Physical Assault, A School Shooting, Being Bullied, Being Tortured, Being Victimized by a Perpetrator Who Was Never Caught, Domestic Abuse, Living in a Dangerous Neighborhood, Living with an Abusive Caregiver, Losing a Loved One to a Random Act of Violence, Witnessing Violence at a Young Age

SCENARIOS THAT MIGHT TRIGGER THIS FEAR

The character having to visit a setting that's typically associated with crime
Having to take public transportation
Their cell phone getting lost, breaking, or running out of juice
Getting stranded far from home
A shooting, mugging, or other act of violence occurring close to home or work
Being stared at by a stranger
Being harassed
Being threatened
A violent person re-entering the character's life
A change that impacts the character's safety (their dog dying, gun laws becoming stricter, etc.)
The character's job requiring them to travel or transfer to a different office
A loved one being targeted and harassed

HUMAN NEEDS THAT COULD BE IMPACTED

Esteem and Recognition: A fearful character may be viewed by others as cowardly, timid, or even paranoid. Their inability to go certain places or interact with some people can cause others to think less of them.

Love and Belonging: A character with this fear may have trouble being intimate or even being physically touched by loved ones. This can cause friction with friends and family members who don't understand the root cause and misinterpret this behavior as a lack of trust.

HOW THE CHARACTER CAN MINIMIZE OR OVERCOME IT

Taking steps to feel empowered to protect themselves (mastering self-defense, etc.)
Maintaining a protocol of keeping in touch with loved ones
Recognizing there are many more good people than bad ones in the world
Seeking therapy to associate this fear with just the perpetrator, not all people

DEATH

NOTES: Most people are afraid of dying; it's part of being human. Often it hits in the moment, say after a near-miss traffic event or a loved one's troubling diagnosis. But it can also linger in the background, particularly around significant birthday milestones or sleepless nights, when it's hard to ignore life's big questions. This fear can be crippling when it becomes an obsession or turns into a phobia that causes panic and anxiety when no logical threat is present.

WHAT IT LOOKS LIKE

Being risk-averse
Frequently checking for signs of illness or disease
Taking vitamins and supplements
Being a very cautious driver
Making purchases based on safety ratings
Making fear-based decisions
An inability to visit people in hospice care
Avoiding cemeteries, funeral homes, and other places associated with death
Checking in frequently on sick loved ones
Refusing to watch movies that show pain, suffering, and death
Avoiding hospitals
Not having a pet (because pets die)
Protecting children to the point of smothering them
Being overly concerned about germs
Shying away from potentially dangerous or thrill-seeking activities (skydiving, storm chasing, running at night, etc.)
Being reluctant to travel far from home
Avoiding travel methods the character deems risky
Not celebrating holidays associated with death (Halloween, the Day of the Dead, etc.)
Running to the doctor for every small thing
Ignoring concerning physical symptoms
Sharing news stories about dangerous places that people should avoid
Exercising obsessively
Putting off getting life insurance, creating a will, etc.
Embracing the belief that existence, in some form, goes on after death
Doing good deeds in this life to balance the scales so they won't be punished in the next one
Insisting on over-the-top safety precautions
Suffering from insomnia or frequent nightmares

COMMON INTERNAL STRUGGLES

The character falling sick and thinking they've contracted a deadly disease
Worrying that they won't be able to accomplish everything they want to before they die
Not being able to rest when loved ones are away from home
Anxiety rising when the character sees a news report about someone dying

Desperately wanting to know the truth about the afterlife but not having any proof
Knowing their actions are driving family members away but being unable to lighten up
Obsessing over exercising regularly and eating healthy
Struggling with paranoia

HINDRANCES AND DISRUPTIONS TO THE CHARACTER'S LIFE
Missing out on opportunities to try new things
Being reclusive and living a life of isolation
Their health being such a priority that they don't have time for other activities
Other people avoiding the character because of their neediness, restrictive rules, and obsessive need for safety
Having to take medication to control anxiety and depression
Spending so much time worrying about death that they lose all joy and happiness

EMOTIONAL WOUNDS IT COULD STEM FROM: A Carjacking, A Child Dying on One's Watch, A House Fire, A Life-Threatening Accident, A Physical Assault, A School Shooting, A Terminal Illness Diagnosis, Accidentally Killing Someone, Bearing the Responsibility for Many Deaths, Being Trapped in a Collapsed Building

SCENARIOS THAT MIGHT TRIGGER THIS FEAR
Experiencing a life-threatening situation, such as a car accident or a tropical storm
The character or their loved one being diagnosed with a terminal illness
A loved one dying unexpectedly
Witnessing someone dying
Having a near-death experience
Suffering a serious injury
Milestone birthdays that represent the passage of time
Seeing signs of aging as they get older

HUMAN NEEDS THAT COULD BE IMPACTED

Love and Belonging: This fear can lead to certain flaws, such as being needy, paranoid, or controlling, that may make friends and loved ones want to avoid the character.

Physiological Needs: Taken to a big enough extreme, the denial associated with this fear can cause a character to forgo wellness visits, reject difficult diagnoses, or refuse treatment for illnesses, ensuring that death arrives sooner than it should.

HOW THE CHARACTER CAN MINIMIZE OR OVERCOME IT
Acknowledging that while death is painful to think about, it's natural and isn't all bad because it ends pain and suffering
Being present and focusing on what's happening, not what will happen
Practicing letting things go by giving cherished items away or donating items to charities
Focusing on living without regret by choosing meaningful goals and working toward them

PHYSICAL PAIN

NOTES: Pain is something we all want to avoid, but it's a part of life that has to be dealt with. A character who fears the discomfort that comes with being injured will live life on the safer side. And if they're unable to rein in their fear, it could develop into a phobia.

WHAT IT LOOKS LIKE

Taking extreme care in all areas of their lives
Being sensitive to hot and cold temperature variations
Choosing safe substitutes—using plastic cups instead of glass, for example
Hiring people to handle home repairs and maintenance
Wearing gloves to wash dishes or clean the house
Not listening to loud music that could induce a headache
Handling pets with care (avoiding teeth and claws)
Avoiding certain textures (prickly, rough, sharp, jagged, etc.)
Avoiding activities that could lead to injury (sports, bungee jumping, working out, etc.)
Being resistant to leaving a place of comfort
Inefficiency due to being very careful and taking more time to complete tasks
Being sidelined by minor injuries or illnesses
Becoming obsessed with safety measures (only driving when traffic is light, installing non-slip strips on the stairs, wearing protective gear, etc.)
Avoiding routine medical procedures
Being afraid of needles
Taking a lot of pain medications
Avoiding treatment measures that would cause pain (physical therapy, getting a massage, stitches, body waxing, etc.)
Being a difficult patient for caregivers
Being a helicopter parent (not allowing their children to do what others are doing, etc.)
Becoming a hypochondriac
Imagining they're in pain when they're not (or believing the pain is worse than it is)
Becoming addicted to painkillers

COMMON INTERNAL STRUGGLES

Catastrophizing
Constantly self-analyzing, looking for areas of pain or discomfort
Wanting to participate in an activity or with a group of people but being too afraid
Knowing they're making themselves look strange to others but not knowing how to stop
Hating that their rules and limits are hurting their relationships with loved ones
Judging others for being reckless
Viewing themselves as cowardly

HINDRANCES AND DISRUPTIONS TO THE CHARACTER'S LIFE

Having to plan everything out rather than be spontaneous
Being unable to participate in certain activities
Constantly worrying that they (or a loved one) will end up hurt

Passing their worry and fear to their children
Inconvenience (due to all the things the character must avoid) making life more difficult than it has to be
Small medical issues becoming big ones because the character refuses treatment options that will inflict short-term pain
The character being unable to accurately assess their physical health because they always envision the worst

EMOTIONAL WOUNDS IT COULD STEM FROM: A Physical Assault, A Terminal Illness Diagnosis, Being Raised by Overprotective Parents, Being Tortured, Being Trapped in a Collapsed Building, Domestic Abuse, Living with a Critical Medical Diagnosis, Living with Chronic Pain or Illness

SCENARIOS THAT MIGHT TRIGGER THIS FEAR

Getting the flu or food poisoning
A new source of physical pain or discomfort
A minor physical problem that requires ongoing treatment
A loved one wanting to participate in an activity that the character deems risky
Being denied access to painkillers
An emergency where pain or injury are likely, such as being caught in a natural disaster
The character learning they're pregnant
Being diagnosed with a chronic illness
Intermittent pain that doctors can't diagnose
Seeing their child start to exhibit the same fear of pain

HUMAN NEEDS THAT COULD BE IMPACTED

Self-Actualization: A character with this fear will avoid things that are commonplace for many people. This can result in them becoming dissatisfied with their life when they realize how limited they are in comparison to others.

Esteem and Recognition: Without context, others may think less of the character because they view them as fearful, weak, or dramatic.

Love and Belonging: Friends can become frustrated with a character who will only spend time with them on their own terms. Additionally, loved ones chafing under the character's unreasonable rules and expectations may grow resentful, rebellious, or defiant as time goes on.

Physiological Needs: For a character who avoids treatments and is unable to objectively diagnose their health, minor maladies can quickly become serious and even life-threatening.

HOW THE CHARACTER CAN MINIMIZE OR OVERCOME IT

Practicing meditation, breathing techniques, or tapping to stave off fear
Following safety measures during activities
Accepting that pain has an important role and it's necessary for survival
Seeking therapy to address trauma and manage the fear so they can live more fully
Trying hypnosis as a therapy
Experiencing pain on a tiny scale to help put it in perspective
Reflecting on what they'll regret if they allow this fear to restrict how they live

Stability and Control Fears

BEING FORCED INTO A PREDETERMINED FATE

NOTES: Because human beings value autonomy, they typically don't appreciate being herded toward a certain destiny. Unfortunately for some characters, their culture, status, or predicament may come with certain expectations, such as ascending a throne, marrying early, or taking over the family business. The fear of being trapped in this way can intensify feelings of not being in control and the desire to push back or escape.

WHAT IT LOOKS LIKE

Living a life that looks different from their upbringing
Holding firmly to personal preferences
Avoiding family members who exert too much influence
Rejecting religious or cultural norms
Engaging in dangerous activities to test fate
Viewing family members as oppressors
Spending a lot of time soul-searching
Criticizing people who follow societal or cultural expectations
Turning to outsiders for support, approval, and validation
Job-hopping to find something that suits their preferences
Avoiding gatherings where people will impose their will or opinions on the character
Pursuing goals that directly oppose what's expected
Coming across as combative or oppositional
Viewing themselves as more enlightened than those around them
Actively exploring religions or cultures other than their own
Refusing to follow the same path as their elders or family members
Building relationships with people outside the family or culture
Dressing in ways that defy cultural or societal expectations
Choosing romantic partners that their loved ones won't approve of
Not asking for help or advice; being staunchly self-reliant
Questioning or fighting everything the people in charge stand for
Looking at their fate in binary terms; seeing only one option or the other
Physically running away to live far from unwanted influences
Joining an activist group that opposes the character's cultural or religious standards
Dedicating their life to finding an alternative to the fate they fear
Hiding their identity (if the character is publicly associated with their fate)

COMMON INTERNAL STRUGGLES

Feeling drawn to some elements of their heritage but fearing that accepting them means also accepting their destiny
Wanting a different future but worrying that pursuing it will harm their important relationships
Feeling selfish or ungrateful for bucking the system and causing problems
Having mixed feelings toward loved ones
Fearing eternal damnation for being disobedient or denying their fate
Feeling misunderstood, lost, and questioning their own identity

Resenting that a predetermined fate puts them in a box
Second-guessing their choices and questioning their own motivations and desires
Wanting to be happy but also wanting to please others
Feeling incapable of handling the pressure of the expectations

HINDRANCES AND DISRUPTIONS TO THE CHARACTER'S LIFE
Being cut off by family members, society, or a religious organization
Rejecting everything tied to their destiny (even good things) and feeling adrift
Becoming stubborn and inflexible
Loved ones being punished because of the character's choices
Being threatened by those pressuring the character to accept their destiny
Having to deal with manipulative loved ones pressuring them to make a certain choice
Making impulsive decisions to avoid their fate that have negative consequences (marrying the wrong person, striking out on their own without financial resources, etc.)

EMOTIONAL WOUNDS IT COULD STEM FROM: An Abuse of Power, Being Bullied, Being Let Down by a Trusted Organization or Social System, Being Treated as Property, Growing up in a Cult, Growing up in the Public Eye, Growing up in the Shadow of a Successful Sibling, Having a Controlling or Overly Strict Parent

SCENARIOS THAT MIGHT TRIGGER THIS FEAR
A prophecy being shared that reveals the character's fate
An approaching milestone that is tied to the destiny
A trusted ally or lover pushing the character to accept their fate
A final option for avoiding the fate being removed
A friend or family member giving in to their own predetermined fate
Escaping the fate, then being forcibly returned to it

HUMAN NEEDS THAT COULD BE IMPACTED

Self-Actualization: If escape requires the character to deny the truth, their heritage, or certain aspects of their identity, they may have a hard time feeling fully actualized.

Esteem and Recognition: If the character is ridiculed or shunned for avoiding their fate, or if doing so causes them to feel shame, it can damage their self-worth.

Love and Belonging: A character whose decision puts them at odds with loved ones or their own culture may struggle to maintain meaningful relationships.

Safety and Security: If the character's resistance puts them (or their loved ones) in danger, their safety will be impacted.

HOW THE CHARACTER CAN MINIMIZE OR OVERCOME IT
Taking control by making decisions for themselves, even if there are limits
Refusing to allow others to have any more control than required (if their fate is set)
Asking themselves what they want, and taking steps to secure it
Leaning into their uniqueness by choosing their own passions, hobbies, etc.

BEING POWERLESS

NOTES: This fear arises when a character worries they could lose a measure of control and be unable to alter their situation, influence outcomes, or make decisions that matter. The anxiety that their agency will be removed (which may be true or merely imagined) is often based on personal experience—a time when they couldn't change their circumstances and had to endure the discomfort of being stuck.

WHAT IT LOOKS LIKE

Experiencing discomfort when thinking about the future
Uneasily taking stock of what they don't have control over or what isn't going well
Identifying disruptive forces that could take things in a bad direction
Looking for possible power dynamics that could put the character at a disadvantage
Always needing to be in charge (and a tendency to micromanage)
Questioning everything and everyone
Preferring to work independently
Setting firm boundaries with others
Being reluctant (or refusing) to marry
Choosing submissive romantic partners
Not going into debt or owing anyone favors
Over-researching any ideas or possibilities that could create a power imbalance
Always having to be strong and at their best
Being fiercely self-reliant
Being hyper-aware of possible dangers
Monitoring the news closely
Actively safeguarding their personal rights as a citizen
Protecting their property and materials (with a security system, dogs, fencing, etc.)
Being hyper-sensitive to being taken advantage of
Going on the defensive when they feel vulnerable
Being confrontational
Setting strict (often unreasonable) rules for their children
Obsessing over their health
Stockpiling resources
Being risk-averse to avoid a setback or loss
Hiding their mistakes
Maintaining careful records of everything (emails, bills, receipts, wills, etc.)
Abstaining from substances that dull the senses (drugs, alcohol, anesthesia, etc.)

COMMON INTERNAL STRUGGLES

Always expecting the other shoe to drop
Wanting companionship but not being able to trust others
Doubting people's motives
Wanting to be more spontaneous but feeling compelled to plan everything
Being intensely uncomfortable with vulnerability
Being paranoid; believing others are trying to oppress the character when they're not

Difficulty relaxing outside of their safe spaces
Struggling with negativity or cynicism

HINDRANCES AND DISRUPTIONS TO THE CHARACTER'S LIFE
Not traveling (to avoid uncontrollable variables)
Working too much so they can build up their savings
Turning down invitations for adventure
Being unable to relinquish control
Clashing with others who have strong personalities
Being seen as controlling, rigid, and unreasonable
Having to avoid crowds
An inability to be vulnerable making deep relationships impossible
Needing to do extensive research before making decisions

EMOTIONAL WOUNDS IT COULD STEM FROM: A Carjacking, A Physical Assault, A Terrorist Attack, An Abuse of Power, Being Held Captive, Being Sexually Violated, Being Treated as Property, Domestic Abuse, Making a Very Public Mistake, Misplaced Loyalty

SCENARIOS THAT MIGHT TRIGGER THIS FEAR
A romantic partner showing signs of being controlling or not respecting boundaries
Encountering a bully
Being arrested under false pretenses
Needing surgery and being given anesthesia
Being scammed or blackmailed
The character's boss making unwanted advances
Suffering physical abuse at the hands of a loved one
Having to quarantine
Being personally targeted in some way
Getting audited

HUMAN NEEDS THAT COULD BE IMPACTED
Self-Actualization: A character who is fearful of being stripped of their freedom or agency may choose low-risk pursuits that give them more control, limiting their options.
Love and Belonging: Deep connections require vulnerability, and someone who's uncomfortable with that will have difficulty taking relationships to an intimate level.
Safety and Security: A character who needs complete control over everything to feel safe will never be truly secure. They'll always feel at risk.

HOW THE CHARACTER CAN MINIMIZE OR OVERCOME IT
Naming the fear to understand it and what's behind it
Taking on small challenges and following through on them
Making independent choices and decisions and owning the outcome
Being accountable for mistakes and fixing them (reclaiming power)
Becoming more mindful and present; focusing on what is, not what could go wrong

BEING RETURNED TO AN ABUSIVE ENVIRONMENT

NOTES: Any character who has been removed from an abusive environment, whether as a child or an adult, will fear having to return to it. The anxiety this possibility triggers can create a host of physical, mental, and emotional reactions, even if the event is unlikely to happen.

WHAT IT LOOKS LIKE

Being careful about their surroundings
Using a pseudonym online and never sharing identifying information
Being careful about who they let into their life
Difficulty trusting or opening up to new people
Heightened self-awareness about their environment and being safe
Rarely going anywhere alone
Staying in touch with police (about an incarcerated abuser or ongoing investigation)
Being triggered by sounds, smells, or other things associated with that environment
Becoming physically ill (nausea, headaches, digestive issues, hair loss, rashes, etc.) at the thought of having to return
Reading into situations and easily believing them to be dangerous
Pleading their case with anyone who will listen
Suffering from PTSD
Taking drugs or using alcohol to manage their fear
Having nightmares about the environment or their abusers
Carrying a weapon
Becoming obsessed with self-defense
Being desperately eager to please their current caregivers and stay in their good graces
Creating an escape plan in case they're forced to return
Hoarding money, travel supplies, and food so they can leave quickly if needed
Threatening to harm themselves if they're forced to go back
Running away if they suspect they're in danger

COMMON INTERNAL STRUGGLES

Having mixed feelings about the abuser (especially if they're a family member or are still in the character's life)
Trying and failing to stop thinking about abusive episodes
Struggling with suicidal thoughts
Fantasizing about neutralizing the abuser
Feeling paranoid that the abuser or someone in his employ is watching the character
Struggling with unearned self-blame (believing they were somehow at fault)
Wanting to move forward but not feeling safe enough to do so

HINDRANCES AND DISRUPTIONS TO THE CHARACTER'S LIFE

Avoiding romance to keep from falling into another abusive relationship
Becoming addicted to alcohol or drugs

Insomnia impacting the character's work or school performance
Being unable to trust the social systems or people who should protect the character
Becoming homebound to avoid their abuser
Having to move frequently to avoid the abuser or people who work for them
Not bothering to build deep relationships because of the ongoing threat of being returned to the abusive environment

EMOTIONAL WOUNDS IT COULD STEM FROM: A Physical Assault, An Abuse of Power, Being Forced to Keep a Dark Secret, Being Sexually Violated, Being Tortured, Being Treated as Property, Childhood Sexual Abuse by a Known Person, Domestic Abuse, Growing up in a Cult, Growing up in Foster Care, Incest, Living with an Abusive Caregiver, Prejudice or Discrimination

SCENARIOS THAT MIGHT TRIGGER THIS FEAR

Being contacted by the abuser or their family members
Suspecting that a friend is being abused
Watching a movie where someone is reclaimed by their abuser
Having to confront the abuser in court
An anniversary date or event that's associated with past abuse
Running into the person (or people close to them) in a social situation
Being contacted by others who were involved in the abuse
Being told by loved ones or friends that the character is overreacting—that the abuse didn't happen, they should move on, etc.

HUMAN NEEDS THAT COULD BE IMPACTED

Self-Actualization: A character in this situation will be driven by fear, limited in where they're able to go, who they can be with, and the activities they feel comfortable participating in. This is not living life to the fullest.

Love and Belonging: If the character's response to this fear negatively impacts the important people in their life, friction and strife will weaken those relationships.

Safety and Security: Even if there is no plausible threat of the character being returned to the situation, this type of trauma leaves a mark. The presence of fear means never forgetting what happened and, quite possibly, never feeling truly secure.

HOW THE CHARACTER CAN MINIMIZE OR OVERCOME IT

Relocating to put distance between themselves and the risk
Pursuing justice so those who hurt the character are held accountable
Applying for a restraining order
Asking for police protection
Joining a survivor's group
Speaking out as a survivor to raise awareness
Seeking therapy for anxiety disorders or PTSD
Cutting ties with anyone who enabled the situation to happen

BEING UNSAFE

NOTES: Safety is a basic human need. When it's lost, everything can feel like a threat. The idiom *being scared of your own shadow* isn't far from the truth for a character with this fear, which can progress to the point of them being unable to leave home. Their unease can be limited to certain places and people or encompass everyone and everywhere, including places that used to feel safe.

WHAT IT LOOKS LIKE

The character being edgy when they're alone
Always erring on the side of caution
Being short-tempered and snappy
Isolating themselves and loved ones from the outside world
Experiencing physical ailments associated with worry (headaches from grinding their teeth, ulcers, fatigue, etc.)
Nervous habits—wringing their hands, biting their nails, etc.
Not going out after dark
Frequently checking locks
Not going anywhere alone
Avoiding certain parts of town
Believing the worst about people
Being obsessed with self-defense and home defense
Being overprotective of loved ones
Becoming confrontational when cornered
Being perceived as unfriendly or standoffish
Identifying exits and possible threats when entering a room
Constant exhaustion from always being on high alert
Carrying a weapon, such as a gun, taser, or pepper spray
Investing in security measures (a dog, a security system, a concealed carry permit, etc.)
Obsessing over news accounts of people being attacked
Distrusting the police or those in authority

COMMON INTERNAL STRUGGLES

Being unable to relax and enjoy life
Questioning the motives of others, never taking friendliness at face value
Feeling compelled to flee a situation despite there being no visible threat
Wanting to go out with friends but being too overwhelmed with worry
Missing opportunities due to a fear of traveling alone, at night, or in a strange place
Being compelled to protect family and friends despite knowing those efforts are pushing them farther away
Not wanting to watch the news but being unable to stop
Feeling like a burden (because they can't stay alone, need someone to drive them after dark, etc.)
Disliking the perception they're creating about themselves but not being able to change

HINDRANCES AND DISRUPTIONS TO THE CHARACTER'S LIFE

Having to schedule their plans around other people's timetables
Being out of touch with the real world
Living as a recluse
Being limited professionally because of their fears
Being pitied, judged, or rejected by others
Difficulty trusting others
Declining health due to poor sleep, an inability to eat, and high blood pressure

EMOTIONAL WOUNDS IT COULD STEM FROM: A Carjacking, A Home Invasion, A House Fire, A Life-Threatening Accident, A Parent's Abandonment or Rejection, A Physical Assault, A School Shooting, A Terrorist Attack, Being Stalked, Domestic Abuse

SCENARIOS THAT MIGHT TRIGGER THIS FEAR

A stranger approaching the character's house at night
Feeling watched in a restaurant or store
A loved one getting involved with someone the character doesn't trust
Being a victim of a home invasion
A car backfiring, fireworks going off, a barking dog, or other unexpected noises
Returning home and discovering an unlocked door or window
Losing a driver's license or other document containing sensitive information
The political climate changing for the worse
Hearing a friend's firsthand account of an attack or violation
Being pulled over by police in an isolated spot
A child not arriving when they were supposed to

HUMAN NEEDS THAT COULD BE IMPACTED

Self-Actualization: A character with this fear will avoid situations that would help them pursue a dream or reach their potential if there's an element of risk involved, making it difficult for them to live life to the fullest.

Esteem and Recognition: The way the character responds to this fear may make them appear needy, clingy, fussy, or paranoid. This can negatively impact the way others perceive them.

Love and Belonging: People close to the character may become frustrated with the character's rules, seeing them as a means of control or a lack of trust.

HOW THE CHARACTER CAN MINIMIZE OR OVERCOME IT

Focusing on what's within their control and letting everything else go
Taking reasonable steps to make their home environment feel safe
Challenging suspicions to determine whether a perceived threat is logical or illogical
Following a routine that helps them feel safe (double-checking locks, closing blinds, parking in a well-lit lot, avoiding certain locations at night, etc.)
Researching places before visiting so the character knows what to expect
Using a comfort item to ground themselves against intrusive thoughts

BEING WATCHED

NOTES: A certain amount of attention is expected or even welcomed—but not by everyone. Some characters develop an aversion to being stared at, scrutinized, or actively watched due to a sensitivity, past trauma, safety concerns, or the need to protect their boundaries. Someone with this fear may be limited in how they interact with people and the wider world, making it more difficult for them to connect with others.

WHAT IT LOOKS LIKE

Physically covering up with layers of clothing
Not making eye contact
Being combative when someone is staring (glaring back at them, calling them out, starting a fight, etc.)
Scanning the room to see who might be watching them
Avoiding roles and responsibilities that would require the character to speak publicly or address a group
Refraining from activities that would draw attention, such as playing a sport
The character connecting with others and expressing themselves creatively through platforms that don't involve face-to-face communication (social media, a blog, etc.)
Adopting a demeanor that doesn't draw attention (head bowed, eyes averted, a quiet voice, etc.)
Attending video meetings with the camera turned off
Being uncomfortable when their picture is taken
Avoiding doctor appointments because of the scrutiny involved
Refusing to eat in public spaces
Difficulty navigating conversations with active listeners who are highly attentive
The character having anxiety or panic attack symptoms when they're forced to endure scrutiny (during an interview, in a police interrogation, while giving a presentation, etc.)
Telling even well-intentioned friends and loved ones to stop looking at them

COMMON INTERNAL STRUGGLES

Being confused when they say they're feeling scrutinized and a trusted friend claims this isn't the case
Struggling with paranoia
Wanting to attend a party or social event but not feeling like they can
Wanting to be free to enjoy the moment yet feeling unable to
Knowing that their fear makes them look strange but being unable to change
Experiencing self-loathing for holding onto an irrational fear
Just wanting to be like everyone else
Feeling weak and defective

HINDRANCES AND DISRUPTIONS TO THE CHARACTER'S LIFE

Friction with friends and loved ones who feel rebuffed when the character tells them not to look at them
Clashing with law enforcement personnel, who see the character as cagey or evasive

Living an isolated life
Avoiding social activities that could bring the character joy and fulfillment
Feeling more comfortable connecting with people on social media than in person
Not living up to their full potential (due to chronic underachieving to avoid attention)
The fear escalating into a mental health issue like social anxiety or a panic attack disorder
Difficulty with physical intimacy

EMOTIONAL WOUNDS IT COULD STEM FROM: A Physical Disfigurement, A Speech Impediment, A Traumatic Brain Injury, Battling a Mental Condition, Being Humiliated by Others, Being so Beautiful It's All People See, Being Stalked, Falling Short of Society's Physical Standards, Growing up in the Public Eye, Social Difficulties

SCENARIOS THAT MIGHT TRIGGER THIS FEAR

Losing a supportive family member or friend who understood the character
Facing a situation where scrutiny can't be avoided (a meeting with Human Resources about a work infraction, being pulled over by a police officer, etc.)
A family member being thrust into the public eye, resulting in reduced privacy for the character
Being asked to do something the character wants to do that involves higher scrutiny
Being told they were seen somewhere (at the mall, out walking, at the grocery store, etc.) when the character didn't know they were being observed
The character suspecting someone is following them

HUMAN NEEDS THAT COULD BE IMPACTED

Self-Actualization: A character with this fear will stay in the shadows and reject opportunities that could thrust them into the spotlight. This narrows their options and may limit their ability to reach their full potential.

Esteem and Recognition: A character who grows flustered or irritated when people look at them may be viewed as insecure or socially awkward. The character may also question themselves, wondering why they react the way they do.

Love and Belonging: Since a certain level of eye contact is normal in most relationships, an aversion to it can put people off or make it difficult for the character to connect with others.

HOW THE CHARACTER CAN MINIMIZE OR OVERCOME IT

Making strategic choices in public (entering the room last, taking a seat at the back, etc.)
Finding ways to feel anonymous (wearing sunglasses, dressing nondescriptly, etc.)
Using an online pseudonym to gain distance from a real life identity
Trying gradual exposure to build up the ability to tolerate being observed
Opting for less intimidating social settings—meeting with one person (not a group) or choosing a restaurant with booths instead of open-view tables
Choosing plastic surgery if altering their appearance will restore their confidence or make them feel more safe
Respectfully sharing their discomfort around staring and scrutiny so loved ones can adjust their interactions with the character

CERTAIN EMOTIONS

NOTES: Not all people are comfortable experiencing a full range of emotions. This could be from not being able to exhibit a feeling as a child, cultural dynamics, or a wounding event they're trying to avoid. Regardless of the cause, a character with this fear will be emotionally stunted and may have difficulty fully relating to others.

WHAT IT LOOKS LIKE

Seeming to have their act together and be in control
Meticulously planning so they know what to expect from any situation
Sticking to a safe routine
Only socializing in large groups (to avoid deep connections)
Refusing to talk about their past
Overcompensating to appear emotionally strong
Avoiding events where the emotion might arise
Being watchful for triggers (people, places, situations, etc.) that could cause them to feel things they don't want to
Faking the expected responses
Steering conversations away from topics that could lead to uncomfortable emotions
Avoiding melodrama and overly dramatic people
Trying to appear carefree
Keeping conversations more surface-level, and moving on if they get intense
Avoiding change
Showing discomfort when the emotion arises or is present in others
Leaving the room when the emotion comes on
Other emotions emerging (anger, fear, anxiety, etc.) if the character tries to express the unwanted one
Using compartmentalization and intellectualization to avoid feeling certain things
Exhibiting unexpected responses to stimuli (not crying when bad news is given, not showing fear in a situation where it would be natural, etc.)
Viewing people who exhibit the emotion as weak

COMMON INTERNAL STRUGGLES

Feeling proud for suppressing emotions while worrying it might not be healthy
Feeling a buildup of internal emotional pressure
Being haunted by the past but knowing that dealing with it would be painful
Being exhausted from constantly policing and burying their emotions
Worrying about what others think
Being overwhelmed with anxiety at the onset of the emotion
Dissociating at the onset of the emotion

HINDRANCES AND DISRUPTIONS TO THE CHARACTER'S LIFE

Avoiding people and situations that are likely to bring the emotion about
Appearing "off" to others, creating worry and concern

Being limited in how deep they can go emotionally in their relationships
Not being able to enjoy what others do (movies, celebratory moments, etc.)
Being isolated from others
Being unable to comfort someone who's struggling
Not being able to fully express their feelings
Wanting to let someone in to explain what's going on but being unable to

EMOTIONAL WOUNDS IT COULD STEM FROM: A Toxic Relationship, A Traumatic Brain Injury, Battling a Mental Condition, Being Forced to Keep a Dark Secret, Being Raised by Parents Who Loved Conditionally, Growing up in a Cult, Growing up in Foster Care, Having a Controlling or Overly Strict Parent, Living in an Emotionally Repressed Household

SCENARIOS THAT MIGHT TRIGGER THIS FEAR
Using drugs or alcohol that lower the character's inhibitions
Having a panic attack
Receiving bad news unexpectedly (a medical diagnosis, becoming pregnant, a loved one dying, etc.)
A situation where the character is expected to be vulnerable
Revisiting a place linked to past emotional highs or lows
A loved one confiding about a traumatic experience
Coming across long-lost items that bring back the past
Having to attend therapy
Witnessing something traumatic
The character being confronted about their inability to express anger, joy, disappointment, etc.

HUMAN NEEDS THAT COULD BE IMPACTED

Self-Actualization: A character with this fear will avoid the things that make them feel certain emotions, restricting them from doing everything they'd like to do.

Esteem and Recognition: A character who recognizes their inability to deal with an emotion that others can easily handle may feel incapable or inadequate.

Love and Belonging: If the character picks and chooses what emotions are safe enough to feel, they'll struggle to be vulnerable, which is a part of all healthy relationships.

Safety and Security: Safety could become compromised for a character who chooses to self-medicate rather than face uncomfortable feelings.

HOW THE CHARACTER CAN MINIMIZE OR OVERCOME IT
Naming the emotion and tying it to what is being experienced in the body
Understanding the emotion's purpose (fear alerts us to danger, anxiety is discomfort over the unknown, etc.)
Acknowledging the event that created the character's difficulty with their emotion(s)
Exploring how repressing this emotion is holding them back
Gentle exposure to the emotion (through books, movies, etc.)
Seeking therapy to help them process the emotion in a safe way

CERTAIN KINDS OF PEOPLE

NOTES: A person who has been traumatized may become fearful of the kind of person who hurt them—men, women, people of a certain race or nationality, members of law enforcement, etc. There can be other causes, such as an irrational fear resulting from a mental health condition or being raised to be afraid of specific people groups. Regardless of where it comes from, a fearful mindset toward a type of person will restrict who the character is willing to interact with, placing limits around what they'll be able to do.

WHAT IT LOOKS LIKE

Attributing one negative interaction to an entire type of person or group
Being hyperaware of their surroundings
Avoiding places where the people they fear are likely to be
The character labeling people they don't really know
Using hurtful stereotypes when speaking about the people they fear
Being watchful of things associated with them—the clothing they wear or certain hangout spaces—and immediately associating danger with them
Speaking disparagingly about this group
Becoming anxious when a person from this group is near
Crossing the street to avoid this kind of person
Gravitating toward media that affirms their bias (watching movies with certain kinds of people as the bad guys, subscribing to podcasts that affirm their beliefs, etc.)
The character's demeanor changing when someone from that group enters their space (falling silent, watching them furtively, becoming confrontational, etc.)
Showing signs of physical distress in their presence: going pale, extremities trembling, accelerated breathing, clenched fists, etc.
The character surrounding themselves with people like them
Taking a work-from-home job to avoid those they fear
Others viewing the character as ignorant, biased, or discriminatory
Strained relationships with family because of the character's ideas about certain people
Warning children away from this group of people (passing on the bias)
Speaking out against that people group to protect others

COMMON INTERNAL STRUGGLES

The character being challenged when they meet someone who breaks the stereotype
Wanting to shelter loved ones from certain kinds of people but being unable to do so, or not understanding why they don't believe that group is a threat
Recognizing their fear may be irrational but not being able to change the fear response
Knowing their fear is interfering with their friendships but clinging to it anyway
Feeling misunderstood

HINDRANCES AND DISRUPTIONS TO THE CHARACTER'S LIFE

Missing out on social interactions where certain people might be present
Having limited work options

Having few friends (because they can't accept the character's bias)
Other people not being able to relate because the character's ideas are so out-there
Having to defend themselves to people who disagree with them
Losing friends because of bigotry
Being fired because their views become known and are unwelcome
Friction with the character's children when other parents won't let their kids associate with them because they don't want them exposed to harmful ideas

EMOTIONAL WOUNDS IT COULD STEM FROM: A Carjacking, A Home Invasion, A Physical Assault, A School Shooting, A Terrorist Attack, A Toxic Relationship, An Abuse of Power, Battling a Mental Condition, Being Bullied, Being Fired or Laid Off, Being Sexually Violated, Being Stalked, Being Treated as Property

SCENARIOS THAT MIGHT TRIGGER THIS FEAR
Having to work with the type of person the character is afraid of
A child, sibling, or other loved one dating "that kind of person"
A person in this group being promoted to a position of power or influence
Being slighted or even marginally disrespected by this kind of person
Being called out for slighting or being disrespectful to a member of this group
Seeing or hearing a story about someone from this group being untrustworthy or dangerous

HUMAN NEEDS THAT COULD BE IMPACTED

Self-Actualization: Most people won't respect or tolerate someone who harbors hatred for a particular group. If the character's viewpoint becomes known, they may be unable to achieve their goals.

Esteem and Recognition: Someone whose fear escalates to bigotry can easily offend friends, family, and peers, who will then look down on the character.

Love and Belonging: The character's narrow ideas can keep them from pursuing relationships with people who could have become mentors, confidants, supporters, and even life partners.

HOW THE CHARACTER CAN MINIMIZE OR OVERCOME IT
Avoiding people who perpetuate the fear through harmful rhetoric
Processing the root event that caused the fear
Learning to separate individuals from potential bias about their culture, role, or other generalization
The character educating themselves about the people group (their culture, community, belief system, celebrations, etc.) to develop a more balanced view
Challenging the bias: Is it based on verifiable fact or hearsay?
Talking to people who have healthy interactions with members of this group
Engaging in safe interactions with this people group

CHANGE

NOTES: Most people are averse to change at some level, so a certain amount of unease is normal. It only becomes a problem when a person is so determined to keep things the same—because they don't want to give up control or are afraid of the unknown—that their quality of life goes down, relationships are damaged, and they're unable to grow and evolve in a healthy manner.

WHAT IT LOOKS LIKE

Dismissing new ideas without considering them
Reacting emotionally rather than logically
Immediately poking holes in a proposed action or solution
Humoring people; giving the appearance of considering something new while planning to reject the opportunity
Avoiding making decisions that require change (so the status quo can be protected)
Using outdated sources or ineffective arguments to make a point
Claiming things are fine the way they are
Accusing people of complicating things or not respecting how things are done
Going to extremes to avoid change (manipulating others, lying, lashing out when a change is suggested, etc.)
Clinging tightly to old-school methods, such as resisting technology, ignoring scientific advances, or rejecting new tools
Being sentimental
Loyalty to people, a job, a community, etc.
Inflexibility
Repairing and fixing material objects rather than replacing them
Living in the same home even when it's falling apart or no longer fits their needs
Sticking close to home; not traveling far or taking long trips
Strife with family members who want to make changes
Resenting others for moving on and leaving the character behind
Being more interested in the past than the future
Trying to discredit the person pushing for change

COMMON INTERNAL STRUGGLES

Feeling stuck in a situation but being unwilling to evolve
Wanting things to be better but fearing change will make things worse
Feeling overwhelmed by new methods and processes
Feeling isolated because they can't embrace the changes needed to keep up with others
Feeling selfish for being so unbending but not knowing how to be more flexible
Wanting to go back in time to when things were happier or simpler
Feeling obsolete
Struggling with anxiety or depression

HINDRANCES AND DISRUPTIONS TO THE CHARACTER'S LIFE

Staying in a situation that makes them unhappy or is unhealthy because it's preferable to facing the unknown
Difficulty making even small changes to a daily routine
Missing out on meaningful activities (a trip with friends, a family reunion, dinner at a friend's house, etc.) because doing so means leaving their comfort zone
Becoming isolated from others
Difficulty utilizing modern advances because the learning curve is too great
Avoiding people who are always trying to "improve" the character's life by changing it
Always needing to do things their own way
Becoming less productive because they insist on doing things the old way

EMOTIONAL WOUNDS IT COULD STEM FROM: A Mental Condition, Being Forced to Leave One's Homeland, Discovering a Partner's Sexual Orientation Secret, Divorcing One's Spouse, Experiencing the Death of a Parent as a Child or Youth, Living with a Critical Medical Diagnosis, Losing a Limb

SCENARIOS THAT MIGHT TRIGGER THIS FEAR

New technology or processes at work that must be learned and used
The character having to move (the house is condemned, needing to downsize, etc.)
A spouse having to move into a retirement home, leaving the character on their own
Grown children moving across the country and asking the character to come with them
The culture shifting to embrace ideas the character disagrees with
Being given a new phone, a computer, or some other tool the character isn't comfortable with but must learn to use
The character's children wanting to deviate from a long-held tradition
Being physically or mentally unable to do something that was never a problem before

HUMAN NEEDS THAT COULD BE IMPACTED

Self-Actualization: A fear of change usually leads to stagnation, with the character not embracing ideas and practices that would improve their life and provide better opportunities.

Love and Belonging: Important relationships can become strained if loved ones are limited by the character's change-averse choices.

Safety and Security: A character who fears change may stay in an unhealthy relationship or unsafe living environment because they prefer the devil they know to the devil they don't.

HOW THE CHARACTER CAN MINIMIZE OR OVERCOME IT

Educating themselves; making the unknown known so the change is less scary
Considering what would make them happier and seeing change as a necessary process to get there
Reflecting on changes that have improved society, made life safer, and benefited the character and their family
Viewing change as an opportunity to learn something new and become resilient
Reminding themselves of past life lessons and how the character is better for learning them
Viewing mistakes or failures as a rite of passage to becoming better

GOVERNMENT

NOTES: Fear is powerful, so it's widely used to manipulate people. When politicians use it to further their ambitions, it builds distrust. This can lead a character to believe that those in power (or the system itself) are inherently corrupt and an enemy of the people. A fear of government will have many layers and can be taken to extremes, so this entry covers a range of possibilities.

WHAT IT LOOKS LIKE

Voicing pessimism about the direction the country is headed
Becoming obsessed with a particular viewpoint
Refusing to believe anything reported by the government
Focusing on abuses of power while ignoring instances when it's used for good
Paying close attention to rumors and what the government tries to deny
Gravitating toward people who voice the same fears
Joining protests
Believing everyone in power is a manipulator
Fearmongering
Jumping to conclusions
Assuming malice—for example, believing that a bill passed because it grants someone more power instead of benefiting citizens
Feeling unsafe (believing the government is failing to protect its people)
Heightened anxiety when watching the news or scrolling news feeds
A tendency to look for a hidden motivation or agenda
Being distrustful of technology because it can be used to monitor and track people
Becoming increasingly agitated during political campaigning and on election day
Refusing to vote because everyone's corrupt, so what's the point?
Becoming more susceptible to related fears
Believing the country is under attack from within
Gravitating to a single source of truth (a TV station, a website, etc.) that confirms the character's bias rather than considering contrasting ideas
Becoming easily provoked (or enraged)
Being pulled toward political outsiders or disruptors (believing that their unconventional ways or outsider status might make them less corrupt)
Purchasing weapons and investing in safeguards because the government can't be trusted
Connecting events to a bigger agenda despite being unable to prove it
Becoming evangelical about a view (and feeling others must be educated to the truth)
Moving off the grid so the government has less control over the character's life
Being drawn to conspiracy theories
Establishing a group of like-minded people to work against the government
Becoming an anarchist
Participating in domestic terrorism

COMMON INTERNAL STRUGGLES

Believing most people are brainwashed but being unable to say it without ruining relationships

Wanting to take the country back but fearing what the government will do
Judging people who see the world differently (and having to hide it)
Fearing for the safety of loved ones and not understanding why they don't share the character's sense of urgency

HINDRANCES AND DISRUPTIONS TO THE CHARACTER'S LIFE
Pessimism limiting the character's ability to enjoy the present
Avoiding social events where conversations are likely to turn political
Friction with family members who are intolerant of the character's views (or vice versa)
Fear about the future making it hard for the character to build toward something better
Using the government as a scapegoat for everything, and missing opportunities to take personal responsibility and grow
The fear pushing the character toward irrational beliefs and ideas
Their social group being small because their ideas scare off potential friends
Losing all objectivity and balance

EMOTIONAL WOUNDS IT COULD STEM FROM: Being Let Down by a Trusted Organization or Social System, Experiencing Poverty, Growing up in Foster Care, Living in a Dangerous Neighborhood, Living Through Civil Unrest, Living Through Famine or Drought, Misplaced Loyalty, Prejudice or Discrimination

SCENARIOS THAT MIGHT TRIGGER THIS FEAR
A family member getting into politics
Political instability that turns violent on home soil
An actual (or perceived) government overreach of power
Seeing a governmental power grab in another country

HUMAN NEEDS THAT COULD BE IMPACTED

Self-Actualization: Fearful characters who fully embrace conspiracy and bias become close-minded, lose their ability to think critically, and allow pessimism and distrust to limit their happiness.

Esteem and Recognition: Society paints conspiracy theorists with an ugly brush. A character with strong negative feelings about the government can soon come to be seen by others as foolish, ridiculous, or even mentally imbalanced.

Love and Belonging: If the character's beliefs keep them from tolerating views outside of their own, it will cause strife with family and friends who believe differently.

Safety and Security: If the character's fears about the government are justified, voicing distrust or contempt may make him or her a target of those in power.

HOW THE CHARACTER CAN MINIMIZE OR OVERCOME IT
Learn and then apply critical thinking skills
Educating themselves on government structure and how it works
Realizing that, to understand actual threats, they must research extensively
Recognizing their own closed-mindedness and seeking to be more tolerant
Joining advocacy groups to come together with others who want change
Being brave enough to seek answers to tough questions they've avoided

LOSING AUTONOMY

NOTES: Autonomy fluctuates throughout life but will decrease with certain milestones, such as getting married, having a baby, and growing old. A character who fears the loss of their independence will look for ways to maintain their freedom, sometimes at the cost of their own happiness or satisfaction.

WHAT IT LOOKS LIKE

Moving out of their parent's home as soon as possible
Fiercely setting expectations to protect their independence in relationships
Maintaining superficial romantic relationships that don't infringe on the character's independence
Putting off having children
Avoiding family members who exert too much influence
Choosing the opposite of what others want
Viewing help as conditional
Declining assistance
Traveling solo (even though it may be unwise or even dangerous)
Living alone
Developing related fears, such as growing old
Refusing to use tools that are meant to help, such as a cane, hearing aid, or glasses
Refusing to move in with a relative, even if doing so makes sense
Doing activities that are inadvisable for someone of their age
Hiding signs of illness or mental struggles from loved ones
Lying about how they are doing to family members
Masking pain so they aren't told what they should do or how to live
Dismissing concerns for their safety or well-being
Being deliberately cantankerous or rude to caregivers
Continuing to engage in activities that have become dangerous (driving, drinking alcohol, running, etc.)
Becoming too focused on their own wants and desires

COMMON INTERNAL STRUGGLES

Feeling pressured to let others help despite a desire to remain independent
Fearing that a loss of autonomy will result in a loss of identity
The character wondering if they're being selfish or stubborn for declining help
Living in denial about their need for assistance
Justifying any loss of cognitive or physical abilities
Feeling like a burden when help is needed
Becoming paranoid about signs of further decline
Resenting the people who are trying to help, then feeling guilty about it
Feeling as if life is no longer worth living once choice is taken away (through a critical illness, age, a difficult diagnosis)

HINDRANCES AND DISRUPTIONS TO THE CHARACTER'S LIFE

Sustaining an injury at home and not having anyone to help
The character missing important events because they're trying to hide a physical or mental decline
Stubbornly refusing helpful advice that would improve their quality of life
Relationships being strained because the character refuses to make concessions that would result in a loss of independence
Lacking deep friendships and community because the character is off on their own
Avoiding long-term relationships that may interrupt the character's lifestyle or routine
Angering or driving away relatives who just want to help

EMOTIONAL WOUNDS IT COULD STEM FROM: A Life-Threatening Accident, A Terminal Illness Diagnosis, Being Held Captive, Being Legitimately Incarcerated for a Crime, Being Raised by Overprotective Parents, Growing up in a Cult

SCENARIOS THAT MIGHT TRIGGER THIS FEAR

Being proposed to
An unexpected pregnancy
A new spouse or child requiring changes in the character's routine
Being diagnosed with a disease that will inhibit the character's mobility
Being diagnosed with Alzheimer's (or pre-Alzheimer's)
Witnessing the neglect of a relative in a nursing home
Being forced to move in with a parent or friend
The character seeing signs of a mental or physical decline
Something happening that forces the character to give up something they enjoy (sustaining an injury while hiking alone, memory problems making a favorite game impossible, etc.)

HUMAN NEEDS THAT COULD BE IMPACTED

Esteem and Recognition: A character with a reason to fear the loss of their independence (such as a worsening mental condition, for instance), may feel badly about themselves for burdening others, even when they have no control over the situation.

Love and Belonging: Strife is imminent when a character who needs supervision refuses to acknowledge it or accept help. The same will be true when someone is expected to take on a caregiver role and is unwilling to do so.

Safety and Security: A character who refuses to accept limitations will unknowingly put themselves in danger.

Physiological Needs: The danger can be so great for a character refusing to make changes that they may put their lives or the lives of others at risk.

HOW THE CHARACTER CAN MINIMIZE OR OVERCOME IT

Accepting that not everything is within their control
Remembering that powerlessness is a temporary emotion that dissipates as soon as they form a plan, make a decision, or act
Appreciating the benefit of letting others in and tackling issues together
Recognizing that depending on others at times doesn't make the character weak
Seeing the value of relationships and having people to rely on

LOSING FINANCIAL SECURITY

NOTES: A character's fear of losing the ability to finance their life can have many causes, such as growing up in a struggling home or living through a global recession. Alternatively, their fear may be the result of a challenge they're facing in the here-and-now, like an illness, job loss, escalating medical bills, or a natural disaster.

WHAT IT LOOKS LIKE

Keeping a strict budget
Taking care of their possessions
Buying used, not new
Being too frugal and not spending money on essentials or small comforts
Picking a career based on salary rather than passion
Marrying for money
Choosing staycations over traveling, or road trips over pricey all-inclusive vacations
Building up and jealously guarding an emergency fund
Working more than one job to maintain a certain income
Pursuing higher education, certificates, and continuous learning opportunities
Buying generic brands
Closely monitoring credit reports and credit card charges
Frequently negotiating for a raise
Always thinking about money (or, conversely, avoiding thinking about money)
Learning how to invest savings
Saying no to extras and making do with what they have
Being risk-averse when it comes to investment; being overly cautious
Getting frustrated when family members overspend or don't follow the budget
Being critical of others who aren't careful with their finances
Refusing to keep up with spend-happy peers
Measuring financial security by an arbitrary goal or comparison (having a certain amount of money in the bank, being wealthier than a sibling or neighbor, etc.)
Being anxious about debt
Making fear-based financial decisions rather than logical ones

COMMON INTERNAL STRUGGLES

Feeling anxious about money concerns
Worrying about running out of money later in life and having to depend on others
Wanting to enjoy life but being too afraid of wasting or running out of money
Worrying about catastrophic and unlikely financial scenarios, such as a house fire, having to support adult children, or being diagnosed with a rare illness
Second-guessing their financial and career decisions
Being paranoid about scams

HINDRANCES AND DISRUPTIONS TO THE CHARACTER'S LIFE

The character losing sleep because they're always worrying about money
Developing high blood pressure from stress (and then having to pay for medication)

Missing out on pleasurable activities that cost money
The character sticking with a dissatisfying job because it's safe
Bypassing lucrative financial opportunities because the character is too afraid of the risk
Suffering the physical effects of too much worrying (headaches, weight loss, ulcers, etc.)
An inability to be content; always striving for more financial security
The character's stinginess or inflexibility straining relationships with a spouse or child
Working an unfulfilling job because it provides financial stability
Being seen as stingy and inflexible

EMOTIONAL WOUNDS IT COULD STEM FROM: Becoming a Caregiver at an Early Age, Becoming Homeless for Reasons Out of One's Control, Being Fired or Laid Off, Crossing Moral Lines to Survive, Declaring Bankruptcy, Divorcing One's Spouse, Experiencing Poverty, Financial Ruin Due to a Spouse's Irresponsibility

SCENARIOS THAT MIGHT TRIGGER THIS FEAR

Being cut off financially (from parents, due to a divorce, etc.)
The character or their spouse losing their job
The boss announcing cutbacks at work
Sustaining an injury or incurring an illness that will be expensive to treat
Losing everything to a scammer or a bad investment
Watching the economy plummet toward a recession or depression
Having to take on caregiving duties for an additional family member
Having to file for bankruptcy
Being sued

HUMAN NEEDS THAT COULD BE IMPACTED

Self-Actualization: A character with this fear will sacrifice nonessentials for financial security. This means they may end up working jobs they don't enjoy and abandoning pursuits that would bring them fulfillment and happiness.

Esteem and Recognition: A character obsessed with financial security even if they are doing well may be judged by others as being stingy and uptight.

Love and Belonging: Money is a common cause of strife between spouses and partners. Big problems can arise in family relationships when loved ones disagree with the character's financial plans.

Safety and Security: A character who foregoes important medical appointments or treatments to save money can put themselves physically at risk. Their emotional well-being can also be impacted if their concerns about money turn into an unhealthy obsession.

HOW THE CHARACTER CAN MINIMIZE OR OVERCOME IT

Creating a rainy-day fund
Developing a good sense of wants vs. needs
Creating a budget with the help of others in the household, so everyone can agree
Talking to family members about spending habits so everyone is on the same page
Balancing frugality with rewards; gaining pleasure in something earned, like a special trip
Investing wisely
Not spending more than the family makes

LOSING ONE'S SANITY

NOTES: The fear of losing one's mind often goes hand-in-hand with other forms of anxiety. Panic can make a character feel like they're going crazy, which, of course, reinforces the fear. This can become a spiraling catch-22 situation that's hard to escape. Some may become so obsessed with appearing whole that they refuse help when they desperately need it.

WHAT IT LOOKS LIKE

Regularly asking, "Does this make sense?" or "Is this normal?"
Making jokes about "losing it" to gauge how others react
Needing reassurance that they're making the right decisions
Researching various disorders and symptoms
Being obsessed with (or obsessively avoiding) people and situations dealing with mental health conditions
Watching for physical or mental shifts, no matter how small
Rehearsing things they know to be true
Using grounding techniques (controlled breathing, tapping, repeating a comfort word, etc.)
Seeking a higher power
Having multiple diagnoses
Withdrawing from others
Becoming homebound
Making excuses to avoid social gatherings
Clinging to the trustworthy people in their life
Seeking (or rejecting) therapy, medication, or other treatments
Frequent panic attacks
Turning to unhealthy coping mechanisms
Hiding any signs of mental illness from others
The character living in denial about their mental health state
The character mimicking others to put on a facade of "normalcy"
Paranoia about being judged

COMMON INTERNAL STRUGGLES

Not knowing which thoughts should be believed and which aren't true
Knowing something is wrong but being too afraid to seek help
The character hiding or lying about what they're going through, then feeling guilt or shame for their dishonesty
Struggling with intrusive thoughts
Worrying over worst-case scenarios—even the ones that are unlikely
Becoming self-conscious of their behaviors and worrying about how others will view the character
Overanalyzing everything
Becoming paranoid
Feeling incapable and broken
The character believing they're alone, that no one else is struggling like they are

HINDRANCES AND DISRUPTIONS TO THE CHARACTER'S LIFE

Having frequent panic attacks and living in fear of the next one
Being unable to truly trust themselves
Living in isolation
Suffering from insomnia, which makes everything harder to manage
Being unable to fully enjoy life
Struggling with low self-esteem
Constantly questioning their own mind and capabilities
The character struggling through their mental health difficulties alone

EMOTIONAL WOUNDS IT COULD STEM FROM: A Toxic Relationship, A Traumatic Brain Injury, Battling a Mental Condition, Being Tortured, Being Victimized by a Perpetrator Who Was Never Caught, Growing up in a Cult

SCENARIOS THAT MIGHT TRIGGER THIS FEAR

Trying yet another treatment that doesn't help or makes the character feel worse
Being chastised or made fun of for saying or doing something odd
Being officially diagnosed with a mental health condition
A friend with a similar condition getting worse or becoming suicidal
Being gaslighted by someone the character trusts
The character losing someone they know they can depend on
Being admitted to a psychiatric hospital
Acting with impaired judgment and incurring dire consequences

HUMAN NEEDS THAT COULD BE IMPACTED

Self-Actualization: A struggling character who is unwilling to seek help may end up living life on the fringes, unsupported and unable to reach their full potential.

Esteem and Recognition: Low self-esteem is a common side-effect of (especially untreated) mental health conditions because the character feels different from everyone else, unable to fit in, and isolated from their peers.

Love and Belonging: A character with this fear may require more support than the people in their life can handle, adding strain to those relationships. Other problems can arise if the character has a serious condition but refuses to seek treatment.

Safety and Security: A character in denial about their mental health may unknowingly and unwillingly endanger themselves or others.

Physiological Needs: Many mental health conditions deteriorate when they go untreated; in extreme cases, this can result in an untimely death.

HOW THE CHARACTER CAN MINIMIZE OR OVERCOME IT

Monitoring diet and sleep habits to understand if these could be a factor
Asking a friend to stay with them and observe their routine and behavior
Consider household dangers (a gas leak, chemicals, etc.) that may be a factor
Asking for a professional assessment
Putting up cameras at home and asking a third-party to review the footage
Journaling symptoms, thoughts, and routines to share with a psychologist

NOT BEING IN CONTROL

NOTES: To varying degrees, every character will desire control because they've seen what happens when they don't have it. The disappointments, frustrations, and even tragedies that can occur when someone isn't in control can cause a fear to develop, creating all kinds of problems.

WHAT IT LOOKS LIKE

Adhering to schedules and routines
Being proactive and prepared
Seeking to be an expert on everything so the character will be as informed as possible
Employing checklists and to-do lists
Anticipating problems before they happen
Being a stickler for rule following and processes
Being a perfectionist
Being rigid and inflexible
Going to great lengths to keep loved ones safe
Exhibiting obsessive compulsive disorder (OCD) tendencies, such as checking locks, making sure the oven is off, excessive hand washing, etc.
Using rituals (counting, breathing techniques, mantras, etc.) to calm down
Seeing things in black and white
Being overly sensitive to criticism
Not taking action without in-depth research and planning
Being risk-averse
Becoming impatient when others won't listen to them or take their advice
Not taking people at their word
Believing they're always right
Suppressing emotions
Monitoring a spouse's emails and calls
Micromanaging coworkers
Being unable to let things go until they align with the character's vision
Believing the ends justify the means when it comes to controlling outcomes
Restricting their child's freedom (with early curfews, limited internet access, having to approve their friends, etc.)
Phobias (of flying, being confined, etc.) arising from the fear of not being in control

COMMON INTERNAL STRUGGLES

Knowing that life is filled with change and uncertainties but being unable to accept them
Wanting to delegate a job but feeling like no one else can do it properly
Struggling with stress and anxiety
Knowing certain things can't be controlled, but trying to control them anyway
Wanting to know the future
Feeling unsafe when things aren't certain
Fearing for the safety of loved ones
Obsessing over situations outside of their control

HINDRANCES AND DISRUPTIONS TO THE CHARACTER'S LIFE

Losing employees due to micromanagement
Driving a child away with nosiness and interference
Being unable to delegate tasks, and becoming overworked as a result
Being unable to live fully in the present
Not taking advantage of good opportunities that can't be controlled or predicted
Struggling with letting others make decisions
Being overwhelmed when unexpected circumstances arise

EMOTIONAL WOUNDS IT COULD STEM FROM: A Carjacking, A Home Invasion, A House Fire, A Nomadic Childhood, A Terrorist Attack, Becoming Homeless for Reasons Out of One's Control, Being Bullied, Being Falsely Accused of a Crime, Prejudice or Discrimination, Sexual Dysfunction, The Death of One's Child

SCENARIOS THAT MIGHT TRIGGER THIS FEAR

A situation arising where the character cannot control the outcome (getting caught in a storm, being stuck in traffic, a parent refusing treatment for a disease, etc.)
A teenager rebelling and wanting more freedom
Hearing about a tragedy that befell a friend's family
Entering a transitional phase of life (going to college, getting married, having a child, menopause, etc.)
Experiencing the unexpected loss of a loved one
Being the victim of a crime
Having to trust someone else (a family member, the judicial system, etc.) for their security

HUMAN NEEDS THAT COULD BE IMPACTED

Self-Actualization: Happiness, fulfillment, and the ability to simply enjoy life can be impacted when certain opportunities or activities are rejected because the character must give up control to participate in them.

Esteem and Recognition: Characters struggling with this fear can exhibit behaviors that are annoying, confusing, or off-putting to others, leading those people to think less of the character.

Love and Belonging: A character with an extreme need for control may impose strict rules and requirements for loved ones. No matter how good the intentions are, loved ones may chafe under the constant watchfulness and worry.

Safety and Security: Characters who refuse to concede control of a situation to someone better suited to handle it could end up risking their health, safety, or wealth.

HOW THE CHARACTER CAN MINIMIZE OR OVERCOME IT

Recognizing that full control isn't attainable
Resisting the urge to cast blame (or take responsibility for things outside their control) in situations where no one is at fault
Recognizing that life's unexpected moments are opportunities for growth and resilience
Making a habit of planning, being proactive, and thinking things through
Deciding to control the controllables and let go of everything else

ONE'S BODY BECOMING A PRISON

NOTES: Characters with this fear are afraid of losing physical mobility and becoming trapped in their own body. This can arise from many events, such as being diagnosed with a degenerative condition, a close friend being paralyzed in an accident, or a mental health condition that causes the character to obsess over this possibility. For a character with this fear, the loss of bodily control may be inevitable or something they're just afraid might happen.

WHAT IT LOOKS LIKE

Researching symptoms online but not seeking medical attention
High anxiety; worrying that something is wrong and obsessing over possible diagnoses
Requesting a second or third opinion
Praying for a misdiagnosis
Leaning into denial
Isolating and pushing family away
Constantly analyzing themselves for signs of mental or physical deterioration
Crashing into depression as reality sets in
Joining support groups
Creating a living will
Taking good care of themselves (exercising, eating healthy foods, giving up smoking, seeing a doctor regularly, etc.)
Staying active
Testing for certain genetic conditions
Becoming fiercely independent
Being overly cautious when it comes to personal risk
Strictly following safety guidelines and road laws
Avoiding activities that could cause an accident (diving, climbing, etc.)
Driving themselves everywhere (instead of trusting someone else to do it)
Avoiding people who have lost their mobility
Exhibiting claustrophobic tendencies
Lashing out at caregivers
Suicidal thoughts (if a debilitating disease is in play)

COMMON INTERNAL STRUGGLES

Being crippled by anxiety and fear
Constantly assessing their physical health and worry over small changes
Struggling to be present with loved ones
Feeling like no one understands them
Being morbidly fascinated with people in this situation while also being terrified of and repelled by them
Knowing that worrying about the future steals their joy in the present but being unable to stop
Struggling with claustrophobia

HINDRANCES AND DISRUPTIONS TO THE CHARACTER'S LIFE

Being so preoccupied with their body that they neglect to focus on other areas of strength (mental, emotional, spiritual, etc.)
Being so independent that the character must face difficult circumstances alone
Being unable to enjoy life
Time and opportunities being lost to worrying over something that may never happen
Developing a negative view about life that drives others away and worsens their own isolation

EMOTIONAL WOUNDS IT COULD STEM FROM: A Life-Threatening Accident, A Traumatic Brain Injury, Battling a Mental Condition, Becoming a Caregiver at an Early Age, Growing up with a Sibling's Disability or Chronic Illness, Living with a Critical Medical Diagnosis, Living with Chronic Pain or Illness, Losing a Limb, Losing One of the Five Senses

SCENARIOS THAT MIGHT TRIGGER THIS FEAR

Receiving a diagnosis of a debilitating disease
Suffering spinal damage that makes paralysis a future possibility
A loved one suffering a stroke or slipping into a coma
A family member being diagnosed with a degenerative genetic disease
Being temporarily confined (being bed-ridden, unable to walk for a time following surgery, etc.)
Losing the ability to see or hear
Growing old and slowly losing mobility
Hearing an account of a person with a degenerative condition succumbing to suicide

HUMAN NEEDS THAT COULD BE IMPACTED

Self-Actualization: A character with this fear will be so focused on avoidance that they'll be unable to move forward and embrace everything life has to offer.

Esteem and Recognition: A common side-effect of this kind of fear is anxiety, which will undermine the character's self-esteem.

HOW THE CHARACTER CAN MINIMIZE OR OVERCOME IT

Spending energy on what can be controlled rather than wasting it on what can't be
Focusing on maintaining a healthy body weight and building muscle
Following a diet for the condition as recommended by doctors
Being diligent about breathing exercises, physical therapy, stretching, and other activities prescribed as part of the character's care
Trying meditation, yoga, and other activities that are helpful for maintaining a positive mental mindset
Being proactive; ensuring supports, equipment, and instructions are ready should communication become difficult
Making a list of activities, movies, audiobooks, and favorite things that will provide comfort down the road rather than trusting others to decide what the character may like
Considering assisted suicide options; speaking with family now about the character's desires

ONE'S GENETICS

NOTES: To varying degrees, every person takes steps to stay healthy because no one wants the discomfort and inconvenience of being sick or injured. But not all maladies are created equal. Imagine a character with a genetic predisposition toward a debilitating physical or mental condition. Not knowing if it's going to crop up or when it will show itself can trigger uncertainty and fear, leading to a host of issues that can greatly impact the character's thoughts and how they approach life.

WHAT IT LOOKS LIKE

Taking a variety of DNA tests
Frequently visiting to the doctor
Requesting tests and bloodwork to look for earmarks of the condition
Maintaining a healthy diet
Exercising regularly
Avoiding potential triggers (alcohol, being out in the sun, etc.)
Heavily researching the condition
Conducting genetic testing to see if the character is at risk
Taking vitamins and supplements
Quizzing family members about their health
Running frequent self-checks for symptoms associated with the condition
Exhibiting hypochondriac tendencies; believing the condition is present when it isn't
Difficulty developing long-term relationships (because the character doesn't want people around when or if their health deteriorates)
Being uncomfortable around people with the condition
Participating in fundraisers to find cures (for cancer, multiple sclerosis, etc.)
Avoiding doctors and testing
Ignoring any symptoms of the condition
Becoming irritated or angry when the subject is brought up
Pretending things aren't as bad as they are
Participating in research studies
Not making plans for the future
Hiding signs that the condition is developing
Deciding not to have children

COMMON INTERNAL STRUGGLES

Wanting to research the condition but being afraid to
The character feeling like their body or mind has betrayed them
Being plagued with visions of what the condition will do to them
Constantly worrying that the condition is appearing
Worrying about what will happen to people in the character's care if the condition develops
Wanting to start a family but being afraid to pass the condition to them
Fearing the future and what it might bring
Wrestling with depression
Struggling to figure out who they are apart from their genetics

Being angry at God
Thinking frequently about death (and possibly having suicidal thoughts)

HINDRANCES AND DISRUPTIONS TO THE CHARACTER'S LIFE

Loneliness
Joy eluding them because they're preoccupied with preventing illness
Overspending on genetic testing, supplements, experimental treatments, etc.
Being unable to enjoy the present because the character is so worried about the future
Not preparing adequately for the future (because the character doesn't see the point)
Making life decisions (about marriage, having kids, the pursuit of a dream) based on the possibility of the condition presenting itself

EMOTIONAL WOUNDS IT COULD STEM FROM: A Loved One's Suicide, Battling a Mental Condition, Being Raised by an Addict, Discovering Hidden Information About One's Ancestry, Experiencing the Death of a Parent as a Child or Youth, Growing up with a Sibling's Disability or Chronic Illness, Living with a Critical Medical Diagnosis, Watching Someone Die

SCENARIOS THAT MIGHT TRIGGER THIS FEAR

Watching a family member suffer with a genetically inherited condition
Experiencing symptoms of the condition
Receiving a call from the doctor's office about test results
Discovering that a family member's devastating condition is genetic
Becoming pregnant
Birthdays that bring the character one year closer to a possible diagnosis
A persistent illness or symptom that can't be explained

HUMAN NEEDS THAT COULD BE IMPACTED

Esteem and Recognition: A character whose life is dictated by their fear of what may happen could be scorned by others who can't understand the character's willingness to be limited by what-ifs.

Love and Belonging: If the likelihood of a devastating condition is high, the character may push others away so they won't witness the character's decline or be burdened by it. The character may also unfairly resent the person who passed the condition along to them, creating strife in that relationship.

Safety and Security: A character living in denial about the condition may prolong a diagnosis and miss out on treatment options that could improve their physical or mental well-being.

HOW THE CHARACTER CAN MINIMIZE OR OVERCOME IT

Recognizing the value of maintaining a healthy mindset
Living in the moment so there's no regrets should the worst come true
Knowing the risk factors and living life with them in mind to lower chances of something cropping up
Practicing gratitude for each moment
Not letting a future possibility control their life or steal happiness
Claiming independence over their actions and choices; choosing empowerment

PERSECUTION

NOTES: Closely related to prejudice, persecution involves an overt attempt to make someone suffer because of their race, religion, gender, sexual orientation, socioeconomic status, weight, looks, political affiliation, alliances, or another arbitrary identifier. If the character has experienced prejudice in the past, witnessed others being persecuted, or has been taught that persecution is a foregone conclusion (and is therefore expecting it), it can develop into a fear with debilitating results.

WHAT IT LOOKS LIKE

Being hyper-aware of their environment and the people in it
Hiding or downplaying certain aspects of who they are
Preparing acceptable responses to questions they could be asked
Changing their beliefs to align with what's popular or accepted
Adherence to habits, rituals, and protocols to keep them safe
Following the rules to keep from drawing attention
Avoiding situations where their personal beliefs might be questioned or highlighted
Expecting prejudicial treatment from others
Sticking with people who are like them
Being hyper-sensitive to criticism
Empathizing with other people groups who are prone to persecution
Being on high alert when they're away from home
Voting for candidates who share the character's ideals, race, gender, etc.
Joining an activist group of like-minded people to fight against persecution
Feeling watched, like the character is being surveilled or spied on
Becoming confrontational (to avoid being mistreated)
Becoming highly anxious
Physically moving, fleeing an area, or quitting a group to avoid persecution

COMMON INTERNAL STRUGGLES

Becoming jaded or cynical about the future
Second-guessing themselves and their suspicions about others
Internalizing other people's negative comments or ideas
Feeling intensely uncomfortable in groups where the character is a minority
Struggling with anger and resentment toward other people groups
Feeling targeted, even when the other person has acted fairly and without prejudice
Fantasizing about revenge

HINDRANCES AND DISRUPTIONS TO THE CHARACTER'S LIFE

Lacking perspective because they've lived in a bubble, surrounded by people just like them
Becoming prejudiced against and distrusting of the kinds of people who have mistreated the character
Allowing the prejudice and stereotyping of others to taint how the character views themselves
Missing out on opportunities because of their avoidance of other groups

Their family moving, and the character having to start over in a new place
Being viewed as easily offended, overly anxious, and possibly prejudiced against others Fearing persecution where there is none
Struggling to know who to trust

EMOTIONAL WOUNDS IT COULD STEM FROM: A Physical Assault, A Terrorist Attack, An Abuse of Power, Battling a Mental Condition, Being Bullied, Being Falsely Accused of a Crime, Being Fired or Laid Off, Being Forced to Leave One's Homeland, Being Raised by Parents Who Loved Conditionally, Being Sent Away as a Child

SCENARIOS THAT MIGHT TRIGGER THIS FEAR

Experiencing prejudice
Being rejected (for a promotion, scholarship, a bid on a house, etc.) without being given a clear reason why
A law being enacted (or removed) that puts the character at greater risk of persecution
Witnessing a hate crime
A close friend leaving a job, neighborhood, or school to avoid being persecuted
Hearing that people like the character are being persecuted locally or around the world
Someone similar to the character being misrepresented or vilified in the media

HUMAN NEEDS THAT COULD BE IMPACTED

Self-Actualization: A character who avoids certain environments or kinds of people for safety reasons will unfortunately find their opportunities limited.

Esteem and Recognition: A character impacted by prejudice and persecution will often internalize it, believing they were to blame or are weak for allowing it to happen, even when this is not the case.

Love and Belonging: If the character sees prejudice where there is none, they may lose out on relationships with people who would have supported and fought for them.

Safety and Security: A character with a fight tendency may become violent or vindictive when they feel persecuted, putting themselves and others physically at risk.

HOW THE CHARACTER CAN MINIMIZE OR OVERCOME IT

Being willing to unpack the source of trauma for the fear, seeking help and managing it as needed
Having a support system or community to be with and gain strength from
Building a routine to help with anxiety
Taking time for meaningful pursuits, especially ones that are creative and bring joy
Finding purpose in helping others who are also struggling
Pursuing advocacy to foster feelings of control and empowerment
Educating others about persecution that's happening

RUNNING OUT OF A CRITICAL RESOURCE

NOTES: Some people live in precarious circumstances where the loss of food, power, medicine, or money could mean disaster. Others may only perceive their situation as insecure. Either way, if a character believes running out of something risks their survival, it becomes a highly motivating fear.

WHAT IT LOOKS LIKE

Spending all their time procuring, maintaining, and protecting the resource
Reducing their reliance on the resource in preparation for a shortage
Looking for viable replacement options—e.g., finding a different medicine that does the same thing but is more accessible
Believing that the resource is likely to become scarce (due to a political, economic, or environmental crisis)
Stockpiling resources
Carefully watching the news for signs of an impending disaster
Working towards self-sufficiency (growing crops, living near a water source, etc.)
Knowing where the resource can be obtained in the case of a scarcity
Being cautious with the expenditure of a resource (placing limits on how much can be used, putting someone in charge of it to control its distribution, etc.)
Not sharing resources with others
Placing strict punishments on the misuse of the resource
Panicking when supplies run low
An overabundance of caution to prevent risk—e.g., a character refusing to go outside because they only have one EpiPen for a bee sting allergy
Safeguarding the resource (by hiding it, placing security measures around it, etc.)
Valuing people based on how much of the resource they have
Seeking leverage to ensure they can acquire the resource no matter what
Constantly inventorying their stockpiles to ensure they still have "enough"
Lying about how much of the resource they have (saying they have a lot to boost their reputation or claiming they don't have much to keep from becoming a target)
Building up supplies of materials they can use to barter for the resource
Prioritizing the resource above anyone and everything else

COMMON INTERNAL STRUGGLES

Catastrophizing and losing perspective; viewing running out of the resource as the worst thing that could happen
Being obsessed with the resource
Being filled with worry all the time
Wanting to help others who need the resource but being too afraid of it running out
Wondering if maybe they're overreacting but being too invested to change their mindset
Wanting to keep the resource to themselves and feeling guilty about not sharing it
Envying people who have plenty of the resource
Thinking about redrawing their moral boundary lines to make certain actions acceptable in the pursuit of the resource

HINDRANCES AND DISRUPTIONS TO THE CHARACTER'S LIFE

Focusing solely on the resource, with no energy for anything else
Being viewed by others as obsessed, callous, stingy, or too serious
Being physically distanced from other communities because living far away makes it easier to protect the resource
Sacrificing other necessities (not seeing a doctor, ignoring critical home improvements, etc.) so the money can be spent on obtaining or protecting the resource
Becoming a controlling person
Relationships suffering because of the character's obsession with the resource
Difficulty relaxing
Being unable to feel or express gratitude

EMOTIONAL WOUNDS IT COULD STEM FROM: A Child Dying on One's Watch, A Natural or Man-Made Disaster, A Terrorist Attack, Being Held Captive, Crossing Moral Lines to Survive, Experiencing Poverty, Living in a Dangerous Neighborhood, Living Through Civil Unrest, Living Through Famine or Drought

SCENARIOS THAT MIGHT TRIGGER THIS FEAR

A shortage of other vital materials (gasoline, medication, toilet paper, etc.)
Current events pointing to an impending crisis
The resource's prices skyrocketing, making affordability an issue
A pandemic straining supply lines and making getting supplies harder
The character's child receiving a diagnosis requiring medication (or refrigeration for it)
Power outages or brownouts becoming more frequent in the character's area
Seeing a news report of people looting to get needed resources
Seeing others with an abundance of the resource when the character is forced to ration it
The character's water source becoming contaminated

HUMAN NEEDS THAT COULD BE IMPACTED

Esteem and Recognition: A character who is afraid of running out of something vital may develop characteristics that are off-putting to others, such as being stingy with their resources or unwilling to share information.

Safety and Security: If the character's access to a necessary resource is limited, they may not feel safe as their supply dwindles.

Physiological: In the case of an antidote, life-saving medicine, or immediate access to healthcare, running out could result in death.

HOW THE CHARACTER CAN MINIMIZE OR OVERCOME IT

Recognizing that running out of the resource, while a possibility, is unlikely and not worth so much time and focus
Supporting initiatives that will protect the resource and keep it from becoming scarce
Maintaining a balance between planning for the future and living in the present
Acknowledging their own resilience—that even if the resource runs out and life becomes more difficult, the character can pivot and adjust
Limiting input from influencers and journalists who will make the character's fear worse

THE FUTURE

NOTES: Feeling anxiety about the future is pretty common. For some, this turns into a fear of THE UNKNOWN, because life is uncertain and no one can see into the future. But what if the character thinks they know what's coming and it involves something catastrophic? In this situation, they'll allow their dread of the perceived event to eclipse logical thinking and sabotage their present.

WHAT IT LOOKS LIKE

Doomscrolling the news
Living in denial about the future event
Difficulty concentrating on mundane activities, such as work or school
Difficulty enjoying leisurely activities
Not making long-term plans, such as scheduling a vacation
Stocking up on food, water, cash, and other resources
Making only low-risk long-term investments
Following social media influencers who agree with the character's view of the future
Seeking information through mediums, psychics, or their horoscope
Being prone to believing conspiracy theories
Staying close to home so they're near their resources when bad things come
Sleeping poorly
Becoming obsessed with politics and current events
Becoming cynical
Warning others about what's coming
Being obsessed with personal safety
Not saving money (or keeping a tight grip on it)
Keeping tabs on the whereabouts of loved ones
Distrusting authority and the establishment
Seeing signs of the impending event everywhere
Relocating to a safer location
Taking extreme measures to stop the event from happening

COMMON INTERNAL STRUGGLES

Overthinking what's happening in the world
Wanting children but fearing to subject them to the future
Struggling with paranoia
Being consumed with cynicism and hopelessness
Being obsessed with the future event and when it will happen
Being overwhelmed by difficult feelings
Knowing people think they're crazy but needing to talk about what's coming
Missing the hobbies and passions they've given up in favor of preparing for the future
Worrying about loved ones who aren't preparing or taking things seriously
Wondering if they've made a mistake but refusing to admit they might be wrong about something so important

HINDRANCES AND DISRUPTIONS TO THE CHARACTER'S LIFE

Difficulty identifying with hopeful or carefree people
Not pursuing an opportunity like a promotion or scholarship because they see no point
Being consumed by fear, anxiety, and depression
Pulling away from people outside their inner circle (because they don't have the energy to invest in those relationships or they need to focus on saving their own family)
Difficulty finding joy, happiness, or contentment
Others viewing the character as illogical, fear-driven, or a conspiracy theorist
Struggling to sleep
Being unable to turn off their brain and relax
Blowing through their savings and running out of money prematurely or having no money when the big event turns out to be a dud

EMOTIONAL WOUNDS IT COULD STEM FROM: A Natural or Man-Made Disaster, A Terrorist Attack, An Abuse of Power, Battling a Mental Condition, Being Forced to Leave One's Homeland, Growing up in a Cult, Living Through Civil Unrest

SCENARIOS THAT MIGHT TRIGGER THIS FEAR

Financial markets plummeting
An adult child going away to college or moving far from home
Something happening that could be a precursor to the big event
Someone coming into political power who could usher in the horrible future
A devastating weather event approaching
A foretold precursor event coming to pass
A conflict breaking out on the world stage

HUMAN NEEDS THAT COULD BE IMPACTED

Self-Actualization: A character with this fear will be focused on preventing or preparing for a frightening future rather than personal discovery and fulfillment.

Love and Belonging: Important relationships may be challenged if other people don't agree with the character or their approach to the future.

Safety and Security: This character will never feel safe with the future event hanging over their head and possibly happening at any moment.

Physiological Needs: In a crusade to prevent an apocalyptic event or one being manufactured by powerful people, the character may face danger that is impossible to survive.

HOW THE CHARACTER CAN MINIMIZE OR OVERCOME IT

Separating logical fears of what may happen from unrealistic ones
Developing critical thinking skills
Challenging conspiracies by investigating the people and agendas behind them
The character controlling what can be controlled and not obsessing over the rest
Not letting future worries steal hope and happiness
Focusing on the now by investing in loved ones and meaningful goals
Preventing regret by taking advantage of opportunities and living life fully
Building a habit of imagining positive possibilities instead of worst-case scenarios

THE PAST BEING DISCOVERED

NOTES: Everyone has secrets. But some past events are traumatic or shameful enough that the risk of exposure generates a compelling fear to keep them hidden. A character in this situation may sacrifice relationships, sabotage their goals, and harm themselves to maintain secrecy.

WHAT IT LOOKS LIKE

Changing the subject when people start talking about the past
Not introducing love interests to family members associated with the event
Being evasive when questions are raised about that event or period in their life
Omitting certain facts or lying about past events
Being ambiguous so people can draw their own (incorrect) conclusions
Focusing intently on the future
Maintaining a quiet online profile
Not being given to sentimentality or nostalgia
Keeping past-related items in a secret location (a safe, the attic, a storage locker, etc.)
Cutting ties with people associated with the past event
Staying busy so they don't have to think about the past
Inventing a fake past
Changing their identity
Moving to a new location
Ghosting people who want a deeper relationship or try to get too close
Abusing drugs or alcohol
Silencing or discrediting people who get close to the truth

COMMON INTERNAL STRUGGLES

Being consumed by shame
Paranoia; worrying that other people know the truth
Missing old friends and family but being too scared to see them
Knowing it's not healthy to ignore the past but feeling incapable of facing it
Berating themselves for choices that led to those regretful events
Overreacting to a question about the past, then being embarrassed or feeling guilty
Recognizing the need to lie but still feeling bad about it
Wanting to be rid of the secret but being unable to bear the shame of others knowing

HINDRANCES AND DISRUPTIONS TO THE CHARACTER'S LIFE

Relocating frequently
Giving up relationships (because they're tied to the past or someone got too close to the truth)
Having to change their name
Avoiding events where they might run into someone from the past
Staying off social media
Slipping up when talking about their fabricated history
Never being able to get close to people
Always being on edge, fearful of revealing the truth
Having to lie to the people they care about

Sacrificing what they really want—such as a career—to protect their privacy
Having to hide things connected to the secret that brought joy and peace, such as a set of skills, a passion, or a relationship

EMOTIONAL WOUNDS IT COULD STEM FROM: Accidentally Killing Someone, Bearing the Responsibility for Many Deaths, Being Forced to Keep a Dark Secret, Being Sexually Violated, Crossing Moral Lines to Survive, Discovering Hidden Information About One's Ancestry, Failing to Save Someone's Life, Having an Abortion, Incest, Poor Judgment Leading to Unintended Consequences

SCENARIOS THAT MIGHT TRIGGER THIS FEAR
Someone from the past being hired at the character's workplace
A family member or old friend coming to visit
Being blackmailed by someone who knows the truth
A burglary of the character's storage unit
Being offered a job that requires a background check
A medical emergency that could reveal the truth
The character being investigated (by the police, a private detective, etc.)
Being dragged into a lawsuit
Experiencing a flashback at the worst possible time
A loved one giving the character an ultimatum to reveal the truth
An offender from the past seeking forgiveness
Seeing someone fall from grace when their past is exposed
An emergency that requires the character to contact the police
Being forced into counseling

HUMAN NEEDS THAT COULD BE IMPACTED

Self-Actualization: It's hard for someone to reach their full potential when they're hiding who they are or pretending to be something they're not.

Esteem and Recognition: People may look down on a character who becomes abrasive, confrontational, or abusive when their secret is threatened.

Love and Belonging: A character whose top priority is protecting the past may feel isolated when they're unable to develop deep, long-term relationships with others.

Safety and Security: If the revelation of the secret threatens the character's or their loved ones' lives, their safety and security will always be at risk.

HOW THE CHARACTER CAN MINIMIZE OR OVERCOME IT
Recognizing if the buried past is causing harm
Realizing the secret needs to come out to lessen its hold on them
Taking accountability for the past (if the character shares blame for the event)
Understanding that they're not at fault, and learning to let go of self-blame
Making peace with the past (acknowledging mistakes, forgiving someone, etc.)
Telling the secret to someone they trust to gain perspective about what to do
Revealing the secret on their own terms

THE UNKNOWN

NOTES: Life is a series of unknowns. When a character finds themselves in uncertain circumstances without enough information to know what's next, it can produce anxiety. But for some people, fearing the unknown can be overwhelming, becoming a fixation that causes them to neglect important aspects of their life.

The situation is slightly different for someone who knows (or thinks they know) something terrible is coming. If this is the scenario for your character, see our entry on THE FUTURE.

WHAT IT LOOKS LIKE

Avoiding risk
Sticking with what's known—staying close to home, adhering to routines, etc.
Avoiding change (unless it's absolutely necessary)
Erring on the side of caution when making decisions
Engaging in habits with predictable outcomes (watching favorite movies, re-reading books, playing the same games over and over, etc.)
Seeing a variety of outcomes and obsessing over which one will occur
Needing lots of information to be comfortable (say, being invited to a wedding and needing to know where it will be, who's invited, etc.)
Creating multiple plans to account for each possible scenario
Impatience caused by waiting and not knowing
Pursuing distractions to keep the character busy as they wait to see what happens
Difficulty focusing on everyday tasks
Interrogating decision-makers or people who might have information the character lacks
Not getting enough (or getting too much) sleep
Always trying to look ahead and predict the future
Becoming very black and white in an attempt to make life simpler and more manageable
Trying to control everything (to avoid uncertainty)
Being paralyzed when decisions need to be made
Preparing for worst-case scenarios (the financial system failing, a natural disaster, being fired, etc.) rather than thinking optimistically
Adopting compulsive coping habits (manically cleaning, overeating, etc.)
Taking actions to force a desired outcome

COMMON INTERNAL STRUGGLES

Being stuck in a cycle of pessimism and negativity
Obsessing over possible outcomes that may never come true
Doubting their ability to handle outcomes
Feeling incompetent to analyze contradictory information or different opinions about the uncertain event
Wishing they could just enjoy the moment and not worry
Resenting the people who are messing with the status quo
Suffering from mental and emotional exhaustion
Having aspirations and desires but being too afraid to set goals

HINDRANCES AND DISRUPTIONS TO THE CHARACTER'S LIFE
Not having long-term plans to work toward
Others accusing the character of being too controlling
Having to hide compulsive or addictive behaviors
People being drained by the character's negativity
Their fixation on the future robbing them of joy in the present
Being ruled by fear
Developing an anxiety disorder

EMOTIONAL WOUNDS IT COULD STEM FROM: A Natural or Man-Made Disaster, A Nomadic Childhood, Being Fired or Laid Off, Being Victimized by a Perpetrator Who Was Never Caught, Financial Ruin Due to a Spouse's Irresponsibility, Growing up in Foster Care

SCENARIOS THAT MIGHT TRIGGER THIS FEAR
Doctors being unable to diagnose a medical condition
Hearing a rumor about possible layoffs at work
A spouse wanting to leave a lucrative career to follow a dream
Being wait-listed for college
Children growing up, and the empty nest approaching
Being sued
Financial markets wildly fluctuating
A family member working in a dangerous field (in the military, as a firefighter, etc.)
The deadline for an uncertain event drawing near
A long-awaited event being further delayed
A high-stakes political election
Unrest and instability growing around the world
A loved one saying they need to talk to the character about something important

HUMAN NEEDS THAT COULD BE IMPACTED

Esteem and Recognition: A character with this fear may view themselves as being poorly equipped to handle life's variables.

Love and Belonging: A character who fears uncertainty in their relationships may drive others away with their constant need for assurance, or they may avoid intimate connections altogether.

Safety and Security: If their fear is focused on an event that could result in great danger, the character's sense of safety and security will be undermined.

HOW THE CHARACTER CAN MINIMIZE OR OVERCOME IT
Engaging in meditation, prayer, mindfulness, journaling, or other healthy de-stressors
Rationalizing that the unknown often holds new possibilities and positive outcomes
Recognizing that no one can know everything; learning to be at peace with uncertainty
Reflecting on happy surprises that have happened in the past
Taking stock of the positive changes they've experienced in their life
Working to be prepared, rather than fearing what might come
Gaining control by imagining the worst-case scenario and creating a plan for it

Relationship Fears

A LOVED ONE DYING

NOTES: Losing a loved one is inevitable, so we all worry about it to a certain extent. For some characters, though, the fear of someone close to them dying can take over their life. Sometimes this is centered around uncertainty about what happens after death. More often, the character believes they can't cope without that person, or they struggle with how their life will change once they're no longer around.

WHAT IT LOOKS LIKE

Being overprotective of a loved one's health (micromanaging their diet, monitoring their activity level, pushing supplements on them, etc.)
Frequently asking the loved one questions to spot risks, liabilities, or health problems
Limiting a child's freedom and independence to keep them safe—not allowing them to drive, stay out late, or visit new places, for instance
Being obsessed with germs and sanitation
Investing in extensive security measures to keep family members safe
Forcing family members to take part in health crazes that promote longevity
Being overly risk-averse when it comes to a loved one's welfare
Researching every symptom, pain, or complaint to see if it's a sign of something else
Booking doctor appointments prematurely rather than letting an illness resolve naturally
Consulting psychics to gain insight into a loved one's well-being and future
Refusing to accept a loved one's illness or terminal diagnosis
Refusing to talk about the possibility of a loved one's death (even if it's likely to happen)
Clinging to people and situations as they are instead of allowing them to evolve
Having panic attacks when thinking about the death of a loved one
Refusing to make contingency plans for a loved one's death—e.g., not buying life insurance or making a will
Arguing with family members or health staff who have a different view on health matters or next steps

COMMON INTERNAL STRUGGLES

Obsessing about a loved one's death and what it would mean for the character
Wanting to hold on tightly to a child while also knowing they need freedom to grow
Experiencing guilt for letting anxiety and fear control decision-making
Fearing the passage of time despite recognizing its inevitability
Knowing their fears are irrational but being unable to overcome them
Worrying about worst-case scenarios despite knowing they're unlikely to occur
Understanding that death is a part of life but being unable to accept it
Wanting to control a loved one (to keep them safe) but fearing it will drive them away

HINDRANCES AND DISRUPTIONS TO THE CHARACTER'S LIFE

Neediness pushing loved ones away
Losing sleep from worry and anxiety
Neglecting their own well-being because they're so consumed with the health of others

Being plagued with worry and unable to enjoy life when the loved one is away
Being unable to watch the news or participate in social media because the stories about people losing loved ones are too upsetting
Relationships with their children deteriorating because the kids are tired of being smothered and not trusted

EMOTIONAL WOUNDS IT COULD STEM FROM: A Life-Threatening Accident, A Loved One's Suicide, A School Shooting, Experiencing the Death of a Parent as a Child or Youth, Failing to Save Someone's Life, Losing a Loved One Due to a Professional's Negligence, Losing a Loved One to a Random Act of Violence, The Death of One's Child, Watching Someone Die

SCENARIOS THAT MIGHT TRIGGER THIS FEAR

A close friend unexpectedly losing a family member
Seeing a TV show or movie in which the character loses a spouse or child
A loved one being admitted to the hospital
A close call (a son experiencing a seizure, their husband falling off a ladder, etc.)
Being told a family member or close friend was in a car accident
A mass shooting or natural disaster resulting in extensive loss of life
A loved one having a near-death experience
Someone close to the character becoming terminally ill
Discovering that a child has been engaging in risky behaviors (racing their car, skydiving, driving under the influence, etc.)
Something terrible happening to a child's same-age friend (almost drowning, being attacked and hospitalized, being present during a robbery, etc.)

HUMAN NEEDS THAT COULD BE IMPACTED

Self-Actualization: A character consumed with this fear may be unable to pursue certain dreams, goals, or passions because their energy is diverted into protecting loved ones from real or perceived threats.

Love and Belonging: If the character is stifling or limiting their loved ones with unreasonable demands, friction may develop that pushes those people away.

HOW THE CHARACTER CAN MINIMIZE OR OVERCOME IT

Recognizing this fear is keeping them from fully enjoying time with their loved one
Focusing on being present in the moment and making the most of time with others
Realizing their behavior, even done out of love, is causing damage
Talking through worrisome what-if scenarios with someone they trust
Seeing the distress they're causing the loved one by trying to control them
Seeking therapy and treatment for irrational fears or anxiety
Talking to the loved one about changes that will help them feel more at ease (checking in more often, avoiding certain activities that are triggering fear, etc.)
Recognizing that, in some cases, death is kinder than living
Shifting focus to helping loved ones live their best life rather than a longer one

ABANDONMENT

NOTES: It's human nature to need others, which is why each character has a circle of people they love and trust. The idea that those loved ones could leave them—by choice or not—causes stress and anxiety. And for characters who have suffered abandonment in the past, the likelihood of them developing a debilitating fear of it happening again is even greater.

WHAT IT LOOKS LIKE

Attaching too quickly to a partner, friend, etc.
Seeking to please and appease
Encouraging dependency
Apologizing for things most people wouldn't worry about
Trying to do everything right and be the perfect partner, friend, daughter, etc.
Seeking reassurance: "You wouldn't rather be with someone else, would you?"
Making demands of the other party that will prove their love or loyalty
Jumping to conclusions when something changes (a friend being too tired to go out after work or a sister spending more time with in-laws) and assuming the worst
Being extremely sensitive to criticism or perceived slights
Struggling with emotional intimacy
Reading too much into the other person's words or actions
Believing that people are going to leave (due to insecurity, feeling unworthy of love, etc.)
Difficulty trusting others
Maintaining shallow relationships to avoid growing close to someone who could leave
Staying in an unhealthy relationship because they believe it's better than being alone
Becoming possessive or manipulative to control the other person and keep them close
Sabotaging promising relationships by pushing the other person away, treating them badly, cheating on them, abandoning them first, etc.
Separation anxiety; needing to be in frequent contact
Reluctance to fully commit to a relationship

COMMON INTERNAL STRUGGLES

Critical self-thoughts eroding the character's worth and esteem
Blaming themselves for things that aren't their fault
Struggling with anxiety or depression
Being tempted to do something they don't want just to keep the other party happy
Feeling worthless or unlovable
The character wondering what's wrong with them (that causes people to leave)
Needing reassurance but not wanting to come off as clingy or desperate
Wanting to relax and enjoy the relationship but being unable to stop looking for signs that the other person is pulling away
A tendency to pick apart their own interactions and find imaginary faults
Feeling defective and unfixable
Worrying that they'll never be happy

HINDRANCES AND DISRUPTIONS TO THE CHARACTER'S LIFE

Having many shallow relationships and few deep, meaningful ones
Being targeted by those willing to use the character's fear to control them
Struggling to engage with new people because the character is too afraid
Getting stuck in a cycle of not wanting to be abandoned but constantly exhibiting behaviors that drive people away
Losing sight of who they are because they're so eager to become the kind of person their partner will stay with
Having to explain to others why the latest relationship didn't work
Living in denial about what's really happening

EMOTIONAL WOUNDS IT COULD STEM FROM: A Loved One's Suicide, A Parent's Abandonment or Rejection, A Parent's Divorce, Abandonment Over an Unexpected Pregnancy, Being Disowned or Shunned, Being Raised by Neglectful Parents, Being Sent Away as a Child, Losing a Loved One to a Random Act of Violence

SCENARIOS THAT MIGHT TRIGGER THIS FEAR

Being asked out by someone
Friends who move away to college while the character stays put
A romantic relationship moving to a new level of commitment (becoming exclusive, moving in together, getting married, etc.)
Being unexpectedly alone—e.g., losing friends in a crowd
A sibling moving out of the house
A friend not returning a phone call, showing irritation, or doing something the character perceives as withdrawal
Experiencing the unexpected death of a parent, spouse, or other close loved one
Being selected as one of the people at work who will be laid off

HUMAN NEEDS THAT COULD BE IMPACTED

Self-Actualization: If a character allows this fear to drive their decision-making (such as not taking advantage of opportunities if it means moving away from a loved one), it will make it harder to pursue passions or achieve their dreams.

Esteem and Recognition: A character who shoulders the blame for being abandoned will think poorly of themselves, and their self-esteem will suffer.

Love and Belonging: Some characters in this situation can become clingy and needy while others push people away to avoid any chance of experiencing abandonment. Their response to this fear could cause difficulties in those important relationships.

Safety and Security: A character who decides that staying with a toxic or abusive person is better than being abandoned by them could put themselves in danger.

HOW THE CHARACTER CAN MINIMIZE OR OVERCOME IT

Examining their trauma and reclaiming their value
Giving people the benefit of the doubt: *Just because they're busy today doesn't mean they don't like me.*
Setting healthy boundaries with other people and focusing on self-worth
Turning to healthy activities (journaling, self-care, etc.) if abandonment is triggered

BEING A BURDEN TO OTHERS

NOTES: This fear can be expressed in any part of the character's life—emotional, physical, etc.—where they don't want to impose on people. While it's natural not to want to be a burden, it becomes problematic when the character suffers because they're unwilling or unable to share their own needs with others.

WHAT IT LOOKS LIKE

The character doing things themselves instead of asking for help
Paying their own way (at a restaurant, on a vacation, etc.)
Being a caretaker for younger siblings or friends
Being highly empathetic
Appearing aloof or private
Cleaning up after themselves (washing their own dishes, throwing away trash, etc.)
Helping others in need but refusing it when it's offered in return
Declining assistance for projects or tasks
Pushing others away
Rejecting monetary gifts (even when they need financial help)
Putting on a happy face even when times are tough
Not asking for advice when it's needed
Not reaching out to someone in a crisis
Difficulty connecting with others on a deeper, intimate level
Putting other people first
Valuing autonomy and independence
Perfectionistic tendencies
Immediately paying back a kindness or favor; being unable to owe anyone
Apologizing for the smallest inconveniences: "Sorry I'm late," or "I hope I'm not taking you away from something more important."
A tendency to take over (not working well on a team)
Making big decisions without input from family members (buying a house, getting surgery, etc.)
Proactively making funeral arrangements for themselves
Seeking euthanasia so no one has to take care of them

COMMON INTERNAL STRUGGLES

Difficulty saying no
Wanting help processing hard emotions but feeling unable to ask
Always striving to be helpful, and it taking a toll on the character
Having to care for themselves and make hard decisions without help or input
Striving for perfection
Feeling isolated from peers and loved ones
Believing their value comes from taking care of others
Feeling unworthy of love
Struggling with a fear of abandonment
Struggling with shame

Taking on more than they can handle
Lying about their needs
Feeling responsible for the thoughts and behaviors of others

HINDRANCES AND DISRUPTIONS TO THE CHARACTER'S LIFE
Rejecting necessary help and suffering as a result
Having to carry their own burdens
A lack of deep relationships because the character won't fully let people in
Being unhappy from loneliness and feeling disconnected
Taking on an impossible challenge because asking for help or admitting defeat is worse
Becoming burned out with the weight of their emotions and responsibilities
Experiencing a crisis that only gets worse when they refuse to reach out for help

EMOTIONAL WOUNDS IT COULD STEM FROM: A Parent's Abandonment or Rejection, A Physical Disfigurement, A Speech Impediment, Crossing Moral Lines to Survive, Falling Short of Society's Physical Standards, Living in an Emotionally Repressed Household

SCENARIOS THAT MIGHT TRIGGER THIS FEAR
The character going through something traumatic without having a support system
Developing a condition that requires a caretaker
Needing more support as they grow older
Falling on hard times and having to accept charity
Making a mistake that impacts other people
Falling apart in front of someone else
Being blamed for something that was not the character's fault
Feeling unneeded by their friends and peers

HUMAN NEEDS THAT COULD BE IMPACTED

Esteem and Recognition: A character with this fear may think less of themselves for needing or wanting to ask for help, resulting in lowered self-esteem.

Love and Belonging: The character's need for self-reliance may result in stubbornness and inflexibility, straining relationships with the important people in their life. Not wanting to burden others also causes emotional distance, disrupting intimacy.

Safety and Security: A character with this fear may ignore signs of a physical or mental condition and unnecessarily compromise their health.

Physiological Needs: Taken to an extreme, the compulsion to not be a burden could cause the character to completely isolate themselves. In this situation, even a minor accident or loss of survival resources could result in a loss of life.

HOW THE CHARACTER CAN MINIMIZE OR OVERCOME IT
Understanding what caused their reluctance to ask for help
Learning to see their own value and understand that they deserve to be cared for
Realizing others get a boost out of helping them just as they do by helping others
Learning that healthy relationships require give and take
Asking for small things to become more comfortable letting others in
Understanding that their personal needs are just as important as everyone else's

BEING SEPARATED FROM LOVED ONES

NOTES: A certain amount of separation anxiety among loved ones is normal; after all, it's easier to control circumstances and feel safe when everyone's close. But people can go to an extreme in this area, becoming panicked, distracted, and unable to function when the ones they care about are out of sight. This can cause obvious problems in those relationships, as well as stunting normal development for people in the character's care.

WHAT IT LOOKS LIKE

Codependency
Difficulty sleeping alone
Difficulty concentrating at school or work
Helicopter parenting
Frequently missing school or work because they must be home with family
Having an extremely limited social life; not wanting to leave loved ones home alone
Frequent calling or texting to check up on others
Refusing to travel far without family
Being unable to stay home alone
Instituting stifling and restricting rules for those in the character's care
Investing in security cameras to maximize home safety (and keep tabs on loved ones)
Difficulty socializing with people who aren't family
Making important decisions based on proximity (working with family members, choosing a job close to a child's school, etc.)
Insisting on accompanying their child everywhere (chaperoning school trips, volunteering at youth group, staying at a party instead of dropping their child off, etc.)
Being nervous when a family member is traveling or out of contact
Obsessively checking location apps to track loved ones when they're away
Devising a plan to unite family members in an emergency
Always doing things together (hobbies, vacations, etc.)
Not allowing anyone else to watch their kids
Following family members who move away
Difficulty accepting new family members, such as a child's spouse, who might take the child away
Encouraging dependency

COMMON INTERNAL STRUGGLES

Worrying something bad will happen to a loved one if the character isn't there
Wanting to become more independent but being too afraid to do so
Desiring stronger friend relationships but not wanting to upset the family dynamic
Mentally warring between wanting to keep loved ones safe and wanting them to be healthy and capable

HINDRANCES AND DISRUPTIONS TO THE CHARACTER'S LIFE

Suffering from anxiety or panic attacks
Being unable to set healthy boundaries (or respect the boundaries of others)

Missing out on social events, retreats, or vacations
Struggling to maintain and strengthen relationships outside of the family
Being unable to form healthy romantic relationships
Worry stealing the character's ability to live in the moment and enjoy life

EMOTIONAL WOUNDS IT COULD STEM FROM: A Home Invasion, A Life-Threatening Accident, A Natural or Man-Made Disaster, A School Shooting, Battling a Mental Condition, Becoming a Caregiver at an Early Age, Being Forced to Leave One's Homeland, Being Raised by Overprotective Parents, Experiencing the Death of a Parent as a Child, Losing a Loved One to a Random Act of Violence, The Death of One's Child

SCENARIOS THAT MIGHT TRIGGER THIS FEAR
Something happening to a loved one when they're away from the character
Impending life changes, such as a move or a family member getting engaged
A catastrophic event occurring while the family is split up
An ex suing the character for custody of the children
A loved one being invited to an overnight trip away from the family
Being alone
A child becoming rebellious and demanding more freedom
A son or daughter pushing back, saying they're being smothered
An adult child meeting someone on vacation and choosing to stay in that country

HUMAN NEEDS THAT COULD BE IMPACTED

Self-Actualization: This fear will drive the character's decision-making, overriding any personal desires, dreams, or goals.

Esteem and Recognition: A character who is unable to be apart from their family may be viewed by others as needy, insecure, incapable, or controlling.

Love and Belonging: Loved ones living with this character will chafe under their strict rules and constant scrutiny. In this situation, the character's desperate need to keep family members close may drive them away.

Safety and Security: A character who can't be separated from their loved ones won't trust others to safeguard them. Their inability to rely on police officers, doctors, teachers, and other caregivers may end up putting their charges in harm's way.

HOW THE CHARACTER CAN MINIMIZE OR OVERCOME IT
Realizing that too much hovering can stunt their loved one's growth
Seeing that distance from someone is an opportunity to show trust and love
Spending time alone in small increments to practice coping strategies and build resilience
Practicing independence through solo activities like reading, painting, or fishing
Spending time with others for companionship (apart from loved ones)
Taking a solo trip with only occasional check-ins
Pursuing self-discovery (trying new things, pursuing interests, trying new hobbies, etc.)
Celebrating small acts of independence

BEING TAKEN ADVANTAGE OF

NOTES: A character with this fear may worry about situations where they could be exploited. These could be serious crimes, such as sexual abuse and identity theft, or a simpler occurrence, like being used by a friend for their personal gain.

WHAT IT LOOKS LIKE

Highly valuing privacy
Being very independent
Living self-sufficiently
Questioning people's motives
Believing that other people can't be trusted
Being slow to volunteer or step up
Asking a lot of questions before committing to something
Not trusting quotes for services (believing the company will take advantage if they can)
Doing extensive research (to avoid scams, find out if someone is reliable, etc.)
Avoiding vulnerable situations, such as running at night or being alone with someone
Setting boundaries that keep others at a distance
Avoiding situations where the character has been burned in the past, such as dating, shopping online, or sharing their creative work with others
Not trusting certain types of people (politicians, salespeople, women, etc.)
Pulling away when people try to get too close
Establishing security measures (locking up documents, changing passwords frequently, giving a false name, etc.)
Demanding payment up front before offering services
Never purchasing something on impulse
Resisting new technologies or advances that carry an element of risk
Being standoffish with strangers and new acquaintances
Resenting requests for favors (e.g., an employer asking them to work an extra hour without pay) when there will be no reciprocity
Difficulty working with a team
Seeing exploitation where there is none

COMMON INTERNAL STRUGGLES

Being unable to trust others
Second-guessing people's motives
Living in a constant fear of betrayal
Feeling unnoticed and underappreciated
Doubting their own judgment (because they've been wrong about people before)
Not wanting to be constantly suspicious, but being unable to change it

HINDRANCES AND DISRUPTIONS TO THE CHARACTER'S LIFE

Career advancement opportunities slipping through their fingers because the character fears they'll be taken advantage of in some way

Being unable to develop meaningful relationship outside of a tight inner circle
Being perceived as paranoid, confrontational, and difficult to work with
Frequently making false assumptions about people
Missing out on friendships or romantic relationships because the character is too afraid to be vulnerable

EMOTIONAL WOUNDS IT COULD STEM FROM: A Toxic Relationship, An Abuse of Power, Being Falsely Accused of a Crime, Being Let Down by a Trusted Organization or Social System, Being Victimized by a Perpetrator Who Was Never Caught, Caving to Peer Pressure, Growing up in a Cult, Having One's Ideas or Work Stolen, Identity Theft, Infidelity, Living with an Abusive Caregiver, Misplaced Loyalty

SCENARIOS THAT MIGHT TRIGGER THIS FEAR

Being asked for a favor
Someone testing the character's boundaries
Being pressured for information, a commitment, or a purchase
Reuniting with someone who has taken advantage of the character in the past
Catching someone in a lie
Someone failing to follow through on a promise
Situations where vulnerability is expected (therapy, a Bible study, a game of truth or dare, etc.)
A loved one falling victim to a scam
Being stalked or followed

HUMAN NEEDS THAT COULD BE IMPACTED

Esteem and Recognition: A character with this fear may be looked down on by others as being paranoid or unreasonable. If the character has been victimized in the past, they also may blame themselves for being taken advantage of.

Love and Belonging: This character will likely have difficulty trusting others and being vulnerable with them, which can cause all kinds of problems in their relationships with close friends and family members.

Safety and Security: A character who distrusts the police, doctors, therapists, or others who are meant to help and protect may put themselves at risk needlessly.

HOW THE CHARACTER CAN MINIMIZE OR OVERCOME IT

Vetting friendships and relationships and setting boundaries
Educating themselves on scams, online safety, and how to fact-check
Giving people the opportunity to prove they are trustworthy in small, safe ways before giving them more access
Practicing awareness by paying attention to people and situations in safe environments
Recognizing the difference between a logical worry and baseless, intrusive thoughts
Learning to read body language
Thinking about how good it feels to be part of someone else's inner circle, and wanting trustworthy friends to share that feeling

BEING TAKEN FOR GRANTED

NOTES: Everyone has something to offer and wants to be appreciated for what they can do, so when their strengths and contributions are taken for granted, it can make them feel devalued. A character who has experienced or witnessed this could develop a fear of it happening to them at home, work, or other areas of life they've invested in.

WHAT IT LOOKS LIKE

Being hyper-sensitive to real and perceived unfairness
Pointing out the value they've added to ensure it's not overlooked
Believing their personal value is tied to being useful or what they contribute
Seeking validation and affirmation from others
Difficulty saying no
Overworking themselves
Offering validation to others (expressing gratitude, complimenting others, etc.)
Taking great care with their appearance
Going the extra mile to be thoughtful, helpful, or caring
Lighting up at the smallest signs of appreciation
Wanting credit for even small things
Soliciting feedback (and hoping it's positive): "Wasn't this a good idea?" or "How am I doing?"
Suppressing their feelings to avoid confrontation
Sulking or retreating when their ideas are rejected or their input is disregarded
The character reminding people about their contributions
Complaining about how much they do
Noticing (and possibly calling out) slights: "You're welcome for holding the door!"
Making passive aggressive comments about being undervalued
Complaining about being underpaid for their work
Resenting special treatment for others when the character feels overlooked
Believing in reciprocity and resenting people who are slow to return favors
Calling out others who are producing lesser quality work or aren't working as hard
Using the silent treatment to express anger or frustration

COMMON INTERNAL STRUGGLES

Feeling devalued or "less than" when someone takes them for granted
Saying yes, even when they don't want to
Mentally keeping score of all they do compared to other people
Feeling guilty about setting healthy boundaries
Struggling with low-level resentment that grows over time
Flirting with burnout
Mentally replaying past instances of being taken for granted
Wanting to be vulnerable with someone but wondering if their efforts will be taken for granted

HINDRANCES AND DISRUPTIONS TO THE CHARACTER'S LIFE

Being perceived as demanding, needy, or difficult
Subconsciously pairing up with takers

Obsessively keeping score (and being unhappy when they come up short)
Having unrealistic expectations (expecting others to give as much as the character does)
Viewing relationships as transactional
Being dissatisfied in relationships because the character gives more than they're given
Struggling with their sense of worth
Other people tiring of constantly having to express gratitude and appreciation

EMOTIONAL WOUNDS IT COULD STEM FROM: An Abuse of Power, Becoming a Caregiver at an Early Age, Being Fired or Laid Off, Being Treated as Property, Growing up in the Shadow of a Successful Sibling, Growing up with a Sibling's Disability or Chronic Illness, Having One's Ideas or Work Stolen

SCENARIOS THAT MIGHT TRIGGER THIS FEAR

A loved one asking the character for money
A spouse failing to express gratitude for the character's household duties
Being expected to work late or work a holiday
A coworker taking credit for the character's work
Siblings expecting the character to care for an ailing parent
Being asked for a free favor that's tied to the character's occupation—e.g., a lawyer being asked to provide extensive legal advice or take on a pro bono case
Having to do most of the work on a group project
A romantic partner taking a trip, leaving the character to handle home responsibilities
Getting a negative performance review at work
A friend only reaching out when they want something
Work duties being expanded without an increase in pay
Being teased or criticized for setting healthy boundaries

HUMAN NEEDS THAT COULD BE IMPACTED

Esteem and Recognition: A character who only feels worthwhile when others are expressing appreciation can find their self-esteem slowly eroding. Likewise, people often won't respect someone who is desperate for affirmation.

Love and Belonging: Without a balance of give and take in their relationships, the character may not feel valued. Relationships may also feel transactional to loved ones if the character is always keeping score.

Safety and Security: Some characters with this fear may be easily manipulated and end up in unhealthy or dangerous circumstances and relationships.

HOW THE CHARACTER CAN MINIMIZE OR OVERCOME IT

Valuing their time and teaching others to respect it—not agreeing to do something the other person can do themselves, for instance
Learning to say no to people
Recognizing guilt trips (including their own) and calling them out
Purposely using good manners with others to set the expectation for politeness
Teaching someone to do a task instead of simply doing it for them
Giving freely to those who do the same

BETRAYAL

NOTES: Being betrayed hurts, and it can take a long time to heal and rebuild trust. But it becomes a problem when the character is unable to trust anyone and constantly doubts the intentions of others.

WHAT IT LOOKS LIKE
Self-sufficiency
Being overly careful about sharing personal details
Having a few close friends, and keeping everyone else at arm's length
Being slow to warm up to new people
Asking pointed questions to suss out true intentions
Refusing to talk with people who hurt the character in the past
Maintaining strict personal boundaries
Demanding information about people's whereabouts or activities (to be sure they're telling the truth)
Utilizing tracking apps to monitor family members' locations
Keeping strict control of their finances
Keeping doors, cabinets, and drawers locked at work
Avoiding people similar to the person who hurt them in the past
Cynicism
The character keeping secrets, not sharing them with others
Not being able to take a joke
Being highly loyal to the trustworthy people in their life
Possessiveness
Testing loyalty by issuing ultimatums and demands
Checking up on a romantic partner to make sure they aren't cheating
Seeing manipulation where there is none
Being oversensitive to perceived betrayals (someone sharing something personal about the character, a friend choosing to sit with another person at an event, etc.)

COMMON INTERNAL STRUGGLES
Difficulty developing deep relationships
Believing the worst about people, even with no proof or provocation
Fearing intimacy
Always being on guard with others
Second-guessing other people's motives
The character knowing they're being irrational but being unable to change
Struggling with self-blame for past betrayals
Mistrusting their "people radar" if it was someone close who betrayed them

HINDRANCES AND DISRUPTIONS TO THE CHARACTER'S LIFE
Being unable to trust the people closest to them
Being emotionally detached from everyone
Refusing to accept help from others, even when it's desperately needed

Relationships being thwarted by the character's paranoia, anger, or possessiveness
Being weighed down with bitterness from being unable to forgive others

EMOTIONAL WOUNDS IT COULD STEM FROM: A Parent's Abandonment or Rejection, A Sibling's Betrayal, Abandonment Over an Unexpected Pregnancy, An Abuse of Power, Being Disowned or Shunned, Being Let Down by a Trusted Organization or Social System, Being Rejected by One's Peers, Childhood Sexual Abuse by a Known Person, Financial Ruin Due to a Spouse's Irresponsibility, Finding Out One's Child Was Abused, Having One's Ideas or Work Stolen, Infidelity, Misplaced Loyalty

SCENARIOS THAT MIGHT TRIGGER THIS FEAR
Running into someone who betrayed the character in the past
Discovering that a friend lied to the character or held back information
Feeling pressured into being vulnerable (having to share a secret, be alone with someone, etc.)
Hearing about an unfaithful partner's engagement
Having to start over with a new set of people (at a job or school, in a new city, etc.)
Needing to rely on a person or organization for help
An acquaintance seeking to gain the character's trust
Overhearing people they know (coworkers, friends, etc.) gossip about a third party
The character believing they've been betrayed but being told they're wrong

HUMAN NEEDS THAT COULD BE IMPACTED

Esteem and Recognition: Characters who have experienced betrayal can blame themselves, even though they've done nothing to deserve it. This leads to them wondering what's wrong with them and why others find it so easy to mistreat them.

Love and Belonging: A fear of betrayal can result in a host of dysfunctional behaviors that spill into many of a character's important relationships, damaging them.

Safety and Security: This fear can cause the character to avoid the people and organizations meant to help them.

Physiological Needs: A deep lack of trust due to an old betrayal can cause a stubborn character to reject life-saving treatment, resources, or aid.

HOW THE CHARACTER CAN MINIMIZE OR OVERCOME IT
Reminding themselves of times when their judgment was sound and they made strong choices (dispelling the lie that their gut can't be trusted)
Challenging the fear: is it being triggered by something in the present or an old memory?
Allowing people the opportunity to earn trust in small ways
Thinking about their own transgressions and how no one is perfect
Using self-improvement to reclaim self-esteem and banish thoughts of being "less than"
Recognizing that most slights happen not because of manipulation or spite, but because the other party is distracted, overwhelmed or tired
Putting the shoe on the other foot: if the character was late, should their partner assume it's because they're cheating?
Healing through forgiveness or letting go of the past

CONDITIONAL LOVE

NOTES: Love should be freely given, but unfortunately, this isn't always the case. For some, love must be earned through performance or achievements, or it can be withdrawn for certain infractions. A character who has experienced conditional love will perceive their value as being tied to specific behaviors or successes, and they'll develop habits meant to ensure acceptance. These thought patterns and actions may continue to plague the character despite their fear and rejection of this kind of love.

WHAT IT LOOKS LIKE

Being a people-pleaser
Being an overachiever and perfectionist
Making choices based on what other people want or like
Difficulty setting or maintaining personal and emotional boundaries
Being oversensitive to signs of anger, disappointment, or disapproval from others
Asking questions to determine what will make someone happiest
Only expressing positive emotions (to avoid driving people away)
Apologizing for the smallest of mistakes
Being slow to open up to new people
Being self-critical
Seeking ways to improve (but for the wrong reasons)
Building up emotional walls
Feeling anxious when they're being watched, evaluated, or critiqued
Finding it almost impossible to ask for help
Needing frequent reminders of a friend or partner's love
Seeking approval for their thoughts, actions, and emotions
Only showing the best side of themselves to others
Being highly obedient or subservient
Being too permissive; not knowing how to love while also providing correction
Loving others unconditionally
Being highly attuned to signs of conditional love in others
Staying in a toxic relationship

COMMON INTERNAL STRUGGLES

Constantly needing to prove themselves to others
Hating their own compulsion to seek approval
Wanting to be in a relationship but being afraid of disappointing the other party
Overthinking interactions
Doubting their own worth
Struggling with the weight of needing to meet everyone's expectations
Being unsure of where they stand with others
Believing they're unlovable
Resenting the imbalance in a relationship but not knowing what to do other than try harder to be better

Recognizing harmful thoughts (like being deeply self-critical) or behaviors (people-pleasing) but not being able to break them
Vowing to never love conditionally but worrying that they still do

HINDRANCES AND DISRUPTIONS TO THE CHARACTER'S LIFE
Difficulty forming intimate relationships
Getting involved in an ongoing cycle of toxic relationships
Not knowing what true love looks or feels like
Struggling to love fully and vulnerably
Viewing minor setbacks as major failures and defining moments
Their frequent questioning of someone's love and constant need for affirmation creating friction with others

EMOTIONAL WOUNDS IT COULD STEM FROM: Being Disowned or Shunned, Being Raised by Parents Who Loved Conditionally, Being Rejected by One's Peers, Being Sent Away as a Child, Failing at School, Getting Dumped, Growing up in the Public Eye, Having Parents Who Favored One Child Over Another

SCENARIOS THAT MIGHT TRIGGER THIS FEAR
Having to interact with a parent, ex, or sibling who loved the character conditionally
Beginning a new friendship and not knowing what's expected
Being asked out
A past abuser or manipulator asking for forgiveness
Realizing they have loved someone conditionally
Making a mistake that hurts someone else
Falling short of someone's expectations
Being blown off or ignored

HUMAN NEEDS THAT COULD BE IMPACTED

Self-Actualization: A character who fears they will be rejected if they don't meet someone's expectations will make decisions based on what those people want rather than what the character wants. Without the freedom to follow their own path, they may never find fulfillment.

Esteem and Recognition: This character is going to have trouble loving and accepting themselves for who they are because their self-worth is tied to the conditions placed upon them by others.

Love and Belonging: A character with this fear may still struggle to set and maintain personal boundaries in close relationships. Their fear of being loved in this way can also result in behaviors that put others off.

HOW THE CHARACTER CAN MINIMIZE OR OVERCOME IT
Recognizing that the person who taught the character that their value was tied to achievement failed miserably as a parent, a teacher, etc.
Experiencing true love and using that as a model for their interactions with others
Avoiding relationships with people who are overly driven and competitive
Affirming their own worth by journaling about their good qualities, small successes, and areas of growth

CONFLICT

NOTES: Disagreements happen, and while most of us don't like confrontation, we understand the need to resolve friction. But for some, the threat of conflict sparks such heightened anxiety that they'll do anything to avoid it. This can create a real problem for characters, who will face conflict often on the path to their goal.

WHAT IT LOOKS LIKE

Being highly agreeable or a people-pleaser
Asking tentative questions
Lying when someone asks if something is wrong
Avoiding touchy topics in a conversation
Changing the topic if emotions start to overheat
Avoiding people who are aggressive and outspoken
Being highly proactive or over-prepared (so nothing will go wrong)
Backing away from people who are emotionally activated
Finding it almost impossible to say no
Letting other people make decisions
Not voicing their unhappiness or dissatisfaction (e.g., not saying anything about an undercooked meal at a restaurant)
Not returning purchases that are broken or under warranty
Putting up with annoyances rather than asking someone to stop
Giving in and letting others have their way
Accepting blame when it isn't deserved
Apologizing to end things (even when they've done nothing wrong)
Letting others take the credit rather than fight about it
Working hard to make up for someone's deficiency rather than talking to them about it
Not rocking the boat
Telling people what they want to hear
Echoing popular opinions
Coming across as overly nice
Withdrawing or becoming quiet when others are upset
Being a perfectionist
Not self-advocating
Becoming flustered, frazzled, or teary when confronted

COMMON INTERNAL STRUGGLES

Wanting to escape when a confrontation happens
Worrying about whether something they're doing is annoying others
Resenting people for making life harder instead of asking them to change
Thinking about the worst-case scenario
Putting their own needs last
Self-directed anger for not standing up for what was right
Being uncertain in the moment
Struggling to manage heightened anxiety symptoms and just wanting to flee

HINDRANCES AND DISRUPTIONS TO THE CHARACTER'S LIFE
Becoming overburdened because others take advantage of their inability to say no
Being viewed as timid and weak by others
Putting up with people they don't like because they can't sever the relationship
Being taken advantage of by others (intentionally or inadvertently)
A lack of assertiveness holding the character back at work
Becoming burned out
Never getting to do what they want
Personal dreams and goals being put on hold
Emotions and tension being suppressed until the character eventually explodes

EMOTIONAL WOUNDS IT COULD STEM FROM: A Speech Impediment, A Toxic Relationship, Being Bullied, Domestic Abuse, Having a Controlling or Overly Strict Parent, Living in an Emotionally Repressed Household, Social Difficulties

SCENARIOS THAT MIGHT TRIGGER THIS FEAR
Receiving criticism (even when it's constructive)
Being asked to pick a side when two friends are fighting
Making a mistake that will be noticed and mentioned by others
Needing to confront a friend (about self-destructive behavior, to stand up for what's right, etc.)
Arguments and yelling
Being asked to lead
Having to deliver bad news
Having to raise a complaint, follow up on a warranty claim, or return an item to a store
A coworker getting angry or frustrated around the character

HUMAN NEEDS THAT COULD BE IMPACTED

Esteem and Recognition: A character who continually backs down and sidesteps friction will eventually think less of themselves. Others will also have less respect for a character who is unwilling to confront wrongdoing.

Love and Belonging: Ignoring problems with others will cause the issues to fester, weakening those relationships.

Safety and Security: Not all conflict is equal. Some situations are more dangerous, hurtful, and toxic than others, and a character who is unable to face conflict may find themselves in unsafe circumstances.

HOW THE CHARACTER CAN MINIMIZE OR OVERCOME IT
Joining a debate team to get more comfortable with conflicting opinions
Roleplaying conflict situations with someone they trust
Understanding the triggers that cause them to shut down (raised voices, violence, etc.) or escalate their anger
Learning how to argue respectfully (actively listening, conveying a clear viewpoint, etc.)
Establishing boundaries with other people
Resisting people-pleasing tendencies when the emotions of others are activated
Preparing for a difficult conversation by planning out what to say in advance

EMOTIONAL VULNERABILITY

NOTES: Relationships are important for all people, and to build them, we have to share our emotions and be honest about our feelings with others. But not everyone is comfortable or even capable of opening up this way. A character who fears rejection or pain may be reluctant to "go there" emotionally. To avoid risking this vulnerability, they'll take on behaviors and habits that keep people at bay, resulting in loneliness and isolation from others.

WHAT IT LOOKS LIKE

Difficulty making eye contact when emotions are high
Sticking to surface-level conversations
Ending relationships before they become serious
Engaging in one-night stands to avoid having to connect
Not volunteering information about their past
Staying busy—always moving—to avoid connecting with others
Knowing their own emotional sensitivities and avoiding triggers for them
Having an exit strategy when they're out with others
Being highly independent and self-reliant
Appearing distant, self-absorbed, or uncaring to discourage others from wanting to get close to and confide in them
Adopting a look that makes them seem intimidating or unapproachable
Wearing earbuds or headphones to avoid small talk in public spaces
Answering questions with as little actual information as possible
Deflecting conversation away from emotional topics
Juggling multiple romantic partners to avoid committing to one
Telling people what they want to hear to stave off conflict or high emotions
Struggling to express their emotional needs
Seeming to be emotionally flat; not expressing highs or lows
Dissociating or checking out during highly emotional moments
Frequently abandoning people, jobs, and hobbies when they become emotionally uncomfortable
Withdrawing from people altogether

COMMON INTERNAL STRUGGLES

Telling themselves they're happy with their life but feeling like they're missing something
Wanting to connect but believing that expressing their true feelings will drive others away
Wanting a spouse and family but not being able to trust anyone to that level
Secretly envying people who are uninhibited and have deep connections with others
Suffering from depression or anxiety
Yearning to offload feelings but suffering in silence
Overthinking their relationships and interactions with others
Always worrying that someone they trust will reject them

HINDRANCES AND DISRUPTIONS TO THE CHARACTER'S LIFE

Always having to keep their guard up

Struggling through personal problems alone; having no one to turn to for help
Avoiding family reunions, weddings, or funerals because of the emotional output they generate
Being viewed as apathetic, cold, or selfish
Having an experience that awakens deep emotion but being unable to show or share it
Stifling certain emotions around others
Going through life without a soul mate or true friends
Having no support system when help is needed
Having to start over often (with new people, a job change, a relocation, etc.)

EMOTIONAL WOUNDS IT COULD STEM FROM: A Parent's Abandonment or Rejection, Being Rejected by One's Peers, Being Sent Away as a Child, Childhood Sexual Abuse by a Known Person, Experiencing the Death of a Parent as a Child or Youth, Getting Dumped, Growing up in Foster Care, Misplaced Loyalty

SCENARIOS THAT MIGHT TRIGGER THIS FEAR
The character learning they're pregnant
A serious medical diagnosis that requires support from others
Being asked to speak at a funeral
Falling in love with someone
Being rejected or betrayed by a trusted friend
A therapist digging around a past betrayal or abandonment
Being catfished
Having to care for an ill loved one
A romantic partner wanting more emotionally from the character
Being asked to mentor someone

HUMAN NEEDS THAT COULD BE IMPACTED

Esteem and Recognition: A character who desires connection but continually sabotages it may wonder what's wrong with them and despise themselves.

Love and Belonging: This fear will cause a character to maintain superficial relationships, preventing them from knowing true love.

Safety and Security: A character with this fear may stay in unhealthy relationships because less emotion or true connection is required from them.

HOW THE CHARACTER CAN MINIMIZE OR OVERCOME IT
A willingness to examine where this fear came from and question the past: *Is this person who taught me to fear emotional openness really a trusted source of truth?*
Reframing vulnerability as the courage to live authentically
Practice openness by sharing an idea, a hope for the future, etc. with someone they trust
Reclaiming power by privately processing emotions rather than locking them away
Pushing back on personal questions that are triggering, setting boundaries with others
Experiencing the lightness (relief) of sharing a problem or anxiety with someone who cares and wants to help
Working with a professional to dispel lies about vulnerability being the same as inferiority or weakness

HEARTBREAK

NOTES: Love requires vulnerability, and that's not easy for everyone. People who open themselves up to others will experience heartbreak at some point, whether through rejection, abandonment, or simply losing someone they care about. This kind of pain is deeply unpleasant, so characters naturally fear it and will try to avoid re-experiencing it.

WHAT IT LOOKS LIKE

Staying busy to keep from building relationships with others
Isolating themselves; not getting too close to people
Using humor as a coping mechanism to suppress emotional pain
Avoiding risk in friendships and romantic relationships
Avoiding places that remind the character of a past heartbreak
Being the life of the party but not making deep connections with others
Engaging in romantic relationships that are safe (because they won't go anywhere)
Avoiding relational commitments
Being emotionally unavailable
Having impossibly high standards when dating
The character prioritizing themselves over others, always looking out for number one
Being vocal about not settling to justify a resistance to dating or commitment
Becoming hardened and skeptical
Being jaded about love—believing it's a fallacy, it never lasts, etc.
Frequently bringing up the past; needing to talk about relationship dysfunction, betrayals, or how someone hurt or abandoned the character
Dumping love interests before they can reject the character
Staying in an unhealthy relationship to avoid a breakup
Becoming overly submissive or compliant to avoid conflict and keep others happy
Growing needy or clingy
Being overly protective with children to keep them from experiencing pain or difficulty
Not having children (because the character can't stand the thought of losing them)
Keeping a pet as a replacement for human connections (or refusing to keep a pet out of fear of it passing away)
Picking fights to stave off intimacy
Encouraging others to avoid situations that could end in heartbreak

COMMON INTERNAL STRUGGLES

Feeling emotionally drawn to someone but being too scared to take a risk
Craving intimacy but fearing vulnerability more
Desiring a variety of close relationships but being unable to fully trust others
Wanting to reconnect with an estranged loved one but fearing rejection
Behaving as if nothing bothers them despite the opposite being true
Difficulty setting or maintaining healthy boundaries
Being held captive by a past heartbreak but not knowing how to move past it
Regretting missed opportunities due to fear-driven choices

Feeling left behind when others make commitments and experience deep connections
Struggling with jealousy when they see other people experiencing love

HINDRANCES AND DISRUPTIONS TO THE CHARACTER'S LIFE
Being unable to trust people
Being viewed as self-involved, apathetic, or abrasive
Difficulty relating to others because the character is single, doesn't have children, doesn't have deep friendships, etc.
Struggling to process or express sadness and grief
Not having support when tragedy strikes
Growing old alone

EMOTIONAL WOUNDS IT COULD STEM FROM: A Miscarriage or Stillbirth, A Parent's Abandonment or Rejection, A Sibling's Betrayal, Being Rejected by One's Peers, Getting Dumped, Infidelity, The Death of One's Child

SCENARIOS THAT MIGHT TRIGGER THIS FEAR
The anniversary of a past heartbreak approaching
Running into someone who broke the character's heart
The character's child losing someone
A significant other saying, "We need to talk."
A spouse's brush with death
A child rebelling and running away from home
A loved one being deployed to a dangerous location
A romantic relationship progressing toward something significant
Suspecting a loved one of betrayal
Investing in a friendship and discovering it wasn't real, that the friend was using the character in some way

HUMAN NEEDS THAT COULD BE IMPACTED
Self-Actualization: This fear creates an aversion to risk and disappointment, which may cause the character to hold back in relationships and many areas of life.
Love and Belonging: The character's inability to pursue or develop deep relationships will lead to a lack of meaningful connection with others.
Safety and Security: A character without meaningful relationships may become vulnerable in an emergency if they have no one to help them through it.

HOW THE CHARACTER CAN MINIMIZE OR OVERCOME IT
Identifying a few people they can trust, and opening up to them
Deciding that the benefit of developing deep relationships outweighs the risk of being vulnerable and possibly being hurt
Remembering that not all relationships are permanent, and moving on is sometimes for the best
Forgiving people for their past actions and letting old hurts go
Shifting their perspective to be grateful for the time they had with someone
Reminding themselves of their strength, capability, and resilience by pushing themselves to try something outside their comfort zone but within their abilities

INFIDELITY

NOTES: Romantic relationships are built on trust and become jeopardized when one party can't depend on the other to stay true. If this becomes a motivating fear (because the character experienced infidelity themselves or watched someone else suffer through it), it may cause them to go to great lengths to safeguard themselves from being blindsided.

WHAT IT LOOKS LIKE

The character doubting their own abilities and attractiveness
Avoiding TV shows and movies that involve cheating
Bending over backward to please a partner
Worrying excessively when a partner is late or doesn't call
Agreeing to bedroom activities they're not comfortable with to appease their partner
Going overboard to maintain their physical appearance (to keep their partner interested)
Being overly jealous or territorial
The character trying to keep their lover all to themselves
Being needy or clingy
Needing constant reassurances
The character paying close attention to the partner's behavior around friends
Asking leading questions: "Is he good-looking?" or "Do you wish I had abs like that?"
Secretly checking up on a partner—accessing their phone without permission, following them, etc.
Trying to trick a partner into confessing to suspected indiscretions
Enlisting friends to spy on the other party
Becoming suspicious when the partner doesn't immediately return calls or texts
Catfishing a significant other online (or having a friend do it)
Accusing a lover of being unfaithful
Not dating at all
Engaging in one-night stands and flings rather than seeking long-term relationships

COMMON INTERNAL STRUGGLES

Wanting to trust a partner but being unable to do so
Comparing themselves to others and coming up short
Feeling insecure, as if the partner is disappointed in them (physically, intellectually, etc.)
Struggling with soaring anxiety for no real reason
Questioning their suspicions (*Is this real or am I being paranoid?*)
Feeling guilty about spying on or checking up on a partner
The character wanting to discuss their suspicions but being afraid to hear the truth
The mind getting stuck on what-if cheating scenarios (*What if he likes his new work partner more than me? What if something happens at the upcoming conference?*)
Feeling like they always have to compete with perceived rivals

HINDRANCES AND DISRUPTIONS TO THE CHARACTER'S LIFE

Relationships ending due to unfounded accusations or spying
Overwhelming worry making it impossible to enjoy relationships

The character's pushy or suspicious behavior prodding their partner toward an affair
Clingy behavior driving the lover away
Losing a friend because the character starts to see them as a potential threat
Unstable, volatile relationships becoming normal for the character
The character being alone because they're afraid to get into a relationship
Inherently distrusting anyone close to the partner who could be a threat
The character isolating their partner and themselves and losing other relationships

EMOTIONAL WOUNDS IT COULD STEM FROM: A Parent's Divorce, Discovering a Partner's Sexual Orientation Secret, Infidelity, Learning That One's Parent Had a Second Family, Misplaced Loyalty

SCENARIOS THAT MIGHT TRIGGER THIS FEAR

The character's lover starting a project with an attractive coworker
A friend's relationship falling apart due to cheating
The character finding suspicious texts or emails
Noticing sudden changes in the significant other (personal grooming habits, a change in schedule, going out with friends more often, etc.)
Catching a partner in a lie
A lover becoming more secretive—hiding a cell phone, locking their computer, or being evasive about where they're going and what they're doing
Unusual charges on a shared credit card statement
The character's spouse requesting more time to themselves
Decreased affection, attention, and physical closeness from a significant other
The character's spouse forgetting an important date, like an anniversary or birthday

HUMAN NEEDS THAT COULD BE IMPACTED

Self-Actualization: Taken far enough, this fear can drive a character to trade meaningful goals and rewarding activities for holding onto their partner at all costs.

Esteem and Recognition: A character who believes their partner will cheat will often blame themselves, as if they're not attractive, interesting, or intelligent enough to keep their partner's attention.

Love and Belonging: A character who fears the possibility of infidelity will adopt characteristics (neediness, possessiveness, jealousy, controlling tendencies) that can undermine the relationship they're trying to protect.

HOW THE CHARACTER CAN MINIMIZE OR OVERCOME IT

Connecting the fear to the person who caused it rather than seeing all partners as potential betrayers
Challenging bias by looking to the healthy, committed relationships around them
Building trust slowly
Being open about the past and the character's triggers to foster open communication and accountability for the character
Assessing triggers as they come up and challenging any fear of infidelity that results (*Is it likely or am I overreacting?*)
Keeping a journal of all the times their partner showed loyalty and trust

LONELINESS

NOTES: The need to be understood and validated is part of the human experience, but some, even surrounded by people, still feel alone. This type of emotional disconnectedness is distressing, so characters may go to unhealthy lengths to forge deep connections. Unfortunately, doing this can inadvertently drive people away.

This fear differs from PHYSICAL ISOLATION—being physically separated from others—so it's important to know which may be in play for your character.

WHAT IT LOOKS LIKE

Politeness
Initiating conversations
Moving close to people to feel connected
Listening in to the conversations of others in public spaces
Lingering at the checkout to enjoy a conversation for a few moments longer
Regularly calling loved ones to check in
Pursuing many social hobbies and interests
Seeking validation from others
Struggling with even constructive criticism because it makes the character feel judged
Participating in online chats and social media to connect with people
Gravitating toward activities that support deeper interactions (therapy, a Bible study, coffee with a friend, etc.)
Preferring small group and one-on-one interactions to large gatherings
Attending many social events
Looking for opportunities to start a conversation
Seeking a sense of true connectedness with people; being dissatisfied with surface-level relationships
Asking personal questions to get to know people more deeply
Oversharing
Not picking up on social cues when someone wants to leave or end a conversation
Trying to persuade people to agree with them
Escalating relationships quickly; going deep early on
Being observant and thoughtful, but it sometimes comes off wrong
Investing more in relationships than the other person does
Low productivity in the workplace due to focusing on relationships

COMMON INTERNAL STRUGGLES

Struggling to be carefree and lighthearted around others
Feeling like no one understands them
Feeling like they're always chasing after others, and no one is pursuing them
Never knowing where they stand with others
Being envious of people who connect easily and deeply with others
Believing their lack of connections means there's something wrong with them
Overanalyzing recent interactions with others to see what the character did wrong
Worrying that if they disappeared, no one would notice

HINDRANCES AND DISRUPTIONS TO THE CHARACTER'S LIFE

Being tied to their phone (so they won't miss a text message or call)
Being viewed as clingy
Getting too serious too soon with potential romantic partners
Often being alone, and struggling to be comfortable with that
Struggling with depression
Becoming anxious in social situations, which makes it harder for them to connect
Being taken advantage of because they're so eager to build relationships
Trying to connect in ineffective or off-putting ways, and not recognizing the problem

EMOTIONAL WOUNDS IT COULD STEM FROM: A Nomadic Childhood, A Parent's Abandonment or Rejection, Abandonment over an Unexpected Pregnancy, Battling a Mental Condition, Being Disowned or Shunned, Being Rejected by One's Peers

SCENARIOS THAT MIGHT TRIGGER THIS FEAR

Being ghosted by someone
A close friend distancing themselves from the character
Attending an event to find friends and seeing others pair up while the character is unable to make a personal connection
Not being invited to a party
Discovering that someone they thought was a close friend doesn't know them at all
Being excluded or overlooked (by a mom group, by classmates, at a team building event)
The character's attempts to connect with a teenaged child being rebuffed
A crisis looming, and the character realizing they have no one to call
Being invited to an event and having no one to go with

HUMAN NEEDS THAT COULD BE IMPACTED

Esteem and Recognition: A character who fears loneliness may become desperate to connect, which can cause others to view them as needy or clingy. The character very often will assume there's something wrong with them (though they may not know what it is), causing their own esteem to plummet.

Love and Belonging: If the character's attempts to stave off loneliness are annoying or off-putting, they won't be able to make the connections they desire and will continue to be lonely and dissatisfied.

HOW THE CHARACTER CAN MINIMIZE OR OVERCOME IT

Investing in friendships
Using different methods to connect with people (chat groups, online gaming, etc.)
Get companionship by becoming a pet sitter or dog walker
Recognizing that building strong relationships is a gradual process that takes time
Engaging in routines and activities so there's less time to dwell on being alone
Volunteering in causes they're passionate about and finding companions that "get" them
Learning to read other people's social cues
Seeing alone time as a benefit rather than a sign of relational failure

NEVER FINDING LOVE

NOTES: Many cultures place a high value on finding a romantic partner, and a character who has struggled in this area or feels they're at a disadvantage can begin to fear they'll never find love. This can erode the character's self-perception, lead them to minimize the benefits of other relationships, and cause a sense of dread about the future.

WHAT IT LOOKS LIKE

Joining many dating websites
Going to clubs and bars to find partners
Attaching too quickly to potential romantic partners
Taking great pains with their appearance
Exercising or working out religiously
Asking people to set them up on dates
Watching movies or shows that focus on romantic relationships
Obtaining nice stuff (cars, homes, jewelry, clothing, etc.) to attract a mate
Being flirtatious and direct
Jumping at any chance for love (any port in a storm)
Avoiding people who inquire about the character's love life
Staying with an incompatible romantic partner rather than be alone
Claiming that all the good ones have been taken
Pretending that being single doesn't bother them
Trying to be what others want
Investing in self-improvement books and courses
Measuring happiness by the state of their love life
Comparing their love life to their friends'
Engaging in activities solely for the purpose of meeting someone
Clinging to nostalgic items from past relationships
Staying on top of fashion and dating trends
Becoming clingy or needy when someone shows an interest
Getting intimate with a romantic partner too quickly
Analyzing a current partner's words and actions to see if their interest is waning
Becoming possessive of a love interest
Prioritizing love over everything else (professional goals, personal interests, etc.)

COMMON INTERNAL STRUGGLES

Romanticizing a past love interest and wondering if they're "the one who got away"
Feeling pitied by others
Losing themselves in their attempt to be what someone else wants
Worrying that life without love isn't worth living
Dreading birthdays that mark another year alone
The character wondering what's wrong with them
Feeling as if they don't measure up
Knowing someone they're currently with is bad for them but not wanting to be alone
Being desperately unhappy but having to pretend everything's fine

Resenting happy couples, then feeling guilt or shame about it
Being overwhelmed with envy when a friend finds love

HINDRANCES AND DISRUPTIONS TO THE CHARACTER'S LIFE
Being targeted by bad players taking advantage of the character's desperation
Having to answer questions from friends and family about their love life
Becoming too serious too soon in romantic relationships
Overlooking red flags, then finding themselves in a dangerous situation
Their professional life being impacted when they get involved with a coworker
Settling instead of waiting for someone who's a good fit
Giving up their own goals to support a love interest in pursuit of theirs
Moving across the country to pursue love
Committing to someone before realizing they're not compatible

EMOTIONAL WOUNDS IT COULD STEM FROM: A Parent's Abandonment or Rejection, Being Rejected by One's Peers, Getting Dumped, Growing up in Foster Care, Infidelity, Social Difficulties, Unrequited Love

SCENARIOS THAT MIGHT TRIGGER THIS FEAR
Being dumped or ghosted
A close friend getting engaged
Being pressured by a love interest to do something the character isn't comfortable with
Learning that an ex has found true love
Discovering a love interest's infidelity
Being catfished
The character's parents divorcing
A love interest having to relocate for family or work
Finding "the one," then learning something about them that makes them unsuitable
Having to attend a friend's wedding alone

HUMAN NEEDS THAT COULD BE IMPACTED
Self-Actualization: A character who chooses to sacrifice their needs, dreams, or identity to make a lover happy will become resentful and feel increasingly unfulfilled.

Esteem and Recognition: Someone may end up with self-esteem issues if they allow this fear to pressure them into choosing someone that others hold in high esteem rather than waiting for a partner who cherishes them for who they are.

Love and Belonging: This fear could generate insecurity that manifests as jealousy, neediness, or a constant need for assurance, driving love interests away.

Safety and Security: This fear can blind characters to the true nature of others, putting them at risk of being taken advantage of.

HOW THE CHARACTER CAN MINIMIZE OR OVERCOME IT
Recognizing that while romantic love is desirable, it isn't necessary for fulfillment
Seeking friendship first (because if love follows, it will be an enduring love)
The character learning to love themselves before finding it with someone else
Being open to different forms of love, not just the romantic kind
Being secure in themselves so they attract people who like them for who they are

NOT FITTING IN

NOTES: As social creatures, we all want to be loved and received by others. When a character fears that they won't fit in with those around them, the need to be accepted—in general or by a specific group—can become obsessive.

WHAT IT LOOKS LIKE

Trying too hard to impress
Overpreparing to be sure social interactions are perfect
Mimicking the actions, speech patterns, and habits of others
Struggling to say no
Pointing out similarities, no matter how small: "I like to skip breakfast, too!"
Telling people what they want to hear
Being too complimentary (or complimenting too often)
Laughing or smiling at things the character normally wouldn't approve of
Seeking out like-minded individuals
Using self-deprecating humor
Sharing personal accomplishments to impress others
Hiding ideas or beliefs that wouldn't be popular with the group
Changing their habits or preferences (clothing, the music they listen to, etc.) to fit in
Over-investing in the opinions of those they want to fit in with (making changes based on their suggestions, quitting things they disapprove of, etc.)
Putting others down if doing so pleases the group
The character being pressured into doing things they don't agree with
Allowing people to mistreat them if it means being part of the group
Being a loner
Being quiet, withdrawn, and content to stay in the background
Proactively rejecting others before they can reject the character

COMMON INTERNAL STRUGGLES

The character wanting to be true to themselves but also wanting to be liked
Losing sight of who they really are and what they believe
Worrying excessively about what others think
The character constantly analyzing their appearance, their responses, etc., and being disappointed
Ignoring their own needs and well-being
The character disliking how the group treats them but not wanting to be alone
Living in a constant state of uncertainty—of being alone, doing something wrong, being laughed at—and hating it

HINDRANCES AND DISRUPTIONS TO THE CHARACTER'S LIFE

Losing any sense of personal identity
Being a slave to the whims and demands of the group
Struggling to think for themselves
Their needs going unmet because they've put others' before their own

Being taken advantage of
Normalizing toxic relationships
Gaining a reputation for being inauthentic, weak-minded, or dishonest
Living a lonely life (because it's too risky to try to be accepted by others)

EMOTIONAL WOUNDS IT COULD STEM FROM: A Physical Disfigurement, A Speech Impediment, Battling a Mental Condition, Falling Short of Society's Physical Standards, Losing a Limb, Prejudice or Discrimination, Social Difficulties

SCENARIOS THAT MIGHT TRIGGER THIS FEAR

Having to start over in a new place (a new school, job, city, etc.)
Attending a party or gathering where friend groups are already established and the character doesn't know anyone
Encountering a barrier to belonging that they can't control (wealth, lineage, etc.)
A friend asking for space because they're being suffocated
Being criticized by someone influential within their group
Having to apply (for a club, to live in a certain building, etc.) and being deemed suitable
Witnessing someone being shunned, belittled, or ostracized by others
Having to sit alone (at lunch, church, etc.)
Seeing a loner become targeted because they have no group to protect them

HUMAN NEEDS THAT COULD BE IMPACTED

Self-Actualization: A character with this fear can easily lose sight of who they are because they're so focused on being who other people want them to be. It's difficult to be fully actualized when your dreams, beliefs, goals, and ideals are no longer your own.

Esteem and Recognition: A character with this fear will likely be insecure about their ability to fit in as their true selves. As such, they won't think too highly of who they really are. If their need to fit in drives them to embrace certain ideas or change who they are, they may also lose the respect of others.

Love and Belonging: A character who isn't fully accepted by others will suffer without a people group and support system of their own.

Safety and Security: Depending on the character's level of desperation, they may be willing to go to dangerous or self-destructive lengths to connect with others.

HOW THE CHARACTER CAN MINIMIZE OR OVERCOME IT

Recognizing where they're insecure or awkward and seeking to strengthen those areas
Setting reasonable boundaries (and respecting other people's)
Resisting the urge to compare themselves to others
Appreciating uniqueness and authenticity
Choosing which groups of people to engage with (and which not to)
Being confident in who they are
Being friendly and approachable
Working on their self-confidence by setting achievable goals and following through

PHYSICAL ISOLATION

NOTES: As social beings, it's common for humans to seek out others for support, companionship, or safety. But alone time is also important for people to be able to rest, reflect, recharge, and be comfortable with themselves. A character who fears physical isolation won't be able to do these things because of the intense discomfort that arises when they're alone. So this entry will explore what the fear of being separated from others can look like.

If your character fears emotional isolation and the feeling of being disconnected from people, see the LONELINESS entry.

WHAT IT LOOKS LIKE

Living in a highly populated area
Having an overly active social life
Always having a significant other
Flourishing in large groups of people
Pursuing a public career or one that requires steady interactions with others
Being the one who coordinates get-togethers
Keeping the TV on at night as background noise
Working in an office rather than remotely
Joining clubs, organizations, gyms, etc. to be around people
Having a large family
Being the last one to leave the party
Going out alone (to bars, a restaurant, etc.) and engaging strangers in conversation
Hanging out in busy, bustling locations
The character volunteering to host events (family dinners, book club meetings, etc.)
Preferring to live with someone (a partner, roommate, etc.) or in close proximity to others (apartment buildings, row housing, or townhouses)
Choosing to live close to family (in the same city, neighborhood, condo building, etc.)
Inviting friends to shop together, run errands, go to the gym, etc.
Making do with surface-level relationships when deeper ones aren't available
Being in multiple romantic relationships simultaneously
The character making efforts to get to know their neighbors
Renovating often or scheduling home repairs so workers are always around
Difficulty respecting other people's boundaries (calling late at night, showing up uninvited, etc.)

COMMON INTERNAL STRUGGLES

Needing downtime to decompress but not wanting to be alone
Being stressed and exhausted by a packed social calendar yet continuing to fill it
Fearing their inner thoughts and emotions when they're alone
Fearing they can't take care of themselves on their own
Negative thoughts and feelings taking over in the absence of other people
Feeling anxious, unsafe, or panicky when alone
Bad memories or insecurities surfacing when no one is around

HINDRANCES AND DISRUPTIONS TO THE CHARACTER'S LIFE

Being unable to enjoy time alone in their own company
Getting behind on personal things (bill paying, cleaning, etc.) because they're always out
Having more shallow friendships than deep and personal ones (because the character is flitting from one group of people to another)
Friends becoming less available because the character's friendship feels suffocating
Engaging romantically with people who aren't a good fit simply because they're available
Past pain going unresolved because the character won't face it
Being over-scheduled
Using drugs, food, or alcohol when alone to combat anxiety
Annoying others by intruding on their time and spaces too often

EMOTIONAL WOUNDS IT COULD STEM FROM: A Home Invasion, Abandonment over an Unexpected Pregnancy, Battling a Mental Condition, Becoming a Caregiver at an Early Age, Being Disowned or Shunned, Being Forced to Leave One's Homeland, Being Rejected by One's Peers, Growing up in the Public Eye

SCENARIOS THAT MIGHT TRIGGER THIS FEAR

A horrible secret or memory surfacing during a quiet moment alone
Getting lost or being stranded (due to a travel issue, a car breakdown, etc.)
Being dumped and having a lot of disposable time
Being sent away (for positive or negative reasons)
A pandemic or environmental disaster that triggers a lockdown
Seeing someone suffering alone with the same issue that plagues the character (depression, anxiety, wrestling with a similar wounding event, etc.)
Plans falling through, leaving the character on their own
An illness or surgery that requires recovery time alone

HUMAN NEEDS THAT COULD BE IMPACTED

Self-Actualization: If a character is uncomfortable being alone, they'll struggle with reflection and self-evaluation, making self-awareness and personal growth difficult to achieve.

Esteem and Recognition: Someone who makes a nuisance of themselves (being needy, popping in unannounced, constantly being a third wheel, etc.) may damage their reputation with those who don't appreciate that type of behavior.

Love and Belonging: Ironically, a character with this fear may struggle to maintain deep relationships if their constant need to be with others becomes off-putting.

HOW THE CHARACTER CAN MINIMIZE OR OVERCOME IT

Remembering times when they needed space and realizing others also have this need
Staying busy when alone: going for walks, gardening, tackling a to-do list, etc.
Visiting wildlife-rich locations with lots of activity (ducks in a pond, deer grazing, etc.)
Celebrating acts of independence
Taking in a pet to make the house seem less lonely
Staying active
Putting energy into learning—taking a class, pursuing a hobby, or refining a skill

REJECTION

NOTES: One of our basic human needs is to be loved, accepted, and valued, so it makes sense that we generally want to stave off rejection. When the desire to avoid it becomes a full-blown fear, it can hinder the character's career, stifle their relationships, keep them from enjoying life, and possibly cause them to lose themselves along the way.

WHAT IT LOOKS LIKE

Being overly agreeable
Being conflict-averse
Taking extra pains with their appearance to look their best
Being a people-pleaser
Adapting to others (their preferences, viewpoints, interests, etc.) to fit in
Not standing up for themselves
Exhibiting a strong work ethic (to prove their worth to others)
Being a perfectionist
Being passive aggressive rather than straightforward about their feelings or opinions
Sticking like glue to the people who accept and love them
Being shy with new people and in new situations
Being evasive or dishonest about beliefs and opinions that others may not agree with
Jumping to conclusions about what others are thinking or feeling
Getting their feelings hurt easily
Choosing isolation over being with others
Avoiding romantic relationships
Staying away from social situations
Underachieving so people won't be disappointed and reject them
Having secret hobbies
Ending romantic relationships and leaving jobs prematurely (rejecting others before they can reject the character)

COMMON INTERNAL STRUGGLES

Wanting to open up to others but being afraid their true thoughts will be criticized
Needing to confide in someone but fearing they'll be rejected for what they share
Wanting to end a relationship but not knowing how
Being afraid of failure or letting people down
Despairing of ever being accepted by others
Obsessing over mistakes made in relationships, viewing them as catastrophic
Longing for a romantic relationship but being too afraid to put themselves out there
Struggling with loneliness but not knowing how to safely build deep connections
Feeling unwanted or unlovable
Constantly worry about what others think
The character wondering what's wrong with them

HINDRANCES AND DISRUPTIONS TO THE CHARACTER'S LIFE

Being consumed with worry about what others think

Trouble making and keeping friends
An inability to form trusting relationships
Burning out from the constant drive to please everyone or be above reproach
Frequently being taken advantage of
Underachieving and falling short of their full potential
Low self-esteem undermining the character's belief in themselves and their capabilities

EMOTIONAL WOUNDS IT COULD STEM FROM: A Loved One's Suicide, A Parent's Abandonment or Rejection, A Sibling's Betrayal, Abandonment Over an Unexpected Pregnancy, Being Raised by Parents Who Loved Conditionally, Being Rejected by One's Peers, Being Sent Away as a Child

SCENARIOS THAT MIGHT TRIGGER THIS FEAR

Any situation where people must choose the character over someone else (a job interview or promotion, a political campaign, etc.)
Meeting someone they'd like to date (but will have to ask out)
The character's work or attitude being criticized
Being fired or laid off
A friend unexpectedly canceling dinner plans
Being wronged by someone (at work, during a family function, etc.) and the character needing to confront them
A spouse asking for space
A child wanting to live with the character's ex

HUMAN NEEDS THAT COULD BE IMPACTED

Self-Actualization: A character who fears rejection will avoid situations where it could occur. This means their dreams will always be shaped by the influence of others and the character must play it safe to ensure acceptance.

Esteem and Recognition: Characters with this fear will often blame themselves for the rejection, leading to lower self-worth.

Love and Belonging: This fear will turn the character into a chameleon—adapting to other people's preferences—to avoid any possibility of rejection. This makes it hard for them to build relationships centered on truth and authenticity.

Safety and Security: A fear of rejection can lead to the acceptance of toxic or abusive behavior, putting the character's physical and emotional welfare at risk.

HOW THE CHARACTER CAN MINIMIZE OR OVERCOME IT

Reminding themselves that rejection doesn't define their worth
Refusing to take responsibility for someone else's rejection of the character
Reflecting on how some relationships are not meant to last and it's okay to move on
Opening up to new people slowly; testing the waters
Recognizing patterns that may contribute to people turning away from the character, and addressing those as needed
Talking through insecurities with a trusted friend to make sure the character isn't missing something (a pattern, behavior that is misconstrued, etc.)

RELATIONSHIP COMMITMENT

NOTES: While many people may struggle with EMOTIONAL VULNERABILITY, others simply fear taking on the responsibilities or expectations that come with a relationship. This fear is common in romance stories, but commitment issues can apply to all kinds of relationships.

WHAT IT LOOKS LIKE

Being good at small talk but avoiding deep conversation
Staying (or merely acting) busy
Preferring to work alone
Not joining groups or clubs
Compartmentalizing relationships (seeing workout buddies only at the gym, etc.)
Setting expectations by often being unavailable for family events or unreliable at work (whether they are or not)
Setting strong boundaries regarding the closeness of certain types of relationships
Brushing off social invitations from people looking to get closer
Not always answering the phone or returning messages
Not keeping a pet
Keeping to themselves (being a quiet neighbor, etc.)
Making it clear that a romantic relationship isn't an exclusive one
Establishing deal breakers to ensure things won't progress: "I don't want kids" or "I travel a lot"
Difficulty trusting others
Abruptly becoming distant or colder when the fear is triggered
Exiting relationships when they become too serious
Keeping things strictly professional with people at work
Not really knowing or engaging with neighbors
Lurking on social media but not engaging much with others
Utilizing dating apps so it's easier to make choices from a distance
Donating to charities rather than volunteering in person
Making excuses about why they can't babysit or pet sit for loved ones
Working alone rather than with a partner
Not dating at all
Not wanting children

COMMON INTERNAL STRUGGLES

Desiring connections but being unable to commit
Feeling selfish or guilty for being unwilling to commit
Wanting to help someone in need but fearing it will lead to more requests for help
Wanting to forgive someone but fearing they may then seek to renew the relationship
Wanting to achieve certain benchmark milestones (getting married, having a child, etc.) but feeling incapable of fulfilling the accompanying responsibilities
Feeling left behind when others hit those relational milestones

HINDRANCES AND DISRUPTIONS TO THE CHARACTER'S LIFE

Missing out on important events with loved ones
Putting up barriers and offending people
Having to attend social events alone
Having no one to turn to when disaster strikes
Not joining a church, and struggling with faith issues alone
Being viewed as detached, unfriendly, or emotionally unavailable
Having no one to share their wisdom and memories with
Growing old alone
Having to be good at everything (because they're on their own and have to do it all)
Growing apart from friends who find true love, get married, or have kids

EMOTIONAL WOUNDS IT COULD STEM FROM: A Child Dying on One's Watch, Bearing the Responsibility for Many Deaths, Becoming a Caregiver at an Early Age, Caving to Peer Pressure, Cracking Under Pressure, Failing to Do the Right Thing

SCENARIOS THAT MIGHT TRIGGER THIS FEAR

An estranged loved one wanting to reconnect
A civil or natural disaster that would be easier to survive if the character was with others
A coworker wanting to go into business with the character
A romantic partner wanting a commitment
A friend asking for something that goes beyond the expectations for their relationship (becoming a godparent, being best man in their wedding, etc.)
Finding an abandoned puppy and having to decide whether to keep it or not
A sibling being incapacitated and asking the character to care for their child
Having to attend a wedding or baby shower

HUMAN NEEDS THAT COULD BE IMPACTED

Esteem and Recognition: If the character is always declining invitations and rebuffing people who try to get close, their actions may be misconstrued as snobbery or unfriendliness.

Love and Belonging: Being afraid to commit will keep the character from connecting deeply and permanently with others.

Safety and Security: Safety is found in numbers, and a lone wolf character will have a harder time overcoming threatening situations that require teamwork and support.

HOW THE CHARACTER CAN MINIMIZE OR OVERCOME IT

Thinking in terms of risk (a relationship ending) vs. reward (love and acceptance)
Starting with low-risk commitments: joining a book club, agreeing to babysit once, etc.
Establishing boundaries that make the character feel more comfortable—i.e., building a deeper friendship with someone but without the pressure to hang out all the time
Considering whether losing someone will cause regret
Making a commitment that has a limited time obligation, such as signing up to coach one season of little league
Testing out a temporary commitment, like fostering a dog instead of adopting one

REPEATING A CYCLE OF ABUSE

NOTES: As human beings, we tend to repeat the behaviors that were done to us, even when we don't want to. Because this is fairly common knowledge, it's likely that a character who suffered abuse would fear the possibility of perpetuating habits they view as abhorrent and destructive. While their intentions may be good, their fear may drive them to extremes or to ineffectual methods that are harmful in their own way.

WHAT IT LOOKS LIKE
Being highly disciplined
Abstaining from drugs and alcohol, since addiction is often tied to abuse
Not trusting themselves enough to get into an intimate relationship
Putting everyone else's needs above their own
Determining to be the opposite of their abuser
Needing to control every aspect of life
Cutting ties with their abuser
Apologizing for getting angry (even when it's justified and their behavior is reasonable)
Withdrawing often to keep others safe or privately deal with intrusive thoughts
Hiding past abuse
Rejecting the ways they're similar to their abuser (personality traits, beliefs, physical similarities, etc.)
Being drawn to people who are unlikely to abuse or allow themselves to be mistreated
Choosing not to forgive an abuser (so the character can maintain a perspective that will keep them from adopting that behavior)
Being too permissive
Not having children
Resisting vulnerability with others (to avoid being mistreated again)

COMMON INTERNAL STRUGGLES
The character repressing certain emotions (anger, frustration, etc.) because they're afraid of what they could lead to
Struggling with unwanted intrusive thoughts about their self-worth or abusing others
The character doubting their ability to break the chain
Fearing losing control and what could happen in that moment
Viewing themselves as a potential abuser instead of someone who is doing right
Obsessively self-checking for risk factors or markers that might lead to abusive behavior
Feeling deep shame over minor behavioral missteps with loved ones (yelling at someone, not respecting a boundary, manipulating them, etc.)

HINDRANCES AND DISRUPTIONS TO THE CHARACTER'S LIFE
Being uncomfortable with certain feelings that are unavoidable
Going to extremes (being too attentive, affectionate, supportive, etc.) and causing new relationship problems
Being too permissive with their children, resulting in them becoming spoiled, undisciplined, or irresponsible

Choosing not to have children or romantic relationships, and missing those intimate connections in later years
Overcompensating by neglecting their own needs
Being ruled by the fear that they will lose control and become what they hate
Needing to control every aspect of their life (which is impossible) to feel confident in their ability to not repeat the cycle of abuse
Trying to achieve this goal without therapy, a support group, or other methods that would provide the character with the tools they need

EMOTIONAL WOUNDS IT COULD STEM FROM: Being Treated as Property, Childhood Sexual Abuse by a Known Person, Domestic Abuse, Growing up in a Cult, Growing up in Foster Care, Incest, Infidelity, Living with an Abusive Caregiver

SCENARIOS THAT MIGHT TRIGGER THIS FEAR

Encountering an abuser from the past
Having intrusive thoughts about abusing someone
Losing control in a small way
Being wronged and experiencing a desire for revenge
Seeing a movie or TV show that contains the kind of abuse the character experienced
Perpetrating a different kind of abuse than what the character experienced and has been guarding against (verbal instead of physical)
The character's child exhibiting traits that are common to an abuser or victim

HUMAN NEEDS THAT COULD BE IMPACTED

Esteem and Recognition: A character with this fear might struggle with deep shame from their abuse. In their efforts to never repeat it, small infractions or personal failures along the way may devastate them.

Love and Belonging: If the character's methods for achieving their goal mean overcompensating in some way, it could lead to new problems and relationship strain.

Safety and Security: While there are many resources available to help people break the cycle of abuse, not everyone takes advantage of them. A character pursuing this goal without addressing their own abuse will continue to struggle mentally and emotionally.

HOW THE CHARACTER CAN MINIMIZE OR OVERCOME IT

Spending time around people in healthy, functional relationships
Taking an anger management or parenting class to learn strategies for dealing with stressful situations
Practicing mindfulness and patience
Working hard to be a safe harbor for others (listening without judgment, thinking before reacting, helping without being asked, etc.)
Learning to communicate well
Practicing self-awareness by labeling sources of anger or frustration as triggers
Reminding themselves of the ways they're different from their abuser (or abusers in general)
Putting a plan in place for when their emotions are activated
No longer associating with abusive or toxic family members

TRUSTING OTHERS

NOTES: Trust is a necessary part of any healthy relationship. It stands to reason, then, that someone with trust issues will struggle to build, maintain, or deepen their relationships with others. This will make emotional vulnerability and physical intimacy difficult.

WHAT IT LOOKS LIKE
Valuing privacy
Being highly independent
Not sharing potentially sensitive information with others
Being suspicious when others ask personal questions
Discomfort with icebreaker-type activities at a conference or party that are meant to help people get to know each other
Not taking others at their word
Having few (or no) close relationships
Being slow to warm up to new people
Taking steps to protect themselves (setting up security cameras, owning a weapon, etc.)
Mistrusting motives, especially when people want to get close or move too fast
Conducting research to verify people's claims
Being argumentative, confrontational, or defensive
Setting boundaries with close friends or partners
Being intensely loyal to friends or loved ones who have proven themselves trustworthy
Maintaining shallow romantic relationships
Sabotaging romantic relationships
Cutting people off for minor offenses; not giving them a second chance
Misreading nervousness as evasiveness
Not fully committing to a relationship (keeping individual bank accounts, the character keeping their own name after marrying, etc.)
Requiring a prenuptial agreement before marriage
Checking up on someone or invading their privacy to be sure they're worthy of trust

COMMON INTERNAL STRUGGLES
Believing that people as a whole can't be trusted
Struggling with self-doubt; the character believing they're responsible in some way for other people's mistreatment of them
Disliking being suspicious and mistrustful but knowing these traits keep them safe
The character suspecting people of conspiring against them
Being uncomfortable with vulnerability
Questioning people's true intentions
Refusing to forgive someone for a betrayal of trust
Wondering if they're being gaslit or otherwise manipulated
Wanting an intimate relationship but being unable to commit to that level of trust
Struggling with loneliness
Feeling like no one truly knows them because they have so many barriers in place

HINDRANCES AND DISRUPTIONS TO THE CHARACTER'S LIFE

Never feeling completely safe or secure with others
Living an isolated life
Carrying grudges and becoming bitter
Being unable to resolve conflict in a healthy way
Not having anyone to lean on when they're in trouble
Being unable to build relationships with people who have new perspectives that could benefit the character

EMOTIONAL WOUNDS IT COULD STEM FROM: Being Disowned or Shunned, Growing up in Foster Care, Having One's Ideas or Work Stolen, Identity Theft, Incest, Infidelity, Learning That One's Parent Had a Second Family

SCENARIOS THAT MIGHT TRIGGER THIS FEAR

Having to trust or rely on someone outside of their intimate circle
Experiencing a betrayal (or a suspected betrayal)
Running into someone who betrayed or manipulated the character in the past
A romantic partner wanting to take the relationship to the next level
Someone asking the character for a favor
Catching someone in a lie (even a trivial one)
Becoming injured or incapacitated and having to rely on someone for care
Someone who hurt the character asking for forgiveness

HUMAN NEEDS THAT COULD BE IMPACTED

Self-Actualization: A character with this fear will minimize their interactions with people overall, narrowing their options for promising opportunities.

Esteem and Recognition: The character will adopt traits and behaviors to help them keep people at arm's length (abrasiveness, cynicism, mistrust, etc.) which will change how people perceive them.

Love and Belonging: A character who can't trust others will struggle to develop lasting relationships. Supporters may distance themselves if, no matter what they do or how they prove themselves, the character continues to shut them out.

Safety and Security: This character may put themselves in danger if they're unable to trust the people who want to help them, such as their parents, well-meaning friends, the police, or doctors.

HOW THE CHARACTER CAN MINIMIZE OR OVERCOME IT

Taking their time to get to know someone, without pressure
Taking it slow and letting people in a little at a time
Sharing a small secret or minor insecurity to test the waters
Choosing to be around people with traits like empathy, kindness, and compassion
Revealing their trust issues to set expectations and avoid being pressured to share
Developing their intuition and instinct through practice, especially if past trauma has left them believing their judgment is off

Identity Fears

BECOMING A PARENT

NOTES: Becoming a parent is a huge adjustment and will naturally come with some anxiety. But for some characters, this natural worry can tip into a motivating fear. It could stem from insecurities around being responsible for someone or act as a trigger relating to a childhood trauma. Whatever the cause, this fear will be the driving factor behind their decisions and steer their life's trajectory.

WHAT IT LOOKS LIKE

Avoiding situations where they would be responsible for children, such as babysitting or volunteering with young people
Becoming a pro-choice activist
Clinging to youthful activities (spending recklessly, partying, hanging out at the bar, etc.)
Being highly independent
Being highly outspoken about the decision to not have children
Becoming defensive when others ask if children are in the future
The character obsessively watching her menstrual cycle to be sure a pregnancy hasn't occurred
The character taking medical steps to avoid pregnancy, such as having their tubes tied or getting a vasectomy
Becoming a pet parent
Relationships fizzling with friends who become parents
Devoting themselves to other pursuits (career, fitness, volunteerism, etc.)
Overachieving in other areas
Choosing a job that requires a lot of travel or unpredictability
Sabotaging relationships that become too intimate
Avoiding sex or being hypervigilant about prevention

COMMON INTERNAL STRUGGLES

The character fearing they would become like their own parents if they had children
Feeling selfish or cowardly for the decision not to have kids
Desiring intimacy in a relationship but being too afraid of becoming pregnant
Desiring children but not wanting to pass on a family history of abuse, mental illness, dysfunction, or addiction
Not wanting kids but feeling a sense of loss at not experiencing the parent-child bond
A desire to have children warring with the fear of being a parent

HINDRANCES AND DISRUPTIONS TO THE CHARACTER'S LIFE

Frequently changing romantic partners before things get too serious
Ongoing strife with a spouse or partner who wants to have children
The loss of close friendships when others start building families
Friends and loved ones not understanding the character's choice to not have kids
Sex being paired with anxiety or fear
Being expected to work holidays, weekends, and extra shifts because the character doesn't have a family to take care of

Strained relationships with parents who want to be grandparents
Being alone because the character is afraid to get into a relationship with someone who wants kids

EMOTIONAL WOUNDS IT COULD STEM FROM: A Child Dying on One's Watch, A Terminal Illness Diagnosis, Battling a Mental Condition, Becoming a Caregiver at an Early Age, Being Raised by an Addict, Being Raised by Neglectful Parents, Being Raised by Overprotective Parents, Learning That One's Parent Was a Monster, Living with Chronic Pain or Illness

SCENARIOS THAT MIGHT TRIGGER THIS FEAR

An unexpected pregnancy
Falling in love with someone who wants to have children
Being asked about when the character is going to start a family
Being expected to produce an heir to continue the family name or business
Not having access to birth control
A close friend dying or becoming seriously ill during childbirth
Being sexually assaulted or abused
Having to parent a friend's child due to unforeseen circumstances
Being asked to raise the child of a sibling after their death
Discovering they have a child from a previous relationship
Experiencing pregnancy symptoms
Being unable to access safe medical care to end a pregnancy

HUMAN NEEDS THAT COULD BE IMPACTED

Self-Actualization: Someone can want something and be afraid of it at the same time. A character in this situation may feel unfulfilled without a child despite being terrified of having one.

Esteem and Recognition: A character whose fear stems from worries about their own capabilities, value, or mental stability will find their self-esteem plummeting as they blame themselves for not being able to start a family.

Love and Belonging: This need can become impacted if the character is partnered with someone who desperately wants to become a parent or has their own children the character struggles to bond with.

HOW THE CHARACTER CAN MINIMIZE OR OVERCOME IT

Realizing that fear is normal and every parent experiences it
A willingness to be vulnerable, talking through fears with their partner
Speaking with other parents about their worries and how they let them go
Taking parenting classes and reading books to feel more capable and confident
Acknowledging that their own parents' failings are not their own
Challenging their fear by spending time with kids and becoming more comfortable with them
Finding joy in being able to give someone the love they deserve
Reaching a place where the decision to not have children is made free of fear

BECOMING WHAT ONE HATES

NOTES: We all know individuals with values, attitudes, or behaviors so foreign to us that we purposely stay away from them, and our characters will too. These people may be monstrous—a murderer, an abusive parent, a psychopath—or just someone the character can't imagine themselves being, like a ruthless venture capitalist or a stay-at-home mom driving a minivan. The fear that they could become like that person can cause misbeliefs about inner weakness and lead to fear-driven, unhealthy decisions. Rather than explore and discover who they are, they focus on who they must not be, hindering the development of their true self.

WHAT IT LOOKS LIKE

Avoiding interactions with the kind of people the character doesn't want to emulate
Having strong, negative opinions about certain types of people
Distancing themselves from family members they view as embarrassments
Cutting ties with anyone who exhibits qualities or preferences the character finds threatening
Voicing criticism of people who represent what the character fears
Becoming defensive if someone suggests the character has something in common with the type of person they disdain
Overcompensating—e.g., if they fear becoming miserly like their parents, they overspend or financially support others to their own detriment
Living a persona (embracing opinions, social groups, etc.) that isn't true to who they are
Hiding certain preferences, interests, or beliefs that make them feel shame
Surrounding themselves with people who think like they do
Being watchful of tendencies or behaviors that indicate they may be slipping
Needing to justify certain choices or actions to others
Developing biases and blind spots
Avoiding situations or people where undesired behavior may be triggered
Attending long-term therapy
Maintaining strict religious practices to prevent unwanted behaviors
The character seeking reassurance that they're not taking on certain traits or attitudes
Allowing a dislike for something to lead to intolerance, bigotry, and discrimination Going to extremes—e.g., someone who struggles with a forbidden sexual desire deciding to live a life of complete abstinence

COMMON INTERNAL STRUGGLES

The character doubting their instincts and motivations
Feeling guilty about secret desires to be the person the character hates
Struggling to avoid losing control and giving in to certain emotions or behaviors
Confusion about why living a certain way doesn't feel authentic
Being drawn to the very people the character wants to distance themselves from
Feeling intense shame and self-loathing (for wanting to engage in certain activities, for being related to someone who exhibits something abhorrent, etc.)
Wanting to be at peace but being unable to accept certain aspects of who they are
Constantly monitoring themselves for signs they're slipping
Living in constant fear that someone will find out their deepest fears or desires

Their thinking being challenged (say, viewing certain people who need help as weak until the character experiences a crisis where they must seek out help)

HINDRANCES AND DISRUPTIONS TO THE CHARACTER'S LIFE

Wrestling with anxiety and depression
Being unable to consider the other side of an issue when it opposes the character's belief
Difficulty developing deep relationships because the character doesn't believe they're worthy or they don't trust themselves to make the right choices
Abusing drugs or alcohol to combat their fears or deal with perceived failures
Living a lie to fit in with others
Being unable to pursue things the character really wants because they're associated with the thing they're trying not to become

EMOTIONAL WOUNDS IT COULD STEM FROM: A Parent's Abandonment or Rejection, Battling a Mental Condition, Being Bullied, Growing up in the Public Eye, Having a Controlling or Overly Strict Parent, Incest, Infidelity, Learning That One's Parent Was a Monster, Living in an Emotionally Repressed Household, Living with an Abusive Caregiver, Prejudice or Discrimination

SCENARIOS THAT MIGHT TRIGGER THIS FEAR

Being around family members who represent what the character is trying to avoid
Seeing media coverage of the type of person they disdain
A joke that suggests they're just like someone they don't want to be
Someone demanding the character prove they aren't just like "those people"
A situation that tempts the character to take a step toward what they're trying to avoid
Wanting something deeply but knowing the only way to get it is to face a difficult truth

HUMAN NEEDS THAT COULD BE IMPACTED

Self-Actualization: A character who actively avoids certain situations, people, or opportunities may not reach their potential or discover their true purpose.

Esteem and Recognition: A character in this situation is going to doubt and second-guess themselves, worrying that they're moving toward an unwanted result.

Love and Belonging: This fear can negatively impact the character's important relationships in several ways, particularly if they are overcompensating, become needy, or their biases and blind spots introduce harmful friction or intolerance.

Safety and Security: A character in denial about certain thoughts, desires, or tendencies may endanger themselves and others by not dealing with those things.

HOW THE CHARACTER CAN MINIMIZE OR OVERCOME IT

Acknowledging how they have been hurt by those they don't want to become
Being honest about why they have this fear and owning any similarities to the people they dislike
Seeking help for behaviors that bother them (like anger issues) so they're no longer a concern
Getting help to see their own value and learn to believe in themselves
Using cognitive therapy to shut out the negative thoughts
Challenging personal blind spots and developing a more balanced view of others

BEING CAPABLE OF HARM

NOTES: Certain destructive thoughts can cause us to wonder if we could harm others, either because of a perceived internal deficit or an obsession with power or success. For most people, common sense prevails, and those thoughts are dismissed. But if they can't be ignored, a deeply embedded fear forms: *I will harm someone if I don't safeguard against it.*

This fear works well for characters who aren't sure where their moral line is. It can also be used to hint at a villain's humanity and the possibility of redemption. Characters with Harm OCD may be especially susceptible to this fear.

WHAT IT LOOKS LIKE

Intrusive, irrational thoughts about harming others
The character being afraid of their own anger
Warning people away and discouraging relationships
Not liking to be surprised
Compulsively pushing an irrational thought of harm away—for example, mentally repeating *I'm a good person. I wouldn't do that.*
Visible shaking, body tension, and panicked breathing
Becoming visibly upset, then exhibiting a flight response such as leaving the room
Having only a few close friends or family members
Creating a buffer of space between themselves and others (just in case)
Avoiding triggers (violent movies, a news report about a sexual assault, weapons, people that tend to make the character upset, etc.)
Seeking assurances from others ("Do you feel safe with me?" or "Do you think I'm capable of harming someone?")
Questioning their actions in the aftermath of an emergency: *What if I didn't run as fast as I could to get help? What if I wanted that man to suffer?*
Avoiding being alone with someone vulnerable, such as a child or an elderly person
Asking for an opinion on a goal, thought, or decision to make sure it's appropriate
Being slow to act because they need to think things through
Avoiding responsibility; not wanting to lead
Explaining their actions or motivations to reassure others that no harm is intended

COMMON INTERNAL STRUGGLES

Wanting something, then becoming anxious about what they might do to get it
Intrusive thoughts around getting something via dark methods (*I'd get full custody if he was dead*) generating shame, fear, or both
An idea forming on how easy it would be to hurt someone in a specific way
An unwanted impulse to use an item violently (cutting a sandwich and imagining using the knife to stab a family member)
Struggling with irrational thoughts, like how forgetting to return a library book must be a sign they want to keep others from enjoying it
Being plagued with flashes of violent images
Fearing that maybe they secretly enjoy violence
Constantly examining and questioning their motives

HINDRANCES AND DISRUPTIONS TO THE CHARACTER'S LIFE

Struggling to build bonds with others (for fear of hurting them)
Choosing to settle or underachieve for fear of big goals activating their dark side
Feeling easily overwhelmed
Having a hard time making decisions
Coming across as needy and dependent (needing constant assurances)
Being susceptible to manipulation and control
Having low self-esteem because they find it hard to love or accept themselves
Carefully subduing their own emotions to stay in control of them (fearing big feelings)
Avoiding conflict whenever possible, leading to fear and a lack of fulfillment

EMOTIONAL WOUNDS IT COULD STEM FROM: A Child Dying on One's Watch, A Life-Threatening Accident, A Traumatic Brain Injury, Being Tortured, Failing to Save Someone's Life, Learning That One's Parent Was a Monster

SCENARIOS THAT MIGHT TRIGGER THIS FEAR

Being responsible for the welfare of others
Having to make a decision where people could be negatively impacted
Encountering a triggering object or situation that brings intrusive thoughts
Being blocked from what they want most by a competitor
Being pulled into an argument
Someone getting aggressive with the character
Experiencing strong negative emotions
Someone the character loves being in danger

HUMAN NEEDS THAT COULD BE IMPACTED

Self-Actualization: A character with this fear may go overboard in setting personal boundaries to keep from acting on those impulses, and those limitations may keep the character from following a certain path or pursuing a goal.

Esteem and Recognition: A character who doubts themselves and is constantly second-guessing their motives won't be comfortable with who they are. Throw guilt or shame into the mix, and they will develop a negative self-view.

Love and Belonging: Characters worried about hurting others may struggle to maintain healthy relationships due to a tendency to keep people at arm's length.

HOW THE CHARACTER CAN MINIMIZE OR OVERCOME IT

Acknowledging they're capable of doing good and bad, which is part of being human
Understanding that negative thoughts and fantasizing are not the same as doing harm
Seeking to manage intrusive thoughts through medication, cognitive behavioral therapy, etc.
Finding ways to practice kindness and self-love
Learning to forgive themselves for whatever may have happened in the past
Believing they're capable of change
Reminding themselves of the progress they're making (they're better now than they were before)

BEING JUDGED

NOTES: The fear of being judged by others is common and at the root of many social anxiety disorders. It can arise when the character thinks people are watching, evaluating, and finding fault with them and their choices (whether this is really happening or not). It's especially sharp when they're with others who tend to be critical in nature. Unchecked, this fear generates tremendous anxiety, sabotages the character's self-esteem, and prevents them from living life on their own terms.

WHAT IT LOOKS LIKE

Shyness or introversion
Speaking in a quiet voice
Not volunteering information or sharing ideas; keeping their thoughts to themselves
Seeking to conform to societal norms
Posting carefully edited photos on social media that show them in the best possible light
Not engaging during meetings, classes, or group outings
The character telling people what they want to hear; not sharing true opinions
Giving noncommittal or vague answers when they're put on the spot
Having a small friend group
Becoming tongue-tied when someone's attention turns to the character
Being highly observant
Avoiding the spotlight
Planning everything carefully so there's less chance of something going wrong
Asking for second opinions, soliciting advice, and doing more research than necessary before making a decision or acting
Taking pains with their appearance
Being uncomfortable with small talk
Not sharing big dreams or goals with others
Avoiding their critics (especially family members)
Not attending events where the possibility of social awkwardness is high
Trying to appear smaller (crossing the arms, standing at the edge of a room, etc.)
Avoiding too much direct eye contact with others
Flying under the radar and trying to be unnoticeable
Being a perfectionist (so others won't be able to criticize them)
Getting sick prior to a performance (a recital, soccer game, speech, etc.)

COMMON INTERNAL STRUGGLES

Being incredibly anxious in social situations
Obsessing over social obligations for days or weeks before they occur
Envying another's confidence and feeling less than for being unable to be that way too
The mind going blank when someone asks a question
Overanalyzing situations; constantly wondering what other people think of them
Wanting to hide but knowing they'll be judged for that too
Wanting to make a physical change (a new haircut, for instance) but being too afraid of what

others might think
Being romantically interested in someone but being too afraid to speak up
Struggling with low self-esteem
Feeling misunderstood
Wanting to open up about anxieties but fearing what people will say

HINDRANCES AND DISRUPTIONS TO THE CHARACTER'S LIFE
Never being able to express themselves
Being unable to handle even the slightest criticism
Lacking close connections and friendships
Being unable to participate in activities that could invite judgment
Having to be perfect to avoid criticism
Being seen by others as shy, awkward, aloof, or stuck-up
Seldom being truly comfortable with others

EMOTIONAL WOUNDS IT COULD STEM FROM: A Speech Impediment, A Toxic Relationship, Battling a Mental Condition, Being Bullied, Being Humiliated by Others, Being Unfairly Blamed for Someone's Death, Failing at School, Falling Short of Society's Physical Standards, Growing up in the Public Eye, Growing up in the Shadow of a Successful Sibling, Making a Very Public Mistake, Social Difficulties

SCENARIOS THAT MIGHT TRIGGER THIS FEAR
Being made the center of attention
Being expected to perform in a play, competition, etc.
Having to organize a wedding, a surprise party, a work retreat, or another event
Being assessed at a job interview or doctor's appointment
Being teased or bullied
Being asked a question they don't know how to answer
Speaking in front of people
The character's creative or professional work being exhibited for others to see
Being the minority in a group

HUMAN NEEDS THAT COULD BE IMPACTED
Self-Actualization: A character who avoids certain people, events, and situations out of a fear of judgment will never be able to do all the things they could or should do.
Esteem and Recognition: Characters who fear being judged or evaluated will have a heightened awareness of how their choices could impact other people's perceptions of them, effecting their self-esteem.

HOW THE CHARACTER CAN MINIMIZE OR OVERCOME IT
Challenging assumptions: *What's the worst thing that can happen if I'm judged?*
Realizing that judgment is fleeting (quickly forgotten), and the character is giving it too much power over them
Asking people they admire how they cope with criticism and judgment from others
Learning that judgment is often subjective and not necessarily true

BEING LABELED

NOTES: It's human nature to label people and things; this helps us understand an uncertain world. Yet no one wants to be forced into someone else's mold. When a character has been labeled in a way that causes offense, is punitive, or puts them in danger, they naturally fear going through that again. As a result, they may hide aspects of their identity that could lead to them being classified a certain way. They might also gravitate toward people who are just like them to minimize the risk of anyone making assumptions about the character.

WHAT IT LOOKS LIKE

Being extremely private
Being careful about sharing personal information
Making friends carefully and slowly to make sure they're safe
Rejecting what makes them different by dressing, talking, and acting like their peers
Giving vague answers to questions about their life
Becoming instantly angry when a stereotype is applied
Embracing a variety of hobbies or activities that don't necessarily fit the stereotype
Working twice as hard as others to offset the bias people have about a label
Quietly accepting jokes made at their expense
The character being the best version of themselves just to disprove the stereotype
Calling out the person doing the labeling
Rebelling when someone tells the character they can't or shouldn't do something
Advocating for inclusion and against typecasting
Throwing themselves into their culture; embracing what makes them different

COMMON INTERNAL STRUGGLES

Keeping something secret (a learning disability, an illness, etc.) despite knowing they need help
Not wanting to lie about their past but feeling unsafe sharing the truth
Learning that a beloved affiliation (to a club, sorority, church, etc.) encourages certain biases about a part of the character's identity
The character struggling to accept who they really are
The character wanting to be true to themselves but feeling the need to change so they'll fit in with others
Resenting what makes them different, then feeling guilty about it
Feeling targeted
Feeling betrayed by friends or coworkers who apply labels to other people groups
Having to hide the labeling from family members who will want to set things right but will only make things worse
Harboring resentment toward those who are silent in the face of discrimination
Struggling to hold in the anger that comes with the unfairness of bias and labeling
Wrestling with unearned self-esteem and self-worth issues

HINDRANCES AND DISRUPTIONS TO THE CHARACTER'S LIFE

Living with shame because of who or what they are
Changing to fit others' expectations
Not being able to live up to their full potential
Becoming prejudiced against the people who are labeling them
Having to do certain things in private (practice a religion, pursue a relationship, etc.)
Standing up for themselves and being labeled as a troublemaker (making things even harder)

EMOTIONAL WOUNDS IT COULD STEM FROM: A Learning Disability, A Physical Disfigurement, A Speech Impediment, Becoming Homeless for Reasons Out of One's Control, Being Falsely Accused of a Crime, Being Rejected by One's Peers, Being So Beautiful It's All People See, Being the Victim of a Vicious Rumor, Experiencing Poverty, Falling Short of Society's Physical Standards, Prejudice or Discrimination

SCENARIOS THAT MIGHT TRIGGER THIS FEAR

The character feeling pressured to reveal what they've been hiding (about their gender identity, personal beliefs, race, etc.)
Public opinion shifting and the character's label being more widely targeted
A tragedy occurring that could result in a new label for the character (losing a limb, developing a chronic illness, etc.)
Experiencing discrimination
The character's children being labeled
A secret hobby or affiliation being discovered

HUMAN NEEDS THAT COULD BE IMPACTED

Self-Actualization: A character will never be fully actualized if they are unable to live as their true self.

Esteem and Recognition: People tend to believe stereotypes about certain kinds of people—meaning, someone with a label may be looked at differently. The character's own preconceived notions about the label may even cause them to think worse of themselves.

Love and Belonging: The character may have trouble connecting to others if they're living a half-life or pretending to be someone they're not. Those close relationships may also be threatened if others realize the character hasn't been honest with them.

Safety and Security: A character denying true labels that indicate a need for medical or psychological interventions may put themselves at risk by refusing to acknowledge the truth.

HOW THE CHARACTER CAN MINIMIZE OR OVERCOME IT

Protecting their privacy not out of shame but the right to be themselves
Practicing self-acceptance to let go of what others think
Claiming a label or labels with pride
Shutting out toxic and unsupportive people who can't accept the character for who they are

BEING PITIED

NOTES: Pity almost always comes from a good place, from people who care. But a character who feels patronized or looked down upon may develop a fear of others feeling sorry for them.

WHAT IT LOOKS LIKE
Independence
Rejecting charity
Downplaying negative life events so others won't think they're so bad
Projecting confidence and strength no matter what the character's feeling
Taking care of themselves when things get rough
Stashing food, money, and resources to prepare for hard times
Being highly adaptable
Always having a backup plan ready
Brushing off the concerns of others
Keeping problems or difficulties to themselves
Becoming defensive or offended when others express pity
Questioning shows of love or concern from others
Avoiding churches, soup kitchens, or other places typically associated with charity or sympathy
Rejecting offers of help even when the character needs it
Minimizing challenges or stressors: "It's not a big deal" or "Everything's fine, really."
Overcompensating to show off their physical, emotional, or spiritual strength
Hiding negative emotions
Refusing to get professional help (in the form of counseling, food stamps, etc.)
Quitting activities they enjoy if they start to perform poorly
Having high expectations for themselves and others
Deftly diverting concern for them to another topic

COMMON INTERNAL STRUGGLES
Wanting to be seen as an equal but secretly resenting people who have an easier life
Believing their worth is tied to their self-sufficiency
Wanting to help others in need but not wanting to show pity
Feeling down about their unhappy life circumstances, then guilty because others are even worse off
The character wanting desperately to prove themselves
Resenting the circumstances that put them in the situation of being pitied by others
Being afraid to show vulnerability to others
Fearing that others will find out about the character's difficult circumstances
Feeling stuck on how to process their feelings or make things better without being able to reveal their situation to others

HINDRANCES AND DISRUPTIONS TO THE CHARACTER'S LIFE
Not getting the help they need because they never ask
Intimacy with others being limited because the character can't be honest about their challenges
Being overworked or resorting to desperate measures to care for themselves
Not being able to cry or express anger around others
Having to keep certain aspects of their life secret
Sustaining a serious injury or developing an illness and having no support system

EMOTIONAL WOUNDS IT COULD STEM FROM: A Learning Disability, A Miscarriage or Stillbirth, A Physical Disfigurement, A Speech Impediment, A Terminal Illness Diagnosis, Battling a Mental Condition, Being Fired or Laid Off, Being Held Captive, Experiencing Poverty, Getting Dumped, Infidelity, Losing a Limb, Losing One of the Five Senses, Social Difficulties, The Death of One's Child, Unrequited Love

SCENARIOS THAT MIGHT TRIGGER THIS FEAR
Being thrust into an unfortunate situation (homelessness, bankruptcy, a job loss, etc.)
Being offered support from well-intentioned friends or family members
Dealing with an overbearing caregiver
Making an embarrassing mistake in public
Being targeted for being weaker or less than everyone else
A situation where the character is expected to be vulnerable
Being used as an example of inequity or an unfair system by someone trying to raise awareness
The character's private situation being made public

HUMAN NEEDS THAT COULD BE IMPACTED

Love and Belonging: Relationships can become strained when the character shuts out loved ones offering support or refuses to share the vulnerable aspects of their life.

Safety and Security: A character who refuses help when they really need it may put themselves in danger needlessly.

HOW THE CHARACTER CAN MINIMIZE OR OVERCOME IT
Separating pity from empathy (and educating others about the difference)
Understanding where feelings of insecurity are coming from
Admitting to personal struggles while acknowledging they aren't the sum of who the character is
Recognizing that people who care feel and show empathy
Setting boundaries to politely decline help that isn't needed
Being secure enough to ask for help when it's needed
Feeling empowered by raising awareness about their situation and eliciting changes that will benefit the character and others like them

BEING RESPONSIBLE FOR OTHERS

NOTES: While some people crave being in charge of others, many shy away from it. The pressure of being responsible for someone else's well-being, success, or happiness can be so great that a character will actively avoid being put in this position. This reluctance is often rooted in personal failures they don't want to repeat or seeing people taking responsibility and not being appropriately supported or valued.

WHAT IT LOOKS LIKE

Putting forth a persona as a poor role model
Manufacturing excuses to get out of responsibilities
Being unreliable (skipping meetings, not following through on promises, etc.) to discourage requests to step up
Avoiding situations where they're put in charge of others
Being neutral or apathetic about social and political issues (because if the character expresses concern, they'll feel compelled to act)
Claiming that social problems aren't real or are someone else's problem
Taking jobs that allow the character to work alone or stay in a supportive role
Gravitating to friend circles, work groups, and organizations led by Type-A personalities who like to take charge
Acting irresponsibly (to keep others from thinking the character is capable)
Selfishness (real or perceived), because the character always seems to prioritize themselves, their own needs and desires, etc.
Reluctance to get involved in a friend's personal problems
Offering advice or recommendations but never being the one to make the decision
Not getting close to people, especially someone needing a protector or provider
Keeping an overloaded schedule, reinforcing the idea that they're not available
Throwing money at problems (because it allows the character to help without getting personally involved or being responsible for individuals)
Staying busy with work, hobbies, personal pursuits, etc.
Not having children

COMMON INTERNAL STRUGGLES

Seeing injustice and wanting to do something but being too afraid to take action
Developing low self-worth for not being there for someone (especially when that person helped the character in the past)
Spotting an opportunity to contribute but being unable to do so because of this fear
Wanting deeper connections but knowing a level of responsibility comes with them
Wishing to be less selfish but feeling powerless to change (because it has become an ingrained defense mechanism)
The character recognizing that they're becoming irresponsible, self-serving, or superficial but needing those traits to protect them from harm
Being mired in feelings of inadequacy, incapability, and insecurity (because they believe they're unable to responsibly care for others)

Recognizing they're being limited (professionally, socially, etc.) by this fear but not knowing how to change course
Wanting to eradicate the fear but being unable to—because they're unwilling to face the past, or the reasons behind it are complicated and hard to unravel

HINDRANCES AND DISRUPTIONS TO THE CHARACTER'S LIFE

Being unable to pursue a dream career that requires leadership and accountability
Not being able to have children (if this something the character wants)
Friction with friends and family members
Missing out on growth opportunities because the character is too scared to act
Having to avoid people who will ask more of the character than they're willing to give
Bypassing an opportunity only to see someone inept or corrupt take on the role of responsibility

EMOTIONAL WOUNDS IT COULD STEM FROM: A Child Dying on One's Watch, Accidentally Killing Someone, Bearing the Responsibility for Many Deaths, Becoming a Caregiver at an Early Age, Being Disappointed by a Role Model, Being Unfairly Blamed for Someone's Death, Choosing to Not Be Involved in a Child's Life

SCENARIOS THAT MIGHT TRIGGER THIS FEAR

Seeing injustice that requires a response
An emergency requiring the character to temporarily care for a friend or family member
The character being the only option to save an orphaned niece from foster care
Being offered a desirable opportunity that would put the character in charge of others
Discovering they're about to become a parent
Being the best option to help, protect, or lead their community in a time of need

HUMAN NEEDS THAT COULD BE IMPACTED

Self-Actualization: A character who deliberately avoids passion projects or areas of giftedness will soon find themselves frustrated and dissatisfied.

Esteem and Recognition: Because of the character's avoidance issues, others may falsely perceive them as being superficial, shallow, selfish, or underachieving.

Love and Belonging: When the character shirks their responsibilities, friends and family members may become hurt and feel marginalized or unappreciated.

HOW THE CHARACTER CAN MINIMIZE OR OVERCOME IT

Taking on a small responsibility that they know they can handle
Using their abilities or skills to help others
Offering to take care of a pet or house sit for a friend
Asking someone to co-lead (sharing responsibility so it's less scary)
Making a promise and keeping it, refuting the lie that they'll always let people down
Forgiving someone else as a step toward forgiving themselves for their own past mistakes that created this fear

BEING VIEWED AS WEAK

NOTES: Weaknesses make people feel vulnerable and ashamed. Whether the character is sensitive to a real or perceived physical deficit, lack of talent, mental deficiency, or other shortcoming, they'll arrange their lives around hiding it.

WHAT IT LOOKS LIKE

Trying to appear physically large (standing tall, squaring the shoulders, etc.)
Exuding bravado
Refusing to accept fault or apologize for anything
Being quick to voice opinions
Taking unnecessary risks
Keeping others at a distance to avoid scrutiny
Controlling others to appear strong or make up for a lack of control in their own life
Avoiding situations that will reveal the weakness (playing a sport, engaging in conversations regarding a topic the character is ignorant about, etc.)
Lingering in group settings so people can't talk about the character
Engaging in rigorous physical exercise
Criticizing or dismissing people who are strong in the character's area of weakness
Refusing to see a doctor when an injury occurs
Suppressing symptoms of an illness or physical debilitation
Not accepting help from others; being staunchly self-sufficient
Being overly competitive with others
Underachieving
Avoiding situations where they've failed in the past
Refusing to compromise or give in
Creating excuses for falling short of expectations
Dismissing criticism
Boasting about their skills and accomplishments
Overcompensating in other areas
Setting unreasonable expectations (too low or too high) for themselves
Self-sabotaging
Self-medicating in situations that could highlight the weakness

COMMON INTERNAL STRUGGLES

Not wanting to think about past failures but being unable to stop obsessing about them
Needing to prove themselves but being afraid of failure
Constantly wondering what other (or certain) people are thinking of them
Struggling frequently with fight-flight-freeze responses
Feeling fake from living a facade
Feeling badly about themselves
Worrying over obligations that may reveal the weakness
Fixating on people the character views as stronger than themselves
Needing help but being afraid to accept it
Wanting to live their life without fear of the judgment of others

Worrying that everyone knows about the weakness and is judging them
Fixating on their own weaknesses instead of their strengths
Constantly comparing themselves to others

HINDRANCES AND DISRUPTIONS TO THE CHARACTER'S LIFE
Sustaining an injury and being too fearful to seek help
Being unable to go deep with others because they're putting on a front
Having to keep up appearances and maintain the strong persona they've created
Being unable to take constructive criticism and grow in important areas of life
Feeling exhausted from the energy expended to appear strong
Limiting themselves personally or professionally because of fear of failure
Gaining a reputation for being cocky or egotistical
Stress and worry making it impossible to rest, recover, and recharge
Ignorance about their strengths causing them to miss opportunities to shine

EMOTIONAL WOUNDS IT COULD STEM FROM: A Physical Assault, A Speech Impediment, Being Bullied, Being Humiliated by Others, Caving to Peer Pressure, Cracking Under Pressure, Domestic Abuse, Failing at School, Living with a Critical Medical Diagnosis

SCENARIOS THAT MIGHT TRIGGER THIS FEAR
A situation that requires the character to step up or act decisively
Being appointed to a leadership position on a team or project
Overhearing disparaging comments about themselves and their weakness
Being pitted against someone who is better in some way
Being publicly confronted or ridiculed
Someone stronger entering the character's school, work, or social environment
Receiving an assignment that requires strengths the character lacks
The character or their skills being put on display
Participating in an activity where vulnerability is expected
Being around a personal critic

HUMAN NEEDS THAT COULD BE IMPACTED

Self-Actualization: Without a willingness to be vulnerable, accept feedback, and self-reflect, the character will struggle to reach their full potential.

Esteem and Recognition: Someone with this fear may fail to view themselves in a healthy and holistic way.

Love and Belonging: An inability to be honest about themselves can affect the character's relationships and make it difficult for them to be fully known by others.

Safety and Security: If the need to be seen as strong causes the character to take risks or act impulsively, they could end up harming themselves.

HOW THE CHARACTER CAN MINIMIZE OR OVERCOME IT
Focus on their strengths and use them to stand out
Owning what makes them unique rather than labeling a difference as a deficiency
Connecting with others who share the character's weakness
Gently correcting people whose actions make the character feel smaller

CRITICISM

NOTES: No one likes to be criticized, but for some people, this kind of disapproval can be intimidating and even demoralizing, sabotaging their self-esteem and leading to an avoidance of any kind of feedback. A fear like this can also be linked to the fear of REJECTION.

WHAT IT LOOKS LIKE

Hesitancy to share their work
Double- or triple-checking completed tasks
Striving for perfection
Being highly self-disciplined
Asking a lot of questions before starting a new project
Conforming to societal norms
Going above and beyond what was asked
Being a good listener
Choosing words carefully
Compensating for a perceived inferiority (bragging, exaggerating, etc.)
Never taking initiative
Self-deprecation
Repeatedly apologizing for perceived wrongdoing
Seeking approval and validation
Being uncomfortable in new environments and activities
Preferring to be alone
A reluctance to take something on that will be evaluated later
Avoiding risks
Becoming defensive when advice or suggestions are offered
Being unable to differentiate between constructive criticism and feedback that should be ignored
Taking things personally
Painstakingly making their appearance perfect
Being very hard on themselves

COMMON INTERNAL STRUGGLES

The character always feeling on edge, as if they're about to make a mistake
Having ideas to share but being too afraid of how they'll be received
Feeling guilt over real or perceived failures
Struggling with low self-esteem
Believing they're inferior or worth less than their peers
Feeling inadequate or incapable
Dwelling on negative feedback
Believing people are waiting for them to make a mistake
Being ashamed of a part of themselves (a physical characteristic, a weakness, an ability, etc.)
Suffering from an anxiety or personality disorder

HINDRANCES AND DISRUPTIONS TO THE CHARACTER'S LIFE

Not growing or improving because they're unable to accept feedback
Never being able to truly express themselves
Not pursuing a passion because of past criticism in that area
Gaining a reputation for being prickly, easily offended, or uncooperative
Envying people who are more talented than the character
Being plagued with insecurity and worry that their efforts aren't good enough

EMOTIONAL WOUNDS IT COULD STEM FROM: A Learning Disability, A Parent's Abandonment or Rejection, A Toxic Relationship, Battling a Mental Condition, Being Bullied, Being Raised by Parents Who Loved Conditionally, Being Rejected by One's Peers, Domestic Abuse

SCENARIOS THAT MIGHT TRIGGER THIS FEAR

Being the odd one out in a group (due to beliefs, preferences, goals, etc.)
Having to change jobs and start over with a new supervisor
The character or their skills being put on display
Being compared to a peer
Being rejected (for a job opening, on a date, when sharing an idea, etc.)
Being assigned to a project without clear parameters or expectations
Being paired with someone whose performance is always lauded
Receiving harsh criticism from a trusted individual
The character's skills being brushed aside or devalued

HUMAN NEEDS THAT COULD BE IMPACTED

Self-Actualization: A fear of criticism will lead the character to avoid opportunities for growth that are challenging or somewhat risky, resulting in stagnation.

Esteem and Recognition: If the character internalizes criticism, they start to doubt their own worth and value.

Love and Belonging: When a character reads criticism into well-meaning advice or accuses loved ones of being unsupportive or overly harsh, friction in those relationships will develop.

HOW THE CHARACTER CAN MINIMIZE OR OVERCOME IT

Giving themselves permission to process emotions associated with judgment rather than denying them
Asking someone safe to weigh in on criticism the character received to get an objective viewpoint and advice
Sharing a flaw or mistake with a trusted friend and seeing that judgment is fleeting

DISCRIMINATION

NOTES: Discrimination doesn't have to be big or obvious for it to hurt; even one thoughtless comment can sting. Experiencing this kind of prejudice can lead to a fear of discrimination, causing a character to hide who they are and fall short of ever reaching their full potential.

WHAT IT LOOKS LIKE

Being hypervigilant
The character associating mainly with people like them (same race, gender, class, etc.)
Staying out of certain neighborhoods or places
Keeping silent when witnessing mistreatment
Going to great lengths to work with and surround themselves with people who are safe or like-minded
Raising their children in a bubble
Hesitating to open up about the parts of their life that may invite discrimination (a mental health condition, sexual orientation, etc.)
Masking anger and frustration (to avoid more mistreatment)
Only being truly comfortable with people like them; putting on a face for everyone else
Conforming to the people around them
Wearing common clothing styles rather than cultural pieces
Being determined to break the norms to prove the character is more than a stereotype
Pretending not to notice microaggressions
Not disclosing certain types of personal information (religion, sexual orientation, etc.)
Making themselves invisible when they're uncomfortable
Perfectionism
Overperforming to disprove stereotypes or gain acceptance
Rejecting the part of themselves that might be discriminated against
Distrusting the justice system
Trying to (carefully) correct a misconception
Advocating for themselves or others

COMMON INTERNAL STRUGGLES

Doubting motives; wondering if people are being discriminatory when they may not be
Being tempted to discriminate against people who have mistreated them
Feeling misunderstood and angry at the unfairness of it all
Believing everyone is against them
Harboring anger or hatred toward a group of people (police officers, the wealthy, etc.)
Struggling with unearned shame
Struggling with self-esteem and identity
Always being on edge, on the lookout for possible discrimination
Wanting to speak out but being afraid (of being hurt, of losing an opportunity, etc.)

HINDRANCES AND DISRUPTIONS TO THE CHARACTER'S LIFE

Discrimination escalating
Repressed anger spilling over into other areas of the character's life

Believing a lie about a person or group of people
Believing the lies that others say about the character (self-fulfilling prophecy)
Missing out on friendships with other kinds of people that could broaden the character's perspective
Living a life that is short of their full potential

EMOTIONAL WOUNDS IT COULD STEM FROM: A Parent's Abandonment or Rejection, A Sibling's Betrayal, An Abuse of Power, Being Falsely Accused of a Crime, Being Fired or Laid Off, Being Forced to Keep a Dark Secret, Losing One of the Five Senses, Prejudice or Discrimination, Telling the Truth but Not Being Believed, Wrongful Imprisonment

SCENARIOS THAT MIGHT TRIGGER THIS FEAR

Witnessing discrimination against someone else
Returning to a place where the character experienced discrimination (a school, family, church, etc.)
Speaking out against discrimination and not being believed
Having to interact with a political or religious group that is known to have questionable or unpopular beliefs
Encountering someone who has been discriminatory in the past
Moving to a new neighborhood, city, or school where the character is in the minority
Seeing a news story about a hate crime
Meeting a person from their own group who has differing opinions or beliefs

HUMAN NEEDS THAT COULD BE IMPACTED

Self-Actualization: Someone with this fear will likely shy away from people and situations where discrimination might (or does) occur, making it difficult for them to achieve goals and be truly free.

Esteem and Recognition: If a character's fear of being discriminated against causes them to hate what makes them unique, this could lead to eroded self-worth and an identity crisis.

Love and Belonging: A character with this fear may have a hard time connecting with others, especially groups, organizations, or settings where the chances of discrimination are high.

Safety and Security: If protections are not in place, the character's fear of discrimination may be realized. They could be targeted in a hate crime, lose access to secure housing, or be denied medical care, due process, or other basic human rights.

HOW THE CHARACTER CAN MINIMIZE OR OVERCOME IT

Learning to value themselves so they can withstand any discrimination that does occur
Surrounding themselves with a supportive, loving community
Seeking out advocacy groups and learning to self-advocate
Educating themselves about their rights
Preparing responses to microaggressions: "I don't know what you mean—can you explain?"
Practicing calm, clear communication to avoid rash responses that may escalate tensions
Focusing on educating others to see past stereotypes

FAILURE

NOTES: Most people have a healthy aversion to failure; it's why we plan, educate ourselves, and weigh options before committing. But a fear of failure becomes problematic when a character is so stymied by it that they limit themselves and become stuck. Someone in this situation will have to work through this fear if they're to meet their relational or professional goals and live their fullest life.

WHAT IT LOOKS LIKE

Being content with the status quo (or telling themselves that they are)
Taking a follower role; letting others lead
Underachieving and setting easy goals
Sidestepping decisions by letting others make them
Not putting out their best effort (because it means risking failure)
Apathy or laziness
Shutting down a coworker's new idea before it can be adopted
Finding faults in potential love interests
Ending a romantic relationship when it starts to get serious
Turning down new projects or opportunities
Doing something reckless or ill-advised the night before an important test or interview—e.g., drinking too much, then falling asleep and missing the appointment
Procrastinating on a school or work assignment
Not finishing projects
Dropping out of something if a competitor emerges
Ensuring they're never around when an opportunity to step up presents itself
Blaming others when a failure occurs
Projecting an image that encourages low expectations from others
Preoccupation with minor tasks (instead of focusing on the important ones)
An inability to analyze past failures and learn from them
Making excuses for underperforming
Handing something off before it reaches a state of completion
Manipulating others to avoid having to take on certain duties
Obsessing so much over making things perfect that an end product is never delivered

COMMON INTERNAL STRUGGLES

The character doubting their abilities or intelligence
The character being certain of their own failure when they're entirely capable of winning
Believing that others think the character is a failure
Worrying that failure will make others think less of the character
Envisioning a desired future but doubting it will ever come to be
Past failures replaying in the character's head on a loop
Struggling with shame and disappointing others
Wanting to take on certain projects or opportunities but being too scared to try
Creating internal arguments against an appealing but risky opportunity

HINDRANCES AND DISRUPTIONS TO THE CHARACTER'S LIFE

Missing out on opportunities that the character would be good at or enjoy
Others looking down on the character (for a lack of ambition or ability)
Being limited in what they're able to achieve in life
Arguing with family members who call the character out for not trying hard enough
Being unfulfilled
Only being able to go so far professionally
Difficulty maintaining a meaningful and healthy romantic relationship

EMOTIONAL WOUNDS IT COULD STEM FROM: A Child Dying on One's Watch, Accidentally Killing Someone, Bearing the Responsibility for Many Deaths, Being Disappointed by a Role Model, Being Fired or Laid Off, Being Humiliated by Others

SCENARIOS THAT MIGHT TRIGGER THIS FEAR

Being assigned a high-profile work project
A work partner calling in sick, leaving the character to handle things alone
Being asked to join a committee or volunteer group
Being asked out by someone the character likes
A romantic relationship escalating to a new level (the other person saying "I love you" or suggesting it's time to move in together)
A person close to the character voicing doubts, echoing their own thoughts
Encountering a scenario like the one that caused the character's fear of failure
Being pitted against someone who is superior and is sure to win
Being rejected by a potential love interest

HUMAN NEEDS THAT COULD BE IMPACTED

Self-Actualization: Because a character with this fear will often avoid opportunities where failure is possible, they'll never fully stretch themselves and grow.

Esteem and Recognition: People who fear failure doubt their ability to succeed and give up easily, both of which contribute to diminished self-esteem.

Love and Belonging: Sabotaging romantic relationships so they end prematurely is one way of avoiding failure, but it creates an unmet need in this area.

HOW THE CHARACTER CAN MINIMIZE OR OVERCOME IT

Reframe failure as something necessary to learn and grow
Reminding themselves of others who failed and how it didn't define them
Accepting that some things aren't within a person's control
Focusing on effort and actions, not the outcome
Planning and analyzing the risks in advance
Choosing their timing carefully, resisting pressure to act before they are ready
Practicing skills and proficiency
Acknowledging mistakes happen and shutting down self-criticism
Avoid catastrophizing by considering how likely the failure is to happen
Asking for help
Celebrating attempts, not just winning

GROWING OLD

NOTES: While growing old is a part of life, it's not always an easy process. Someone who has always looked young, whose identity is tied to their perceived attractiveness, or whose occupation relies on mobility and independence can develop a fear in this area. Whether they're triggered by their changing looks, a potential mental decline, a physical weakening of the body, or death itself, someone with this fear may become driven to do everything in their power to keep the inevitable at bay.

WHAT IT LOOKS LIKE
Incessantly working out
Eating healthy
Following a strict skin care regimen
Investing in cosmetic surgery
Wearing a lot of makeup to cover the signs of age
Staying out of the sun
Seeing doctors often for preventive and corrective measures
Hanging out with people younger than them
Heightened awareness of mental and physical changes
Adopting youthful practices, speech, and activities
Needing constant reassurance about their appearance
Being obsessed about staying physically and mentally active
Avoiding reminders of old age, such as nursing homes or a retirement party
Constantly testing their mental or physical acuity for changes
The character avoiding having their picture taken
Refusing to wear reading glasses (even if they need them)
Taking many supplements that support memory and improved neurological functions
Trying fringe skin care regimes that promise youthful results
Following skin care and fitness influencers on social media
Spending money on products and gadgets that promise to wind back the clock
The character comparing themselves to others their age
Being sexually active even if desire isn't always there
Remaining stubbornly autonomous; turning down help or refusing to admit that an activity is beyond their ability
Refusing to change their ways—e.g., continuing to drive even when it's dangerous for them to do so or refusing help when it's offered
Avoiding doctors altogether (being in denial about growing old)

COMMON INTERNAL STRUGGLES
The character obsessing over shifts in their appearance or mental capabilities
Worrying that others also notice the changes
Seeing deficiencies where there are none
Constantly wanting to look in mirrors but being afraid to
The character comparing themselves to others and finding themselves lacking
Becoming deeply insecure about their appearance

Knowing that aging is a normal process but feeling compelled to fight it anyway
Being in denial about changes that are happening
A fear of death emerging

HINDRANCES AND DISRUPTIONS TO THE CHARACTER'S LIFE
Overspending on maintaining their appearance, creating a budget crisis
Frequent surgeries and recoveries stealing the character's free time
Difficulty relating to people their own age
Having to put more time and effort into hiding the signs of aging
Being exhausted by the effort to always prove themselves and their capabilities to others

EMOTIONAL WOUNDS IT COULD STEM FROM: A Physical Disfigurement, Being So Beautiful It's All People See, Watching Someone Die

SCENARIOS THAT MIGHT TRIGGER THIS FEAR
A friend or associate passing away (especially one who is the same age)
Seeing a drastic change in an older friend's appearance
Experiencing a physical change associated with aging, such as gray hair, age spots, or a drop in metabolism or libido
Hitting a milestone birthday (40, 50, 60, etc.)
Experiencing memory problems due to medication side effects or not enough sleep
The character having trouble doing something they've always excelled at
Being rejected or discriminated against and believing it's due to their age
Realizing they cannot command attention the way they used to
Realizing they're attracting the interest of partners older than they're used to dating
Experiencing the onset of menopause or other conditions that come with age

HUMAN NEEDS THAT COULD BE IMPACTED

Self-Actualization: Aging is part of the human experience. A character who is unwilling to accept it will be unfulfilled because they are denying who they truly are.

Esteem and Recognition: A character fearful of aging may think less of themselves due to changes to their appearance or an increased need to rely on others.

Love and Belonging: This insecurity will cause problems with loved ones if the character projects their obsession onto other impressionable (younger) family members, causing self-esteem issues to emerge in them.

Safety and Security: A character in denial about growing old may put themselves in danger by continuing activities that are no longer safe for them.

HOW THE CHARACTER CAN MINIMIZE OR OVERCOME IT
Probing this fear for the unhappiness or disappointment beneath it, and adjusting goals to meet personal needs so the character can focus on living and loving their life
Acknowledging how trying to stop the clock steals time and money from other things
Focusing on the present, and the people and experiences that make life worth living
Looking forward to the positives: grandchildren, retirement, a freedom to travel, etc.
Considering regrets should tomorrow not arrive and prioritize removing them

GROWING UP

NOTES: While many young people welcome the freedom and independence of adulthood, some see only increased pressure, impossible expectations, and the loss of the ease of childhood. This fear can develop if the character feels incapable of fulfilling adult obligations or faces overwhelming expectations about being a grown-up.

WHAT IT LOOKS LIKE

Holding onto childish things, such as toys, hobbies, or interests
Escaping into daydreaming, video games, books, etc.
Dating for fun only; not pursuing a long-term relationship
Making only vague plans
Allowing others to make the important decisions
Focusing on leisurely or fun activities
Going through the motions when it comes to adult milestones—e.g., attending college only to have fun and not caring about getting a degree or education
Feigning illness to get out of school, work, or other obligations
Procrastinating
Being unreliable; not following through
Being left behind by peers
Losing touch with friends who move on to a new stage in life
Living a party lifestyle
Maintaining the appearance (clothing, hair styles, etc.) of a younger person
Being perceived as immature, selfish, or entitled
Spending time with younger people
Setting goals that are unattainable or impractical
Engaging in codependent relationships where the character is cared for by another
Reluctance to lead or be responsible for others
Pretending to be incapable of adult skills (balancing a bank register, keeping a job, etc.)
Choosing jobs that don't pay enough to support the character
Expecting their parents to bail them out of difficulties
Struggling to keep a job; bouncing from one opportunity to another
Manipulating parents to maintain access to their resources

COMMON INTERNAL STRUGGLES

Feeling anxious as coming-of-age milestones approach (getting a license, moving out of a parent's home, starting their first job, getting married, etc.)
Not wanting to live at home but being afraid of losing their parents' financial support
Feeling stuck between childhood and adulthood
Feeling incapable of taking care of themselves or doing important things
Struggling with confidence and self-worth
Envying peers who have crossed successfully into adulthood
Living in denial about the inevitable future
Wanting independence but being too scared to give up comfort and familiarity
Being paralyzed by big decisions that will determine the character's future

Feeling overwhelmed by the prospect of adult responsibilities
Wishing they had a purpose but not knowing what it is

HINDRANCES AND DISRUPTIONS TO THE CHARACTER'S LIFE
Missing out on opportunities to fulfill their personal and professional potential
Relationships frequently petering out as the other person moves on to the next stage of life and the character is left behind
Being unable to relate to their peers' adult struggles and successes
Lacking age-appropriate social and life skills
Irresponsibility and lack of self-discipline causing problems in many areas of life
Living only for themselves and missing out on the joys of serving others
Friction with family members who challenge the character about their future

EMOTIONAL WOUNDS IT COULD STEM FROM: A Traumatic Brain Injury, Battling a Mental Condition, Being Raised by Overprotective Parents, Cracking Under Pressure, Experiencing the Death of a Parent as a Child or Youth

SCENARIOS THAT MIGHT TRIGGER THIS FEAR
Watching someone suffer through an adult trauma (being fired, getting divorced, etc.)
Being pressured about future plans (choosing a career, starting a family, etc.)
Being offered a promotion that requires more work and responsibility
Being pushed to get a driver's license
An unexpected pregnancy
Reaching a milestone birthday
Being given an ultimatum tied to being kicked out of the house
A romantic partner wanting to take the relationship to the next level
A friend who shared the character's superficial desires deciding to pursue an adult goal
A younger sibling taking adult steps before the character (moving out first, etc.)

HUMAN NEEDS THAT COULD BE IMPACTED

Self-Actualization: A character who fears growing up will deny an essential part of their identity, making it difficult to accept themselves for who they truly are.

Esteem and Recognition: Refusing to grow up will inevitably draw criticism from others and impact how the character is perceived.

Love and Belonging: A character with this fear will struggle to maintain or create healthy relationships with their peers. Their inability to commit, along with the behaviors they adopt to keep from transitioning to the next stage of life, can also create tension with loved ones who find it difficult to support them.

HOW THE CHARACTER CAN MINIMIZE OR OVERCOME IT
Setting achievable goals so the character can practice following through and succeeding
Choosing to solve their own problems instead of asking for a bailout
Moving on from friendships that are stunting the character's maturity
Seeking the advice of old friends who have moved forward in their lives
Envisioning the future they want for themselves and planning for it

HUMILIATION

NOTES: Humiliation is embarrassment on steroids—a lingering sense of disgrace and wounded pride that's often brought on by a public shaming. It's naturally something to avoid, but when a character develops a fear of humiliation, they'll constantly be watching for it, seeing it where it doesn't exist and going to great lengths to keep it at bay.

WHAT IT LOOKS LIKE

Overcompensating to prove their worth
Obsessing over their appearance
Seeking to do everything perfectly so no one can find fault
Holding themselves to unrealistic standards
Being suspicious of people and their motives
Sticking close to people they know they can trust
Overplanning or over-practicing when they fear they will be scrutinized
Second-guessing themselves
Staying in the background
Being uncomfortable in the limelight
Needing to know what will happen (hating to be surprised)
Overreacting to playful teasing or being unable to take a joke
Seeking respected opinions and reassurance before making choices
Being reluctant to meet new people and develop new relationships
Not making a move romantically until the character knows the other person will say yes
Making fun of themselves before others have a chance to do so
Acting tough and impervious to embarrassment
Avoiding people who have caused humiliation in the past
Avoiding people who witnessed the character's humiliation
Taking remarks out of context (assuming humiliation was intended when it wasn't)
Becoming flustered when someone responds with skepticism or criticism
Becoming reserved and cautious in public (to avoid a social misstep)
Declining social or work opportunities where a public mistake is possible
Mentally replaying conversations to see if the character said something embarrassing

COMMON INTERNAL STRUGGLES

Having trust issues
Feeling paranoid that people are out to get them
Wanting to pursue a new friendship but fearing what could happen
Assuming the worst despite knowing how unlikely it is
Being unable to let go of mistakes or failures, no matter how small
Being plagued by a past humiliation; seeing it repeatedly in their mind
Wondering if the humiliation was justified (self-blame)
Self-loathing undermining the character's sense of worth
Feeling like there's no escape from an ongoing humiliation, such as bullying
Fantasizing about revenge

HINDRANCES AND DISRUPTIONS TO THE CHARACTER'S LIFE
Experiencing performance anxiety in many areas of their life
Missing out on good opportunities that include a public aspect
Being unable to view feedback critically and move on (which leads to quitting rather than learning and growing or moving forward)
Lashing out at perceived humiliation, causing problems in relationships
Being stuck, unable to move past a former humiliation
Avoiding places where past indignities occurred
Feeling unseen because they're too afraid of ridicule to voice their own thoughts or opinions
Having to see their humiliator regularly (at school, work, in the neighborhood, etc.)
The character's fear progressing into an anxiety or panic disorder
Low self-esteem becoming a limiting factor in the character's life

EMOTIONAL WOUNDS IT COULD STEM FROM: A Physical Disfigurement, A Speech Impediment, Being Bullied, Being Disowned or Shunned, Being Humiliated by Others, Being the Victim of a Vicious Rumor, Failing at School, Sexual Dysfunction, Social Difficulties

SCENARIOS THAT MIGHT TRIGGER THIS FEAR
Being set up on a blind date
Being intimate with a partner for the first time
Having to give a speech
Being caught in a lie (no matter how small)
The person who humiliated the character becoming a coworker or part of the family
Someone bringing up a humiliating event from the character's past
Seeing someone's embarrassing blunder on social media, TV, or in person
Being pressured by a friend or partner to do something that carries an element of risk
The character's feelings about a humiliating event being minimized by others
The character's child being rejected by their peers or picked on by a bully

HUMAN NEEDS THAT COULD BE IMPACTED

Self-Actualization: If the character's fear causes them to avoid situations where they'll be scrutinized, this can hold them back professionally and academically, robbing them of many enrichment and fulfillment opportunities.

Esteem and Recognition: A character whose fear stems from past humiliations may wonder why they were targeted and end up blaming themselves.

Love and Recognition: A character with this fear may have difficulty being vulnerable and maintaining healthy, trusting relationships.

HOW THE CHARACTER CAN MINIMIZE OR OVERCOME IT
Signing up for a speech club like Toastmasters to become more comfortable in a crowd
Engaging in situations where the character will be in the public eye
Joining a comedy class so they can reframe laughter as approval instead of contempt
Attending social functions with a friend (for support)
Joining inclusive groups built on acceptance and respect
Revisiting the site of a humiliation on a happy occasion to give it a positive framework
Regain control by confronting a tormentor instead of hiding from them

INADEQUACY

NOTES: The silver lining of personal shortcomings is that they provide opportunities for growth and teach us the importance of asking for help. But not everyone is comfortable admitting their weaknesses. A character who fears inadequacy (or the perception of it) will engage in behaviors that distance themselves from others and limit their success—ironically, bringing about the very thing they fear.

WHAT IT LOOKS LIKE

Staying in their comfort zone
Choosing safe goals
Driving conversations toward the topics they know a lot about
Making excuses for turning down ambitious opportunities
Privately consulting self-help resources
Lying to cover up their shortcomings
Needing to know exactly what's expected of them before they commit
Avoiding activities and situations that don't play to their strengths
Avoiding people who excel in areas where the character is weak
Striving for perfection to prove their capability
Double- and triple-checking their work before submitting it
Using social media to highlight their successes and show how they're living their best life
Overspending to create an appearance of having it all
Clinging to past accomplishments
Avoiding competitions or contests they're unlikely to win
Overly inflating their strengths to hide their weaknesses
Not seeking advice or help from others; handling everything on their own
Difficulty regulating their emotions
False bravado
Having unrealistic expectations (about their abilities, the life they should be living, etc.)
Fretting over public appearances
Not responding well to criticism (lashing out, being defensive, falling apart, etc.)
Fight or flight responses kicking in when a personal insecurity is triggered
Building themselves up by diminishing the accomplishments of others

COMMON INTERNAL STRUGGLES

Being consumed with negative self-talk
Constantly comparing themselves to others
Needing to confide in someone but not wanting to show their shortcomings
Obsessing over real and perceived inadequacies
Feeling uncomfortable around the successful people in their circles
Wishing for more than they currently have or are
Being exhausted by having to act more confident than they feel
Wrestling often with jealousy and envy
Wanting to pursue a certain goal but doubting their abilities
Focusing on negatives rather than positives

HINDRANCES AND DISRUPTIONS TO THE CHARACTER'S LIFE

Being limited professionally and romantically
Needing to avoid competitors or people who are overly critical
Being obsessed with what others have instead of looking at themselves and making the changes that would get them what they want
Hiding an injury, illness, or whatever they think makes them look weak
Being too afraid to pursue opportunities that would improve their life
Missing out on chances to turn their weakness into a strength and overcome it

EMOTIONAL WOUNDS IT COULD STEM FROM: A Child Dying on One's Watch, A Learning Disability, A Physical Disfigurement, A Speech Impediment, Accidentally Killing Someone, Being Bullied, Being Fired or Laid Off, Making a Very Public Mistake, Poor Judgment Leading to Unintended Consequences

SCENARIOS THAT MIGHT TRIGGER THIS FEAR

Being fired from their job
Receiving a promotion that requires more responsibility and leadership
Being attracted to someone the character feels is out of their league
Being pressured to join a competitive team
Facing an important decision with long-term ramifications
Someone close to the character achieving a major accomplishment
Being paired with someone "perfect" whose presence shines a light on the character's weakness
Making a poor financial decision
Making a public mistake
Being given an opportunity to pursue a risky dream
Being pitted against someone they feel they could never defeat

HUMAN NEEDS THAT COULD BE IMPACTED

Self-Actualization: This fear embodies self-doubt and will keep a character from pursuing a dream because, deep down, they'll believe they're incapable of achieving it.

Esteem and Recognition: Self-esteem will be compromised for a character who constantly feels less capable than others.

Love and Belonging: A character with this fear may settle for unhealthy relationships because they believe they can't do better and don't want to be alone.

HOW THE CHARACTER CAN MINIMIZE OR OVERCOME IT

Separating feelings of inadequacy from actual identity and worth
Choosing to celebrate achievements instead of downplaying them
Starting by taking small risks that challenge the character's insecurities
Setting out not to master something but just get better at it
Looking back often to remind themselves how far they've come
Building skills and knowledge
Focusing on personal goals and growth, not what others are doing
Targeting a weakness and seeking to improve it or make it a strength
Avoiding competitive people and environments
Replacing people who tear each other down with friends who build each other up

LEADING

NOTES: Leading is not easy. It requires responsibility, accountability, being scrutinized, and making decisions that have a wide impact. The weight of this burden can cause some characters to avoid stepping forward when asked (or needed). And if they must take charge, this fear will cause them to resent having the role thrust upon them.

WHAT IT LOOKS LIKE

Resistance to being in charge
Avoiding making a final decision
Not speaking up (since this could cause others to see the character as a leader)
Being risk-averse
The character pointing out their own flaws and lack of leadership potential
Avoiding conflict and arguments
Working with a partner who likes to be in charge
Indecisiveness and hesitation
Putting decisions to a vote instead of being the sole person to decide
Pulling back or hiding out in stressful times
Communicating through email or other remote means instead of face-to-face
Having someone else make the speeches and be the face of the operation
Overanalyzing when a choice needs to be made
Wanting to stick to what's known rather than innovate and experiment
Setting smaller goals that are easier to achieve
Not feeling up to big challenges
Resisting growth (of a movement, a business, a community) to keep things manageable
Pushing people away
Finding reasons to stay in the comfort zone rather than think about what's next
Seeing drawbacks instead of potential
Viewing failures or lackluster progress as proof of an inability to lead
Focusing on what could go wrong, not what could go right
Worrying about the repercussions when they have to make the final call
Pretending things are okay when they're not
Hiding relief when someone offers to take charge
Self-doubt pushing the character to keep things smaller and less complicated
Taking criticism personally
Becoming prickly when they don't know an answer
Self-sabotage (to keep from doing well and being viewed as someone capable)

COMMON INTERNAL STRUGGLES

Wanting to hide from responsibility and feeling cowardly about it
Wanting to make things better but only being able to see their own shortcomings
Believing leading would be a disaster
Wanting to do right by others but fearing their efforts will only cause disappointment
Feeling unworthy of the belief others have in them
Feeling like an impostor

Wanting to go back to simpler times
Having a closed (instead of a growth) mindset
Focusing on mistakes and failures rather than successes
Believing successes are due to luck, not skill
Having good ideas but not wanting to be blamed if something goes wrong
Feeling cowardly for not having the strength to step forward
Being unhappy in a follower role (but not wanting to lead, either)

HINDRANCES AND DISRUPTIONS TO THE CHARACTER'S LIFE
Withholding ideas out of the fear of being singled out and asked to lead
Being stuck in a less-than-ideal status quo
Having to deal with bad leaders and situations that don't improve
Feeling like they're living beneath their potential
Leading, but with a fear-based mindset that catastrophizes
Being pessimistic about the future
Not being able to see their own ideas come to fruition

EMOTIONAL WOUNDS IT COULD STEM FROM: A Learning Disability, A Speech Impediment, Bearing the Responsibility for Many Deaths, Caving to Peer Pressure, Cracking Under Pressure, Failing to Do the Right Thing

SCENARIOS THAT MIGHT TRIGGER THIS FEAR
Being asked to take something over or oversee a project, committee, or event
A survival situation where the character is the best suited to lead
Being the oldest in an emergency, so siblings look to the character for direction
Someone coming to the character in dire need of help
A death in the family that makes the character a successor
The character knowing that not stepping up will result in a great harm

HUMAN NEEDS THAT COULD BE IMPACTED

Self-Actualization: A character who has a knack for leading but shies away from it may chafe under the leadership of someone less capable. This character also may become dissatisfied living life as a follower and always answering to others.

Esteem and Recognition: A fear of leadership often indicates an insecurity or self-doubt about the character's abilities, resulting in the belief that they can't succeed or do what other people can do.

Safety and Security: Some situations require a person to step into a leadership role to right a wrong or keep others safe. If the character refuses, they (or the people around them) may suffer.

HOW THE CHARACTER CAN MINIMIZE OR OVERCOME IT
Viewing the role as a necessity to making things better
Surrounding themselves with talented and dedicated people invested in success
Expecting mistakes as part of risk-taking, and deciding to learn from them
Viewing the only failure as being unwilling to try
Finding a mentor to help guide the character to informed decisions

LETTING PEOPLE DOWN

NOTES: As a rule, people don't like to disappoint others. Maybe it comes from the belief that doing so is rude. Or we want to be viewed as capable and reliable, and letting people down doesn't achieve that goal. Sometimes it comes from a deep need to please others. There's nothing wrong with these motivations—until they're taken too far. When a character's fear of letting others down results in the formation of unhealthy behaviors or patterns, it can lead to a whole host of problems.

WHAT IT LOOKS LIKE

Paying attention, going the extra mile, and making good use of their time
Thinking ahead, trying to be prepared for what might be needed
Asking clarifying questions to be sure they understand what's expected
Always following through on responsibilities
Consistently receiving high grades or performance reviews
Doing chores, running errands, etc. without being asked
Spending free time on pursuits meant to make the character better (studying, taking on an internship, reading self-help books, etc.)
Obsessing over small details
Taking care of their appearance
Being sensitive to others' emotions and needs
Being on the lookout for vocal patterns or behavior that indicates disappointment
Making sacrifices to put the needs of others first
Not agreeing to commitments unless the character is sure they can deliver
Always agreeing to everything so they won't disappoint others
Being supportive, not contrary
Seeking to put others at ease: "It's no problem, I'm happy to do it."
Arriving to meetings or appointments ahead of time
Going out of their way to not make others feel uncomfortable
Working harder than everyone else
Being a perfectionist
Overachieving
Thinking carefully about how to answer before answering a question
Blaming themselves when someone is disappointed

COMMON INTERNAL STRUGGLES

Wanting to follow a passion (for a career, etc.) that other people don't approve of
Putting on an emotional front to hide "unacceptable" emotions
Needing to turn down a request and feeling terrible about it
The character feeling that they're not enough
Wanting to speak the truth but not wanting to disappoint or upset the other person
Feeling unappreciated or taken for granted
Struggling (with a deadline, responsibility, pressure, etc.) but being unable to talk about it
Wondering if someone is taking advantage of them
Feeling worthless when they fall short of someone's expectations

HINDRANCES AND DISRUPTIONS TO THE CHARACTER'S LIFE

Being exhausted from working too much and always needing to be the best
Being unable to do what makes them personally happy because they're always doing what others want
Being taken advantage of
Constantly flirting with burnout
Frequently falling ill due to a lack of self-care
Believing that their own opinions and ideas aren't as important as another person's
Not knowing their own needs and desires

EMOTIONAL WOUNDS IT COULD STEM FROM: A Child Dying on One's Watch, A Loved One's Suicide, A Parent's Abandonment or Rejection, A Parent's Divorce, Bearing the Responsibility for Many Deaths, Being Legitimately Incarcerated for a Crime, Being Raised by Parents Who Loved Conditionally

SCENARIOS THAT MIGHT TRIGGER THIS FEAR

Receiving a poor grade or performance assessment at work
Being asked to do a very large or difficult task
Learning that someone wasn't happy with their work
Not being chosen (for a promotion, to be best man in a friend's wedding, etc.)
Being paired with someone who is never satisfied
Getting invited to two events at the same time and having to choose one
Being given an opportunity to do something important for themselves or someone else, but it means asking for a day off, requesting to push back a deadline, etc.
Being asked or pressured to do something the character isn't comfortable with
Knowing they're not well-suited for an important task

HUMAN NEEDS THAT COULD BE IMPACTED

Self-Actualization: A character who gives into other people's wishes will put their own needs and desires on the back burner, and dissatisfaction and discontent will grow.

Esteem and Recognition: A character who takes responsibility for the happiness of others will blame themselves when someone becomes upset, sabotaging their own self-esteem.

Love and Belonging: In this situation, the character could easily become needy and over-attentive, putting people off.

Safety and Security: A character who doesn't maintain healthy boundaries may put themselves in harm's way in their efforts to keep from letting others down.

HOW THE CHARACTER CAN MINIMIZE OR OVERCOME IT

Setting time aside to understand what they want, and prioritizing that
Having honest conversations with loved ones about the unfair weight of expectations
Learning to say no
Learning to ask for help
Setting boundaries and asking others to respect them
Viewing "not helping" as a way to encourage others to discover their own capabilities

LOSING ONE'S HERITAGE OR CULTURAL IDENTITY

NOTES: Cultural differences—ones we adopt or are born into—define us. Losing that aspect of identity can shake the foundation of who the character is and threaten the connections they have with others from their culture. This is an enormous loss. While it's normal and healthy to embrace one's heritage, a fear of losing that sense of identity—whether the possibility is real or perceived—can drive the character to great (even unhealthy) lengths to keep it from happening.

WHAT IT LOOKS LIKE

Holding firmly to personal traditions
Observing cultural rituals to keep them alive and relevant
Educating their children about their culture: engaging in traditions, telling them stories about it, speaking their native language at home, etc.
Educating others about the character's culture—forming a club at school or a committee at work, for instance
Becoming an activist
Living a life at home that looks different from the character's life outside of the home
The character seeing offense or slights against their culture where none were intended
Resisting assimilation or integration into a different culture
Condemning family members who choose to integrate with other cultures
Only associating with people within the character's cultural group
The character sheltering their children from influences outside of their community
The character unintentionally passing their fear of others to their children
Requiring loved ones to choose spouses from within their cultural group
Scorning those outside of the character's community (rejecting them before they can reject the character)
Developing an us vs. them mentality

COMMON INTERNAL STRUGGLES

Wanting to maintain their cultural identity but also wanting to fit in with others
Feeling conflicted about their identity
Being drawn to the practices of other cultures and feeling disloyal
Fearing certain people groups outside of the character's community
The character fearing that they're losing their children to another culture
The character wanting to protect their children from being drawn away by other cultures but recognizing that doing so may damage their relationship
Wanting to challenge harmful cultural practices (genital mutilation, child marriage, honor killings, homophobia, etc.) but fearing reprisals
Only feeling safe and understood when the character is within their own community

HINDRANCES AND DISRUPTIONS TO THE CHARACTER'S LIFE

Facing barriers if a common language is needed to access opportunities and help
Missing out on valuable experiences, learning opportunities, and advances from other cultures

that could benefit the character
Experiencing discrimination or harassment
Strained relationships with family members who want to integrate with the rest of the world
Living life feeling like an outsider
Becoming judgmental or prejudicial about people from other cultures

EMOTIONAL WOUNDS IT COULD STEM FROM: A Terrorist Attack, Being Bullied, Being Disowned or Shunned, Being Forced to Leave One's Homeland, Discovering Hidden Information About One's Ancestry, Finding Out One Was Adopted, Living Through Civil Unrest, Prejudice or Discrimination

SCENARIOS THAT MIGHT TRIGGER THIS FEAR

A natural disaster or human conflict destroying a sacred site
Seeing other people's children abandon their heritage
A child choosing to date someone from another culture
Witnessing the passage of laws that target their culture or heritage (prohibiting certain headwear, a form of worship being forbidden, etc.)
Being targeted because of their heritage
Being pressured to fit in
A bad apple within the character's culture committing a crime, creating animosity toward the character's heritage

HUMAN NEEDS THAT COULD BE IMPACTED

Self-Actualization: Taken to an extreme, this fear can cause a person to hide within their cultural community, rejecting anything outside of it. This can limit the character's options and opportunities.

Esteem and Recognition: A character who is paranoid or fearful of other cultures may garner ire or a lack of respect.

Love and Belonging: A character who is rigid or overly strict in their desire to preserve their culture may unintentionally drive loved ones away.

HOW THE CHARACTER CAN MINIMIZE OR OVERCOME IT

Learning how to honor one's culture while fitting in with the wider world
Fostering positive cultural beliefs and practices at home so children want to embrace their heritage (rather than feeling forced to do so)
Not letting guilt or shame pressure the character into doing things that don't feel right
Encouraging cultural progressiveness; advocating for certain traditions, practices, or ideas to be adapted for the modern age (so the culture continues to flourish)
Speaking and writing in their native language so it isn't lost
Studying history and sharing it with others
Sharing cultural beliefs, stories, recipes, and music so they can be enjoyed by all
Being open and answering questions about their heritage
Addressing assumptions and misconceptions so people understand the culture better
Recognizing that embracing aspects of other cultures isn't a rejection of their own
Joining organizations and events that focus on diversity to join with other cultures in a common goal to promote education, acceptance, and inclusion

LOSING ONE'S SOCIAL STANDING

NOTES: As social creatures, characters gravitate toward certain groups, and it's human nature to want to climb to the top of the pack in those circles. Unfortunately, while social success is exhilarating, it's also tenuous. The fear of losing their standing and everything that comes with it can drive a character to cling to their status regardless of the cost.

WHAT IT LOOKS LIKE

Marketing themselves well by making the most of their strengths and downplaying weaknesses
Gaining validation from the admiration and approval of their peer group
Distinguishing themselves through a talent, skill, or other advantage
Celebrating successes and achievements
Joining certain clubs and societies
Always networking; making choices that will put the character in the same space with influential people
Working hard to be the best (at a sport, their profession, in their appearance, etc.)
Portraying an image the group would approve of
Conforming to the ideals and behaviors of the group
Hiding or downplaying information that would impact their reputation (a physical challenge, family secret, etc.)
Overspending to impress others and maintain their status
One-upping others
Choosing romantic partners with their income and status in mind
Throwing lavish parties
Engaging in activities to keep up appearances (not because the character is passionate about them)
Seeing relationships as transactional
Viewing newcomers as potential competition
Subtly (or overtly) undermining people who threaten their social standing

COMMON INTERNAL STRUGGLES

Worrying about what others think
Being ashamed for embracing certain attitudes or actions that are necessary to stay on top
Not feeling valued by the people closest to them
Feeling superficial and empty, without real purpose
Wondering who they are without their money, talent, or status
Struggling with peer pressure
Wanting to be true to themselves while needing to hide certain aspects of who they are
Disliking their peers but needing their acceptance

HINDRANCES AND DISRUPTIONS TO THE CHARACTER'S LIFE

Going into debt to maintain the reputation of having it all together
Having shallow relationships based on social standing and possessions rather than authenticity and accountability
Being stuck in an unhappy marriage

Having to continue in a lucrative but unfulfilling career
Losing good friends who wouldn't be accepted by the character's social group
Living behind a facade that doesn't reflect who the character truly is
Being surrounded by people the character doesn't really like
Developing stress-related ailments (eating disorders, anxiety, insomnia, etc.)
Alienating loved ones who would speak truth to the character and challenge them to be better

EMOTIONAL WOUNDS IT COULD STEM FROM: Becoming Homeless for Reasons Out of One's Control, Being Bullied, Being Humiliated by Others, Declaring Bankruptcy, Experiencing Poverty, Falling Short of Society's Physical Standards, Financial Ruin Due to a Spouse's Irresponsibility

SCENARIOS THAT MIGHT TRIGGER THIS FEAR

A friend slipping down the social ladder and being shunned by their peer group
A devastating financial setback (making a bad investment, being scammed, etc.)
A secret coming to light that threatens the character's status or reputation
A competitor joining the social group and rising quickly through the ranks
Seeing a friend be replaced by someone "better"—e.g., a friend getting divorced because her husband had an affair with a younger woman
Sustaining an injury that mars the character's physical appearance

HUMAN NEEDS THAT COULD BE IMPACTED

Self-Actualization: If social success depends on the approval of others, what the character wants will always take a back seat to the desires and values of the group.

Esteem and Recognition: The character will often have to conform to stay in their peers' good graces. Ironically, if others see that the character is being inauthentic, they may disapprove of them for being hypocritical or dishonest.

Love and Belonging: It's difficult to build truly supportive relationships that are built on deception, flattery, and insincerity.

Safety and Security: A character who is willing to do anything to maintain their social standing may make choices that put them at risk.

HOW THE CHARACTER CAN MINIMIZE OR OVERCOME IT

Recognizing the need for true friends who will support the character through thick and thin
Finding value in their individuality and ideals rather than in the approval of others
Deciding what's really important and shouldn't be compromised
Finding great joy in an activity the group wouldn't approve of, and deciding to openly pursue it
Realizing that everyone has value, regardless of their wealth or social standing
Seeking to serve the people around them; becoming more other-focused
Wanting to develop authentic relationships, and realizing that authenticity is required

LOSING THE RESPECT OF OTHERS

NOTES: Having the respect of our peers is a core need; even people who claim they don't care what others think desire respect on some level. The fear of having it and losing it can be devastating to a character's mindset. Depending on their personality (like many fears), it will show up in a variety of ways.

WHAT IT LOOKS LIKE

Paying attention to what peers perceive as being important and investing in those areas Projecting an air of confidence
Being a high achiever
Volunteering to take on work, projects, or responsibilities
Pushing themselves past reasonable limits to make a good impression
Exhibiting workaholic and perfectionistic tendencies
Not taking on tasks unless they believe they can accomplish them well
Taking on other people's responsibilities to help out
Avoiding confrontations to keep the peace
Mimicking others to stay within the status quo
Changing personalities depending on who they are with
Choosing a partner who will meet the approval of others
Being susceptible to peer pressure
Being a rule follower
Being thoughtful and considerate to the point of annoyance
Apologizing for perceived missteps
Taking on the submissive role in relationships
Often being perceived as a teacher's pet or brown-noser

COMMON INTERNAL STRUGGLES

Berating themselves over mistakes
Replaying previous conversations obsessively and imagining what they should have said
Being afraid to take chances whether in work or their personal lives
Fearing change and new expectations
Obsessing over worst-case scenarios
Needing help but being unable to ask
Being afraid to speak up for fear of peers thinking less of them
Not trusting their intuition; believing others know best
Feeling powerless, as if the opinions of others control their lives
Self-loathing over their inability to stand up for themselves and their own wishes
Having an irrational fear of failure
Struggling with indecision from overthinking all the possible outcomes of a situation
Constantly worrying that someone will realize how inept they are

HINDRANCES AND DISRUPTIONS TO THE CHARACTER'S LIFE

Developing stress-related health conditions from the constant pressure to be the best
Sacrificing their social life to make a good impression at work

Overcommitting because they can't say no or want to impress people with all their activities
Dating or marrying someone because it's who their parents approve of
Obeying the wishes of others instead of following their heart
Succumbing to peer pressure instead of standing on their own ideals
Losing sight of who they are and what they believe (because they're always giving in to others)
The character's own needs going unmet while they're performing for others
Constantly competing with others to maintain someone's respect (a parent, boss, mentor, potential love interest, etc.)

EMOTIONAL WOUNDS IT COULD STEM FROM: A Parent's Abandonment or Rejection, Being Bullied, Being Fired or Laid Off, Being Humiliated by Others, Being Raised by Parents Who Loved Conditionally, Being Rejected by One's Peers, Domestic Abuse

SCENARIOS THAT MIGHT TRIGGER THIS FEAR

Changing schools or jobs, and the character having to make new friends and figure out their preferences
Seeing another person fall from grace
Overhearing others gossip about someone's mistakes
Being challenged by peers to do something that defies the character's moral code
The character's social standing falling because of a new and popular arrival
Making a social blunder
Having to make a decision where either choice will disappoint someone important
A sibling distinguishing themselves, making the character feel as if they must do something exceptional to stand out

HUMAN NEEDS THAT COULD BE IMPACTED

Self-Actualization: Some characters may go to extremes to maintain the respect of parents, bosses, etc.—even to the point of pursuing goals and dreams that are more aligned with those people's desires than with what the character really wants. In this situation, the character may end up changing who they are; they may feel unable to be true to themselves without losing the respect of those important people in their life.

Esteem and Recognition: A character who is desperate to be respected may be driven to this place because of a past failing that damaged their esteem, putting even more pressure on them to not fall from grace again.

Safety and Security: Someone with this fear may push themselves to extremes and compromise their own safety in order to impress.

HOW THE CHARACTER CAN MINIMIZE OR OVERCOME IT

Admitting to mistakes or making amends to be accountable
Leaning into authenticity rather than choosing to people-please
Remembering that respect is a two-way street and must be earned by all parties
Realizing that having to sacrifice identity or self-esteem for respect is not a fair trade-off
Looking at themselves in the mirror and liking what they see becoming more important than what others may think
Having confidence in being a good friend, husband, coworker, and person negating the character's need to seek approval

MAKING THE WRONG DECISION

NOTES: Most people weigh decisions before choosing how to proceed, so over time, considering the pros and cons of different outcomes is normal. But a fear of making the wrong decision can cripple a character, rendering them unable to decide or take risks.

This fear can paralyze even when it comes to making simple decisions, differentiating it from the fear of BEING WRONG ABOUT SOMETHING IMPORTANT.

WHAT IT LOOKS LIKE

Asking a lot of questions
Being risk-averse
Not thinking quickly on their feet
Over-researching before deciding
Changing their mind often
Procrastinating; waiting until the last minute to make a choice
Using self-talk to work through the options
Having a backup plan
Being easily swayed by what others think
Deferring to others to make the decision
Asking for more time
Obsessing over trivial details
Projecting irresponsibility or unreliability so people will ask someone else
Giving ambiguous answers when pressed for information
Keeping their options open (dating multiple people, accepting two jobs, etc.)
Being reluctant to commit in case something better comes along
Riding other people's coattails (so the character isn't responsible if things go wrong)
Looking for answers in unconventional places (a horoscope, fortune cookies, etc.)
Blaming others when the decision goes south
Refusing to make a move without certainty
Preferring to make no decision and stay where they are

COMMON INTERNAL STRUGGLES

Overthinking and overanalyzing options
The character doubting their own instincts
Being haunted by past missteps
Blaming themselves when they feel the wrong decision was made
Feeling paralyzed when there are too many options
Viewing decisions through a binary lens (either right or wrong)
Feeling the weight of their decision; feeling responsible for how it will impact others
Envying others for the ability to be decisive
Being overwhelmed with worry or anxiety
Feeling incapable and struggling with their self-worth
Becoming highly neurotic

HINDRANCES AND DISRUPTIONS TO THE CHARACTER'S LIFE

Missing out on new opportunities because it's safer to do nothing
Being viewed as uncertain, indecisive, or flaky
Making changes frequently (in their work, in relationships, etc.) because they're afraid of missing an opportunity
Preoccupation with their own dilemma making it impossible for the character to be present for others
Being easily stressed
Needing a lot of input to make a decision
People becoming annoyed by the character's constant requests for advice
Being inefficient; squandering time and money
Loved ones being frustrated by the character frequently changing their mind
Remaining stagnant—relationally, professionally, spiritually, emotionally, etc.

EMOTIONAL WOUNDS IT COULD STEM FROM: Caving to Peer Pressure, Cracking Under Pressure, Crossing Moral Lines to Survive, Failing to Do the Right Thing, Failing to Save Someone's Life, Making a Very Public Mistake, Misplaced Loyalty

SCENARIOS THAT MIGHT TRIGGER THIS FEAR

Receiving multiple options for a high-stakes decision (jobs, school admission, financial investments, a big purchase, etc.)
A loved one going into hospice, and the character needing to act on their behalf
Someone voicing doubts about the character's decision
A family member seeking the character's advice
Hearing rumors about a possible disaster
Taking someone's advice and things turning out badly
Having to vote in an election
Being given an ultimatum
A family member bringing up one of the character's past mistakes
Facing a choice with no good outcomes
Making a decision and realizing afterward that it was the wrong one

HUMAN NEEDS THAT COULD BE IMPACTED

Self-Actualization: Reluctance to make choices will cause the character to follow rather than lead, leaving their fate in the hands of others.

Esteem and Recognition: A character with this fear will struggle with chronic self-doubt and an inability to trust themselves. Their indecision may also cause others to doubt them.

Safety and Security: A character with this fear might stay in unhealthy or unsafe situations rather than make a decision that requires change.

HOW THE CHARACTER CAN MINIMIZE OR OVERCOME IT

Using cognitive behavioral therapy to overcome their negative inner voice
Putting small decisions into context so the stakes don't become larger than life
Remembering that making mistakes is how people learn
Seeking advice only for high-stakes decisions
Being accountable if they make an error, and then moving on

MEDIOCRITY

NOTES: The fear of mediocrity has two sides. On one hand, it can drive the character to define themselves by challenging ideas and shooting for big, audacious goals. But it can also do damage when it's based on external validation. Needing the admiration of peers to feel exceptional instead of basing their success and value on their uniqueness and strengths is a recipe for disaster.

WHAT IT LOOKS LIKE

Having a large ego
Having unrealistic expectations
Challenging ideas and the way things are done
Being a risk-taker
Pushing boundaries (and causing friction with people because of it)
Wanting to be extraordinary
Overachieving—not out of a desire to grow, but to do something others will admire
The character being hypercritical of themselves
Being a perfectionist
Never settling for good enough
Needing external validation
Desiring superiority over others
Looking down on people who are average or stick with the status quo
Refusing to accept mediocrity in others
The character basing their value on the opinions of others
Being envious of other people's accomplishments
Exhibiting narcissistic tendencies
Choosing discomfort to prove strength
Becoming anxious as deadlines approach
Unfairly comparing themselves to others
Fearing criticism and judgment (because it suggests they're not at their best)
Pointing out other people's flaws to counteract their feelings of inferiority
Going to extremes to stand out (getting plastic surgery to improve their appearance, amassing debt to maintain a certain lifestyle, etc.)

COMMON INTERNAL STRUGGLES

Needing things to be perfect and knowing they never will be
Not choosing a desired career path because it's too ordinary
The character wrestling with depression when they fall short of a goal
Feeling demeaned at the slightest criticism
Berating themselves over simple mistakes
Becoming resentful when they don't receive recognition they feel is warranted
Being overwhelmed with self-doubt and feelings of inadequacy
Worrying that they will be forgotten or eclipsed by others

HINDRANCES AND DISRUPTIONS TO THE CHARACTER'S LIFE

Being dissatisfied with significant accomplishments
Constantly being plagued with self-doubt about their abilities
Needing the praise of people they admire before they can claim success
Being unfulfilled socially because they're focused on achieving goals
Others being put off by the character's ego and unrealistic expectations
Constantly measuring themselves against people who are exceptional and coming up short
Frequently burning out

EMOTIONAL WOUNDS IT COULD STEM FROM: Being Bullied, Being Disowned or Shunned, Being Raised by Parents Who Loved Conditionally, Growing Up in the Shadow of a Successful Sibling, Losing a Limb, Misplaced Loyalty

SCENARIOS THAT MIGHT TRIGGER THIS FEAR

The character losing a competition or contest
Being told they will never amount to anything
Being passed over for a promotion
A physical or mental health condition diagnosis
Seeing an ex-partner with someone the character perceives to be better than them
Observing someone being showered with accolades and desiring the same
Being assigned a ho-hum role or project where there is no chance to shine
A sudden burden of responsibility—e.g., needing to step into a parental role while a sister is in rehab
Being teamed up with a partner who is superior to the character (in an area of giftedness, with other people, etc.)

HUMAN NEEDS THAT COULD BE IMPACTED

Self-Actualization: A character who fears mediocrity may reject hobbies, interests, or relationships in favor of chasing pursuits meant to make them feel good but that ultimately won't satisfy.

Esteem and Recognition: A character in this situation may be very successful externally but internally battle negativity, criticism, and feelings of inferiority.

Love and Belonging: If the character critically judges others for not being "better," this will cause offense and a trail of broken relationships.

Safety and Security: Characters who fear mediocrity can push themselves incredibly hard to succeed, compromising their physical and mental well-being.

HOW THE CHARACTER CAN MINIMIZE OR OVERCOME IT

Understanding that life isn't all-or-nothing
Striving for balance and not letting any one goal create regret in other areas of their life
Focusing on the now, and living life in full, and seeing that as a true accomplishment
Embracing being a jack-of-all-trades and having a versatile skill set rather than mastering just one thing
Appreciating people who show up consistently, and seeing value in being someone others can depend on

NOT BEING BELIEVED

NOTES: This fear often arises from a character making themselves vulnerable to someone (a relative, a corporation, the media, etc.), then being accused of dishonesty or worse. There is nothing like an abuse of power to send a person spiraling into a dark abyss that takes years to escape.

WHAT IT LOOKS LIKE

Never making assumptions
Making people state what they want openly (preferably when others are around) to be sure the expectations are clear
Recording interactions with others (having security cameras at home or using a cell phone to video a conversation)
Carefully documenting important events so the character doesn't forget the details
Staying silent unless they have a witness or an abundance of proof
Being honest to a fault—refusing to tell even a little white lie
Needing constant assurance that people believe them, even in insignificant situations
Questioning everything that is said or presented to them
Following rules and obeying the law
Being able to read others and recognize dishonesty
Searching for the truth in all things
Keeping quiet about abuse or unfairness (because speaking up won't do them any good)
Harboring a healthy distrust of other people and institutions
Asking someone to back them up, even over something small
Extreme self-reliance (because the character can trust no one but themselves)
The character often accusing people of lying to them or to loved ones
Always believing anyone who claims injustice or abuse
Becoming angry if their word is questioned
Withdrawing from friends and family
Giving up and only saying what others want to hear
Being loose with the truth (because no one will believe them anyway)
Having nightmares related to the incident

COMMON INTERNAL STRUGGLES

Wanting to speak up about an injustice but worrying they won't be believed
Feeling guilt or shame despite having done nothing wrong
Being paranoid that everyone is conspiring against them
Hating the isolation but not knowing how to make themselves vulnerable again
Wanting to confide in someone but not knowing who can be trusted
Wanting to expose a bad situation but being deterred by society's reaction to a similar public event
The character second-guessing themselves, doubting their ability to remember details correctly
Negative self-talk (berating themselves for not being brave enough to speak up)

HINDRANCES AND DISRUPTIONS TO THE CHARACTER'S LIFE

Living in isolation
Struggling professionally because the character has trouble trusting those in authority
Being ruled by fear or anger
Quitting jobs rather than enduring or fighting workplace injustices
Difficulty relating to or accepting people who resemble the ones who didn't believe the character (men, women, police officers, doctors, religious people, etc.)
Living with self-doubt because the character doesn't trust their own instincts
Never knowing who can be trusted

EMOTIONAL WOUNDS IT COULD STEM FROM: A Parent's Abandonment or Rejection, A Sibling's Betrayal, A Toxic Relationship, An Abuse of Power, Being Bullied, Being Disappointed by a Role Model, Being Falsely Accused of a Crime, Being the Victim of a Vicious Rumor, Being Unfairly Blamed for Someone's Death, Having Parents Who Favored One Child Over Another, Misplaced Loyalty

SCENARIOS THAT MIGHT TRIGGER THIS FEAR

Spotting favoritism in the family, at work, etc.
Being met with skepticism when sharing an idea, viewpoint, or piece of information
Watching someone in a similar situation go public and be attacked by the media
Witnessing behavior at work that should be reported
Their word being questioned in court as they testify about a crime
Seeing a victim be blamed or shamed
Being told by an abuser that no one will believe the character if they talk
Telling authorities about wrongdoing and seeing nothing happen
Innocently witnessing a crime, then being questioned as a suspect
Hearing about an injustice that makes the character doubt the account, making them question everything

HUMAN NEEDS THAT COULD BE IMPACTED

Esteem and Recognition: A character who fears that others will automatically not believe them may think poorly of themselves, as if the character is perceived as untrustworthy or they've done something to deserve the distrust of others.

Love and Belonging: In this situation, trust issues are common, and when characters close themselves off, it's difficult for deep and healthy relationships to grow.

Safety and Security: If the character is too reluctant to speak up about a dangerous or hurtful situation, they may experience physical or emotional harm.

HOW THE CHARACTER CAN MINIMIZE OR OVERCOME IT

Becoming a strong communicator so they can articulate themselves clearly
Practicing emotional control so their responses are measured and reasonable
Remembering that a past event cannot be a reflection for every future encounter
Learning to give people the benefit of the doubt so biases don't take hold
Being careful who to trust
Self-advocating when it comes to respect and fair treatment (without being rude)
Learning to dismiss, instead of internalizing, unfounded accusations

NOT BEING ENOUGH

NOTES: This fear is intricately tied to self-esteem because, at its core, the character worries they aren't good enough for others or are incapable of satisfying them. Similar to LETTING PEOPLE DOWN, the character may be driven to perfectionism or actively avoid people and situations that carry high expectations.

WHAT IT LOOKS LIKE

Seeking frequent feedback and reassurance
Comparing themselves to others
Not engaging in activities that would pit the character against someone else
Using self-deprecating humor to temper how others view them
Making excuses for failure in advance (setting the stage, in case things don't work out)
Deferring to others in collaborative situations
Blaming themselves when they don't measure up
Bypassing opportunities that come with high expectations
Wilting in the presence of critical people
Accepting all criticism; difficulty differentiating constructive feedback from what's unnecessary
Gravitating toward low-expectation activities and people who don't ask for much
Difficulty taking compliments
Apologizing for insignificant things
Engaging in unnecessary professional development or attempts at improvement
Closely monitoring the activities of rivals
Constantly trying to up their game
Disparaging others to boost themselves up
Setting unrealistic goals and being devastated when they aren't achieved
Harshly judging themselves
Striving for perfection
Having a one-foot-out-the-door mentality in relationships because the character expects them to end prematurely

COMMON INTERNAL STRUGGLES

Wanting to pursue an opportunity but being too afraid of failing to do so
Internalizing even constructive criticism as a personal failure
Getting stuck in negative self-talk
Being unable to embrace and celebrate successes
Feeling as though they should be someone other than who they are
Obsessing over ways to improve themselves
Struggling with self-loathing
Feeling like they're to blame for everything that goes wrong
Being unable to see their own strengths
Always worrying that a romantic partner is going to leave them for someone "better"

HINDRANCES AND DISRUPTIONS TO THE CHARACTER'S LIFE

Missing out on new opportunities or chances to lead

Being viewed as insecure, incapable, or clingy
Missing deadlines because of their drive for perfectionism
Staying noncommittal in romantic relationships
Staying in an unhealthy relationship because they think it's the best they can do
Being stuck in a job that's beneath their skill set
Always believing the worst about themselves
Becoming a target because they won't stand up for themselves
Believing they're to blame when things go wrong

EMOTIONAL WOUNDS IT COULD STEM FROM: A Loved One's Suicide, A Parent's Divorce, Being Fired or Laid Off, Being Raised by Parents Who Loved Conditionally, Being Rejected by One's Peers, Failing at School, Falling Short of Society's Physical Standards, Learning That One's Parent Had a Second Family

SCENARIOS THAT MIGHT TRIGGER THIS FEAR

Being passed over for a job or promotion
Being rejected by a romantic partner
A child choosing to live with their other parent
Being cheated on
Disappointing a teacher, coach, or other mentor figure
Finding out about an important social gathering the character wasn't invited to
A situation evolving into a competition
A romantic partner voicing dissatisfaction with the character's sexual performance
A promising relationship petering out because the other party pursued friendship with someone else
Sustaining an injury or sickness that severely debilitates their physical or mental capacity
Being pitted against a rival whose talent or skill surpasses the character's

HUMAN NEEDS THAT COULD BE IMPACTED

Self-Actualization: A character with this fear may self-sabotage fulfilling opportunities if they believe their shortcomings could be highlighted.
Esteem and Recognition: A character with this fear will always believe they're to blame for failing to meet an expectation, resulting in low esteem for themselves.
Love and Belonging: A character will struggle to connect with others if their fears cause them to sabotage or avoid deep relationships.

HOW THE CHARACTER CAN MINIMIZE OR OVERCOME IT

Recognizing validation comes from within, not from other people
Being the best person the character can be, and loving themselves for it
Seeing that chasing relationships or approval won't lead to happiness
Calling out a partner or coworker who makes the character question their worth
Not letting others invalidate what they feel
Resisting the urge to smooth things over or people-please
Focusing on progress, not perfection
Increasing esteem through meaningful goals, skill-building, and healthy growth

PUTTING ONESELF OUT THERE

NOTES: Have you ever voiced an idea or offered to step up only to be met with a scoff or outright dismissal? If so, you know what it's like to feel minimized, and each time it happens, it becomes harder to put yourself out there.

Characters who have been shot down repeatedly may start to fear it will always happen, so they stop speaking out or stepping forward. This fear can lead to severe frustration at feeling stymied, as well as low self-worth.

WHAT IT LOOKS LIKE

Staying in the background or in their comfort zone
Keeping their head down at work
Doing what they're told, even when they disagree with it
Not speaking up or sharing ideas unless they're forced to
Not sharing passions, interests, or ideas because they don't want to be mocked
Not sharing achievements or personal good news
Avoiding people with big personalities and egos
Not wanting to talk about themselves; shifting the focus to someone else
Avoiding risky topics of conversation (to keep the status quo)
Not volunteering because they believe they won't be wanted
Only sharing ideas with people who will take the character seriously
Giving feedback or suggestions anonymously
Avoiding situations that could lead to being in the spotlight
Self-monitoring their behavior to make sure it aligns with what others do
Having a hard time saying no
Becoming a perfectionist
Seeking out extra training or education to the point of becoming over-qualified
Not approaching others in social situations
Avoiding arguments
Hesitating and reading the room before voicing thoughts or suggestions
Waiting to be noticed instead of actively entering a conversation
Doing what others want rather than making suggestions that can be shot down
Being sensitive to jokes or friendly jabs
Choosing to stay home rather than go out
Underachieving to avoid failures that others might judge
Struggling to self-advocate
Not bidding on a job or applying for a promotion
Avoiding competitive situations

COMMON INTERNAL STRUGGLES

Frustration from feeling held back, especially when a bias is at work (not being taken seriously because of their age, gender, or other identifier)
Having to keep anger in check
Feeling stuck and not knowing how to move forward

Wanting something specific but being undermined by self-doubt
Wanting to be more assertive but not knowing how
Beating themselves up for what they should have said and done but didn't
Believing the lies (that they aren't qualified, they're too young, etc.)

HINDRANCES AND DISRUPTIONS TO THE CHARACTER'S LIFE
Making excuses for why they don't want to hang out with friends
Envying what others have (fulfilled dreams, relationships, achievements, etc.)
Missing out on a promotion or job position the character is perfect for
Being romantically interested in someone but not acting on those desires
Well-meaning friends trying to "fix" the character (coaching them to be more assertive, stand up and be noticed, swing for the fences, etc.)
Being taken advantage of because they can't set boundaries

EMOTIONAL WOUNDS IT COULD STEM FROM: A Learning Disability, A Physical Disfigurement, A Speech Impediment, An Abuse of Power, Being Humiliated by Others, Being Rejected by One's Peers, Cracking Under Pressure

SCENARIOS THAT MIGHT TRIGGER THIS FEAR
Being assigned a task that will be scrutinized
Hearing about a competition with a reward that would bring a dream within reach
Being financially strapped and having to ask for a raise
Asking someone to go out on a date
Having to market and promote a product they created
Meeting a partner's family for the first time
Being asked their opinion about a controversial topic
Being paired with someone who has been dismissive or mean in the past

HUMAN NEEDS THAT COULD BE IMPACTED

Self-Actualization: A character whose fear keeps them from pursuing fulfilling hobbies, careers, or relationships will always live short of their full potential.

Esteem and Recognition: Others may look down on a character who avoids risk or ambitious opportunities, thinking they have no drive or confidence. The character may also think less of themselves for allowing their fear to hold them back.

Love and Belonging: A character in this position might avoid putting themselves out there romantically, resulting in them never finding true love or making the deep connections they desire.

HOW THE CHARACTER CAN MINIMIZE OR OVERCOME IT
Building up self-belief and confidence through knowledge and skills
Thinking carefully about how to convey an idea or solution
Practicing in advance—knowing what to say and having answers to questions or criticisms that could come up
Learning to recognize which dismissals can provide learning opportunities and when they shouldn't be taken seriously

SUCCESS

NOTES: Most people seek out success, but the high expectations and changes that follow can make it a frightening prospect for some. While this fear is often associated with a character's career, it could also apply to their love life, hobbies, and parenting.

WHAT IT LOOKS LIKE

Self-sabotage
Avoiding competition
Seeking to maintain the status quo
Making self-deprecating comments
Deferring to others (on a work project, when parenting, etc.)
Turning down raises or promotions
Being risk-averse
Choosing background roles so the character can stay out of the spotlight
Procrastinating
Prioritizing things that won't lead to success
Pursuing small, safe goals
Avoiding big responsibilities (parenting, marriage, leadership, etc.)
Being indecisive; waffling over decisions
Lacking vision (for work projects, their family, etc.)
Obsessing over past mistakes
Retreating during stressful times
Dismissing compliments and encouragement from others
Making excuses for failures or stagnation
Underachieving
Focusing on weaknesses instead of strengths
Giving off a vibe that will ensure low expectations from others (irresponsibility, superficiality, foolishness, etc.)
Not sharing their passions, interests, or ideas with others
Pessimism; expecting failure
Being drawn to friends and lovers who hold the character back

COMMON INTERNAL STRUGGLES

Wanting to be esteemed by others but fearing to lead
Not being able to overcome the fear of what could go wrong
Doubting themselves
Feeling like an impostor
Fearing that success will cause them to leave others behind
Worrying that things will become complicated beyond what they can manage
Worrying that they couldn't repeat success should they achieve it
Being concerned that success in one area will shoehorn them into that single endeavor
The expectations of others feeling like a heavy weight on the character's shoulders
Being afraid their ideas are worthless or stupid
Not wanting success but resenting when people close to them achieve it

HINDRANCES AND DISRUPTIONS TO THE CHARACTER'S LIFE

Not branching out into new hobbies or interests
Being perceived as incompetent or lazy
Never achieving great things
Their world being small
Not learning from their mistakes
Being stuck professionally
Staying in unfulfilling romantic relationships
Never reaching their full potential
Being unaware of their strengths and areas of giftedness
Falling behind on new technology or techniques
Not being taken seriously by others

EMOTIONAL WOUNDS IT COULD STEM FROM: A Toxic Relationship, Being Disappointed by a Role Model, Growing up in the Shadow of a Successful Sibling, Living with Chronic Pain or Illness

SCENARIOS THAT MIGHT TRIGGER THIS FEAR

Someone seeing potential in the character and setting high expectations for them
Being nominated for a prestigious award
Being asked to do something the character doesn't feel qualified to do
Succeeding at something and experiencing an unwanted change
Being put in the spotlight
Being asked to join a coworker in a new business venture
Beginning a new relationship and not knowing the other person's expectations
A survival situation where success must be achieved
Someone taking credit for the character's work

HUMAN NEEDS THAT COULD BE IMPACTED

Self-Actualization: Staying in their comfort zone will greatly reduce the character's chances of reaching their potential in personal or professional endeavors.

Esteem and Recognition: A character who avoids success won't distinguish themselves and will never gain respect from their peers. Their lack of achievement may also make them feel badly about themselves.

Love and Belonging: A character who doubts their own value may gravitate toward people who don't value them, resulting in unhappy, toxic, or even abusive relationships. They could also experience friction with friends and loved ones who are frustrated with the character's lack of ambition.

HOW THE CHARACTER CAN MINIMIZE OR OVERCOME IT

Focusing on the journey instead of the result—e.g., seeing value in sharing stories with the world rather than becoming a best-selling author
Building up self-worth by looking at the dedication, grit, and sacrifice that brought the character to this point
Looking just one step ahead instead of focusing on the end goal

Existential and Moral Fears

BEING DISAPPOINTED

NOTES: People tend to hope for the best in their relationships, work, and personal pursuits, and when those expectations aren't met, the letdown can be difficult to process. This disappointment can be so uncomfortable that a character may avoid situations where it could arise and adapt their mindset to expect less, reducing its likelihood.

WHAT IT LOOKS LIKE

Underachieving; avoiding high-risk situations
Sticking to a routine and preferring structure over the unknown
The character reminding people repeatedly of their expectations
Choosing what's known over what's new (eating at the same restaurants, shopping at the same stores, etc.)
Avoiding situations that trigger excitement, anticipation, optimism, or hopefulness
Providing opportunities for people to back out of commitments
Avoiding competitions and contests
Analyzing online reviews before committing to a purchase
Keeping their expectations low
Gravitating toward situations they can control
Micromanaging others
Expecting a new romantic relationship to go nowhere
Not setting goals
Labeling people by their most prominent weaknesses
Expecting loved ones to not follow through on commitments
Frequently complaining
Not liking surprises or spontaneity
Always requiring a trial period before hiring someone
Analyzing someone's emotional state to better understand their response to the character
Reading too much into the responses of others
Staying busy; working too much
Reading into circumstances and always seeing an impending disappointment
Failing to give others grace
Having a backup plan in case someone fails to come through

COMMON INTERNAL STRUGGLES

Needing to decrease stress but being unable to delegate tasks to others
Being pessimistic about the future
Prior disappointments cycling through the character's mind on a loop
Not wanting to be rigid but desperately needing control to manage expectations
Wanting a romantic relationship but having no faith in other people
Being jealous of people who can bounce back from disappointment
Envying those who can take risks
Knowing their pessimism is bringing others down but being unable to change
Feeling dissatisfied with their life
Wanting good things to happen but rejecting that they will (tempering expectations)

HINDRANCES AND DISRUPTIONS TO THE CHARACTER'S LIFE

Only being able to rely on a small set of trustworthy people
Missing out on meaningful activities with others
People avoiding the character because of their cynical attitude
Not pursuing professional opportunities that would further their career
Being unable to commit unless the perfect conditions or circumstances are in place
Quitting activities early
Missing out on cooperative efforts to do good (not voting, not volunteering, etc.)
Their controlling or rigid behavior driving people away
An inability to take risks robbing the character of opportunities to grow
Missing out on new experiences they might enjoy

EMOTIONAL WOUNDS IT COULD STEM FROM: A Miscarriage or Stillbirth, Being Disappointed by a Role Model, Being Let Down by a Trusted Organization or Social System, Growing up in Foster Care, Unrequited Love

SCENARIOS THAT MIGHT TRIGGER THIS FEAR

Needing to share a secret that makes them vulnerable
An event that naturally causes heightened expectations (a birthday and the possibility of a surprise party, a dating anniversary when the other party might propose, etc.)
A lover saying they need to talk to the character
Being asked to give someone a second chance
Being told about a promising new treatment for the character's illness
A friend or loved one breaking the character's trust
Being stood up by a friend or date
Being put on the short list for a promotion at work
Applying for a job and having to compete with many applicants
Experiencing a major setback in pursuit of a life goal

HUMAN NEEDS THAT COULD BE IMPACTED

Self-Actualization: A character who is afraid to take risks will never live up to their full potential and won't be satisfied with the path they're on.

Esteem and Recognition: People may be put off by a character who is overly cynical, pessimistic, or jaded.

Love and Belonging: A character who fears being disappointed may settle for someone who is safe and reliable but also doesn't excite them.

HOW THE CHARACTER CAN MINIMIZE OR OVERCOME IT

Viewing life as a mix of highs and lows, with disappointments happening at times
Setting realistic expectations
Considering negative outcomes and planning for them to lessen the risk of disappointment
Reminding themselves of opportunities they missed out on because of their fear
Believing that trying and failing is better than avoidance and regret
Learning to laugh disappointments off and not take them as seriously

BEING STILL

NOTES: Stillness and quiet are important practices that provide the chance for recovery, self-reflection, intimacy in relationships, and emotional processing. But for some, this is the last thing they want. A character who is afraid of their own thoughts, of being unproductive or "lazy," or of facing a past, present, or future event may do everything in their power to stay busy, letting the joys of life pass them by.

WHAT IT LOOKS LIKE

Juggling multiple tasks at the same time
Being easily distracted by new ideas and opportunities
Workaholic tendencies
Perfectionism
Frequenting busy places (the mall, urban areas, restaurants, etc.)
Stacking their schedule with back-to-back commitments
Sleeping less than other people
Fulfilling obligations even when the character is sick or needed elsewhere
Being in constant motion
Avoiding being alone
Jumping into a new relationship when an old one ends
Difficulty falling asleep (because their brain won't turn off or they're afraid of certain thoughts)
Being unable to relax
Filling free time with mindless activities (scrolling on their phone, watching TV, etc.)
Showing frustration or defensiveness when people tell the character to slow down
Proposing new ideas often
Difficulty giving others their full attention
Having poor time management
Dropping the ball because they have too much going on
Making excuses for failing to follow through on responsibilities
Being obsessive (at work, when exercising, planning, etc.)
A pattern of working feverishly, then collapsing from exhaustion

COMMON INTERNAL STRUGGLES

Having unrealistic expectations
Being overwhelmed but feeling compelled to keep taking on tasks
Wanting to be there for others but being unable to slow down and really listen
Struggling with burnout
Knowing they're avoiding certain things and feeling guilt and a sense of failure about it
Feeling torn between conflicting or competing duties
Feeling guilty about letting others down or not being available to them
Struggling with physical and mental fatigue
Feeling dread when they don't have enough to do

HINDRANCES AND DISRUPTIONS TO THE CHARACTER'S LIFE

Being unable to enjoy accomplishments because they need to move on to the next thing

Failing to face something they need to address
Missing out on going deeper in relationships
Loved ones being frustrated by the character's frenetic pace
Being unable to adequately or accurately process their emotions
Being distracted and missing important information
Losing out on opportunities to self-reflect and grow
Not recognizing a problem or when change is needed
Experiencing health problems from inadequate sleep and rest

EMOTIONAL WOUNDS IT COULD STEM FROM: A Traumatic Brain Injury, Battling a Mental Condition, Bearing the Responsibility for Many Deaths, Being Tortured, Finding Out One's Child Was Abused

SCENARIOS THAT MIGHT TRIGGER THIS FEAR
Relocating to a remote or rural setting
Their computer or phone breaking
Being forced to participate in therapy, meditation, or mindfulness
Going on vacation
Suddenly losing a job
Moving to a place where slowing down is highly emphasized
Losing electricity (and access to distractions)
A car breaking down in a remote area, forcing the character to wait for a tow truck
Needing to quarantine
Having to attend a funeral
Receiving a medical diagnosis that requires the character to reduce their stress
Family members holding an intervention for the character

HUMAN NEEDS THAT COULD BE IMPACTED

Self-Actualization: A character who is always moving from one task to the next will struggle to value their accomplishments and may never be satisfied.

Esteem and Recognition: This kind of character might feel badly about themselves if they know they're living in avoidance.

Love and Belonging: The character may prioritize projects over people, creating friction with loved ones or even a habit of actively avoiding vulnerability with others.

Physiological Needs: Frenetic motion and constant stress will take a toll on the body and the mind, impacting the character's physical and mental health over time.

HOW THE CHARACTER CAN MINIMIZE OR OVERCOME IT
Journaling, so they can be still while doing something
Practicing breathing exercises and meditation
Taking a camping trip far from civilization and connectivity
Breaking unhealthy routines, scaling back on activity, and setting boundaries
Carefully probing past pain, especially any tied to expectation and worth
Practicing self-care until it feels more natural
Become curious and exploratory without setting goals (going for a drive without a destination in mind, trying new things, etc.)

BEING UNABLE TO ACHIEVE A DREAM

NOTES: We all have dreams, and we know how much work they require. For some characters, achieving that goal can be all-consuming, overshadowing everyone and everything else. This becomes a problem when the fear of falling short causes the character to abandon other aspects of their life, sideline people who should be a priority, or give up on the pursuit rather than risk failure.

WHAT IT LOOKS LIKE

Being a visionary (but internally stressing, thinking it might not be enough)
Wanting desperately to leave behind a legacy
Working long hours to achieve the dream
Having very little free time
Being achievement-driven
Obsessing over the goal to the point of ignoring everyone else
Forgetting about appointments, dates, and outings with friends
Sacrificing their basic needs in pursuit of the dream (giving up on personal hygiene, going without sleep or food, etc.)
Researching and learning new skills
Ignoring good advice if it doesn't support the goal
Skipping school or work to focus on the dream
Developing unhealthy sleep patterns
Networking to acquire necessary contacts
Sensitivity to criticism
Being paranoid about competitors or others who could reach the goal first
Going to great lengths to bring down a competitor (spreading rumors, sabotaging them, etc.)
Procrastinating on short-term goals that are needed to achieve the dream
Cutting corners by skipping necessary steps, borrowing another's research, etc.
Refusing to listen to advice or counsel
Obsession leading to a loss of objectivity and self-sabotage
Taking stimulants to stay alert and productive
Giving up on the goal prematurely
Resenting those who succeed in areas where the character was too scared to try

COMMON INTERNAL STRUGGLES

Struggling to balance personal responsibilities with the demands of the dream
The character comparing themselves to more successful people and finding themselves lacking
Telling themselves the results will be worth the sacrifice
Feeling overwhelmed
Wrestling with self-doubt and insecurity about their ability to succeed
Envying people who are succeeding at the dream
Fearing failure
Crossing a moral line and being plagued with guilt
Worrying that if they don't succeed, they're letting others down
Believing that their value is tied to their success

HINDRANCES AND DISRUPTIONS TO THE CHARACTER'S LIFE
Falling into depression or struggling with substance abuse
Personal relationships suffering because they're no longer a priority for the character
Burning out
Sacrificing something important in pursuit of the goal (a marriage, scholarship, job, etc.)
Suffering health issues from pushing themselves too hard
Giving up on or failing to achieve the dream, and ending up with nothing and no one

EMOTIONAL WOUNDS IT COULD STEM FROM: A Terminal Illness Diagnosis, Battling a Mental Condition, Becoming a Caregiver at an Early Age, Declaring Bankruptcy, Failing at School, Growing up in the Shadow of a Successful Sibling, Living with a Critical Medical Diagnosis, Losing a Limb, Losing One of the Five Senses, Prejudice or Discrimination, Social Difficulties

SCENARIOS THAT MIGHT TRIGGER THIS FEAR
Suffering a financial blow that puts the dream on hold (losing funding, a spouse being fired, being hit with an unexpected expense, etc.)
Developing an injury or condition that prevents success
Being assigned an unexpected responsibility that steals time from the pursuit of the dream
Losing an ally
A competitor entering the scene
Making a mistake that threatens success and generates a confidence crisis

HUMAN NEEDS THAT COULD BE IMPACTED

Self-Actualization: A large part of a character's self-actualization is wrapped up in achieving dreams and being all they can be. If they're too afraid to try or their obsession handicaps them in other ways, they may never be fulfilled.

Esteem and Recognition: A character whose worth is tied to their success in a certain area will see any setback as a personal failure. The longer they go without achieving their dream, the worse they'll feel about themselves.

Love and Belonging: It's common for a character with this fear to put all their energy into pursuing the goal and ignore or minimize the people in their life.

Safety and Security: If the dream becomes all-important for the character, they may unintentionally sacrifice their physical and mental health.

HOW THE CHARACTER CAN MINIMIZE OR OVERCOME IT
Learning to value the process (and resulting personal growth) over the outcome
Not being derailed by setbacks or failures; seeing them as part of the process
Creating a sustainable, realistic plan for achieving the goal
Setting goals the character can achieve rather than impossible ones
Remembering that self-worth should be tied to effort, not be a result of it

BEING WRONG ABOUT SOMETHING IMPORTANT

NOTES: Few people like to admit to being wrong, but the stakes are especially high when it comes to deeply held beliefs. Being wrong about something meaningful can be devastating—shattering a character's confidence, affecting self-worth, and damaging their standing with those they respect. As you can imagine, being wrong when it matters is something they'll go to great lengths to avoid.

WHAT IT LOOKS LIKE

Overthinking to be sure they're right
Doing a lot of research before committing to a way of thinking
Overexplaining their viewpoint to convince others they're right
Avoiding debates because they aren't confident in their ability to back up their belief
Downplaying their beliefs (in case they're disproven)
Being hesitant to share deep beliefs
Sticking to popular talking points rather than elaborating or going deeper
Making a small concession—"Okay, maybe *that* situation is different"—but refusing to admit they were wrong
Changing the subject when someone challenges their viewpoint
Doubling down when challenged by others
Getting defensive when challenged
Demanding evidence from naysayers
Making sweeping judgments about people who think differently
Inflexibility; being unable to even consider an idea that goes against their beliefs
Surrounding themselves with people who share their ideas
A flight response in the face of discomfort (refusing to engage, walking away, etc.)
Sending people one-sided articles, studies, and other "proof" to support their belief
Avoiding new experiences
Limiting news sources to ones that echo what they believe
Spinning false narratives to retain their views
Resistance; becoming confrontational, deploying intimidation tactics, or being verbally abusive if an uncomfortable truth seems to be emerging
Trying to sway others to their way of thinking
Becoming zealous about their ideals

COMMON INTERNAL STRUGGLES

Secretly being unsure but refusing to admit it to others
Doubt causing them to wonder what else they might be wrong about
Becoming obsessed with proving themselves right
Feeling driven to convert others to their way of thinking
Having a me vs. them mentality
Being black or white in their thinking
Dismissing any doubts that come up
Feeling personally attacked when their ideas are challenged

HINDRANCES AND DISRUPTIONS TO THE CHARACTER'S LIFE

Limiting their romantic life to people who agree with them
Spending an inordinate amount of time researching to support their ideas
Ending relationships with people who challenge them
Being limited to only activities and ways of thinking that are tied to their beliefs
Being closed off to new or alternative ways of thinking

EMOTIONAL WOUNDS IT COULD STEM FROM: Being Disappointed by a Role Model, Being Humiliated by Others, Having a Controlling or Overly Strict Parent, Making a Very Public Mistake

SCENARIOS THAT MIGHT TRIGGER THIS FEAR

A loved one suffering a loss after following the character's advice
Needing help from someone who holds an opposing view
Learning that a mentor was wrong about something important
A loved one changing their position and embracing an opposing viewpoint
A major life change (relocating, a catastrophe, etc.) forcing a shift in perspective
Being asked a question they don't know how to answer
Someone with the same beliefs falling from grace
Being confronted with a fact or data they can't refute
Having a lapse in judgment and doubting their instincts
Finding a flaw in the belief or ideal they've been clinging to
Researching a belief for confirmation only to discover it's been thoroughly debunked

HUMAN NEEDS THAT COULD BE IMPACTED

Self-Actualization: A character who is afraid to entertain ideas that oppose their own will become stuck in certain areas, unable to apply critical thinking or grow in vital ways.

Esteem and Recognition: While some people judge others for their beliefs, most reserve judgment for how discussions around those beliefs are handled. Characters who lash out when they're challenged will appear insecure or weak-minded, and others will think less of them for it.

Love and Belonging: Some people can't help but view people differently for clinging to certain ideas. This can strain or even break a relationship.

Safety and Security: A character who sticks blindly to a belief may fail to see or avoid a dangerous situation until it's too late.

HOW THE CHARACTER CAN MINIMIZE OR OVERCOME IT

Separating past failures from current actions
Addressing the past and being accountable for mistakes
Sharing informed opinions from a place of knowledge
Fact-checking as a practice
Reading up on something from several sources before sharing it
Taking a seek-to-understand approach; learning as much as they can about a situation before making a decision or acting on it
Appreciating differing viewpoints instead of viewing them as threats

DISCOVERING AN UNCOMFORTABLE TRUTH

NOTES: The truth isn't always pleasant. It can evoke uncertainty, fear, and anxiety—especially when the discovery runs contradictory to what the character believes. If they suspect that a truth could showcase loved ones in a difficult light, reveal personal shortcomings, or be otherwise hurtful, the character may (even subconsciously) choose to ignore or avoid it.

WHAT IT LOOKS LIKE

Ignoring phone calls and text messages from certain people or groups
Avoiding the news
Disengaging when a conversation gets too close to an uncomfortable topic
Quitting social media
Not asking about a particular person and what they may be up to
Not tracking expenditures or paying attention to financial accounts
Dismissing the advice of loved ones around the topic
Developing false narratives to contradict the truth
Gathering "evidence" to support what they believe
Making excuses for why something (or someone) is the way it is
Surrounding themselves with people who support their version of the truth
Going on the offensive when people disagree
Avoiding medical practitioners (if the truth involves a medical condition)
Fully devoting themselves to their version of the truth; not considering anything else
Throwing away unopened mail
Making a big change for no obvious reason (getting a new phone number, moving, quitting their job, etc.)
Refusing to hear anything negative about a certain person or organization
Avoiding gatherings specific people will be attending
Pointedly not asking questions about or showing interest in the uncomfortable topic
Being nonconfrontational in general
Not asking certain questions
Striving to maintain the status quo
Viewing people who try to broach the truth as the enemy
Distracting themselves with unhealthy habits, such as too much shopping, drinking, or sleeping
Withdrawing into the safety of fantasies and daydreams

COMMON INTERNAL STRUGGLES

Feeling cowardly for suspecting something isn't quite right but not being able to face it
Experiencing overwhelming anxiety when faced with the truth
Wanting to know the truth but doubting their ability to handle it
Developing a mental condition from being unable to face facts
Fearing change
Viewing a threat to their belief as a threat to their identity
Suspecting they're becoming closed-minded or fixed in their thinking, and despising themselves for it

HINDRANCES AND DISRUPTIONS TO THE CHARACTER'S LIFE

Ignoring certain things (finances, health, a relationship, etc.) and ending up in trouble
Looking foolish or ignorant for not facing facts
Being ruled by fear instead of being freed by the truth
Having to avoid certain people, topics, or ideas
Physically suffering because they won't seek medical attention
Relationship friction with people who want the character to face the truth
Living in a false reality
The character's safety and peace depending on them believing a lie or remaining in ignorance about certain things
Not knowing what's happening in the world due to willful ignorance
Fear or denial making it difficult to engage in certain conversations

EMOTIONAL WOUNDS IT COULD STEM FROM: Discovering a Partner's Sexual Orientation Secret, Discovering Hidden Information About One's Ancestry, Learning That One's Parent Was a Monster

SCENARIOS THAT MIGHT TRIGGER THIS FEAR

A spouse acting suspiciously
Unexpectedly running low on money (a card being declined, a check bouncing, etc.)
Someone insisting on revealing the truth to the character
Hearing rumblings about a trusted organization's corruption or cover-up
An emergency that forces the character to face the truth (having a stroke, war breaking out, being evicted, becoming a scapegoat, etc.)
Stumbling across the truth in a public forum
The topic arising in a conversation the character can't avoid or escape from

HUMAN NEEDS THAT COULD BE IMPACTED

Esteem and Recognition: A character who is unable to face facts may lose the respect of others who see them as foolish, illogical, or living in denial.

Love and Belonging: If loved ones try to enlighten a character who is determined to ignore the truth, the relationship may suffer irreparable harm.

Physiological Needs: If the uncomfortable truth is related to the character's health, their inability to face it may contribute to their own death.

HOW THE CHARACTER CAN MINIMIZE OR OVERCOME IT

Going through what-if scenarios to get comfortable with possible truths
Recognizing that knowledge is power, and being kept in the dark can actually be harmful
The character surrounding themselves with a support system so they feel empowered to handle the truth, no matter what it is
Realizing that knowing the truth is the key to letting go and moving on

DIVINE RETRIBUTION

NOTES: Believing in a higher power can bring comfort, peace, and an inner strength. But it also comes with certain behavioral expectations. A character who is hyper-focused on divine judgment or punishment for stepping out of line won't experience comfort or peace. Their fear will not only inform their choices as they try to live within rigid parameters, but it will taint their view of their god and other people, so they see everyone and everything through a lens of judgment and disapproval.

WHAT IT LOOKS LIKE

Abstaining from punishable offenses
Holding themselves to an impossibly high moral standard
Perfectionist tendencies
Highly valuing justice
Exceeding expectations when it comes to religious activities (attending services, praying, confessing, fasting, serving others, etc.)
Proselytizing
Making all their decisions through the lens of religious guidance
Surrounding themselves with like-minded people
Fearing death and the afterlife
Pointing out the sins of others
Reveling in someone else's downfall to feel better about themselves
Avoiding people and places that may lead to temptation (parties, people from other religions, etc.)
Refusing to acknowledge doubts about the faith
Blindly following religious leaders
Doing penance when they've done wrong
Frantically seeking to balance the scales for wrongdoing
Seeing divine punishment in every bad thing that happens
Warning others of God's wrath
Only wanting to please their god; not caring about other people
Difficulty relating to people outside of their religion
Being hypocritical; objecting to some sins while secretly embracing the ones they want to engage in or have difficulty resisting
Having an us vs. them attitude
Having nightmares about hell and punishment

COMMON INTERNAL STRUGGLES

Losing the joy and comfort of their faith because they're so obsessed with adhering to a list of dos and don'ts
Wrestling with temptations
Wanting to show compassion to others but feeling compelled to uphold justice
Seeing their god as wrathful and critical instead of loving and forgiving
Always worrying about where they stand with their god
Seeing themselves as worthless or beyond redemption
Comparing themselves to others

Being haunted by past decisions and mistakes
Being paralyzed by decisions that have eternal consequences
Experiencing panic when their foundational religious beliefs are questioned
Developing depression or an anxiety disorder

HINDRANCES AND DISRUPTIONS TO THE CHARACTER'S LIFE
Being highly self-critical; blaming themselves unfairly
Missing out on enjoyable activities because they might be sinful
Being perceived as intolerant, self-righteous, judgmental, or out of touch
Frequently clashing with friends or family who don't share their beliefs
Struggling to find a romantic partner with the same values
Viewing the world in a binary fashion (black or white, good vs. evil, etc.)
Feeling guilty for actions, thoughts, or ideas that aren't actually a problem
Being unable to think for themselves
Being unable to see other perspectives or consider ideas that contradict their own

EMOTIONAL WOUNDS IT COULD STEM FROM: Bearing the Responsibility for Many Deaths, Being Forced to Keep a Dark Secret, Crossing Moral Lines to Survive, Having a Controlling or Overly Strict Parent, Having to Kill to Survive

SCENARIOS THAT MIGHT TRIGGER THIS FEAR
Being tempted to sin
Being asked to cover up a close friend's transgression
Discovering an interest or hobby that their faith doesn't embrace
A near-death experience or terminal diagnosis that brings death and judgment close
A loved one leaving the faith
Facing a question or doubt about their religion that they can't dismiss
Falling in love with a non-believer
Someone finding out about the character's hidden sin
Facing a new situation and not knowing right from wrong
Having to choose between their god and a loved one

HUMAN NEEDS THAT COULD BE IMPACTED
Self-Actualization: Someone this preoccupied with avoiding judgment will struggle to find joy and contentment.

Esteem and Recognition: A character who feels judged and unable to live up to an impossible standard will struggle with their own feelings of value and self-worth.

Love and Belonging: This fear can make tolerance for others a challenge, impacting the character's ability to form and maintain healthy relationships. Likewise, others may find the character's hyper-religious beliefs insufferable and seek distance from them.

HOW THE CHARACTER CAN MINIMIZE OR OVERCOME IT
Reminding themselves that their religious teachings include the forgiveness of sin
Seeking help to deprogram toxic religious teachings
Practicing self-forgiveness
Reexamining their ideas about their god, judgment, and sin

EXTINCTION

NOTES: The fear of extinction is very similar to the fear of death, but on a larger scale. A character in this situation could worry about their race or species being annihilated in an apocalyptic event. They may also be scared that their culture or legacy will be targeted and eradicated or otherwise lost. Because of the high stakes involved, this fear is one that can drive a character to extremes.

WHAT IT LOOKS LIKE
Actively passing their culture, beliefs, and ideals to the next generation
Teaching others their language and customs
Becoming an activist in extinction-related causes (environmentalism, gentrification, etc.)
Raising awareness of the perceived danger
Fighting propaganda that denies a threat exists
Speaking out against colonization and the erasure of cultures
Studying lost cultures to identify the signs leading to extinction
Sharing pieces of their culture with others through music, clothing, traditions, language, food, etc.
Looking for signs that society is becoming aggressive toward the character's culture
Obsessively checking news sources
Watching for shifts in the weather, animal behavior, or human activity (crime levels, the stock market, people leaving certain areas, etc.)
Scouring old texts and prophecies
Being triggered by apocalyptic movies
Becoming paranoid
Loudly proclaiming their fears as a warning to others
Having an escape plan in place
Praying fervently for preservation
Making procreation a priority (to ensure the continuation of their line, culture, etc.)
Believing in ideas that others may consider conspiracy theories (a zombie apocalypse, sentient AI, aliens, etc.)
Dreaming about or pursuing extreme escape options (space travel, virtual realities, etc.)
Stocking food, resources, or weapons in case of an apocalypse
Complaining that younger generations have lost their connection to the past
Conveying history through oral or written storytelling so it isn't forgotten
Gathering a tight-knit group to survive together as a remnant
Isolating from the rest of the world

COMMON INTERNAL STRUGGLES
Having an us vs. them mentality
Grieving what hasn't yet been lost
Feeling anger toward people the character considers a threat
Struggling with despair, as though the character is fighting the inevitable
Worrying that their life won't amount to anything
Wanting to be remembered for something

Being mired in a wistful nostalgia for times past
Feeling insignificant and ineffective

HINDRANCES AND DISRUPTIONS TO THE CHARACTER'S LIFE
Difficulty enjoying the present because they're so concerned with what's coming
Becoming obsessed with stopping something that may never happen
Focusing on surviving rather than thriving
Falling into depression and despair
Not making plans for the future (because what's the point?)
Being seen by younger generations as irrelevant, and losing influence with them
Traumatizing their children through fearful, erratic behavior
Being labeled or stigmatized for having fringe beliefs

EMOTIONAL WOUNDS IT COULD STEM FROM: A Natural or Man-Made Disaster, A Terrorist Attack, An Abuse of Power, Battling a Mental Condition, Growing up in a Cult, Living Through Civil Unrest, Living Through Famine or Drought

SCENARIOS THAT MIGHT TRIGGER THIS FEAR
Reports of an impending global or planetary catastrophe
Laws changing that put the character's people group at a disadvantage
Being one of a few remaining masters of a craft and learning that a peer has passed on
The character's concerns being teased or scorned
A natural disaster that destroys much of the character's homeland
A war that breaks out, targeting the character's people
Books or movies about an apocalypse
Witnessing genocide

HUMAN NEEDS THAT COULD BE IMPACTED

Self-Actualization: When survival is the only priority, everything considered less important—hobbies, downtime, passions—will be sidelined.

Esteem and Recognition: People will likely look down on someone with this fear as being paranoid, sensationalist, and a conspiracy theorist. They may not even be taken seriously inside their own people group.

Love and Belonging: Those who don't share this fear will struggle with the character's beliefs and restrictions, resulting in relationship friction.

Safety and Security: A character who fears extinction will never feel safe, always worrying that the end is near or eventually coming.

HOW THE CHARACTER CAN MINIMIZE OR OVERCOME IT
Focusing on daily needs of survival, connection, and esteem, not wider fears
The character caring for others, focusing on living a meaningful life in the present
Safeguarding or distributing cultural objects, practices, beliefs, etc., so these will live on
Being willing to consider these fears may not be grounded in truth and seeking help
Acknowledging how this fear may be hurting relationships or restricting loved ones, and whether this is fair

HAVING NO PURPOSE

NOTES: Everyone wants to believe they have purpose and exist for a reason. Fearing that their life has no real meaning can wreak havoc with a character's self-esteem and identity.

WHAT IT LOOKS LIKE

Taking inventory and personality tests to determine aptitudes
Bouncing from one activity to another, trying to find one that feels significant
Being overly committed so the calendar is full and the character feels busy
Tending toward perfectionism
Working long hours just to have something to do
Volunteering with different charities
Fundraising for various causes
Trying new things but quitting them when they don't seem to satisfy
Job-hopping to find the perfect role
Joining different organizations and social groups to find the best fit
Dismissing accomplishments that aren't deemed important or meaningful
Seeking outside approval or validation (to make up for internal feelings of inadequacy)
Turning to self-help professionals for guidance
Becoming more religious or faith-oriented
Drifting through life with no meaningful connection to their inner self
Having unrealistic expectations about what they can or should have accomplished by certain points in life
Dreading birthday milestones (because they accentuate what the character hasn't been able to accomplish)

COMMON INTERNAL STRUGGLES

Struggling to stay hopeful and optimistic
Constantly feeling as if they're not good or productive enough
Feeling as if nothing they do matters
Feeling insignificant among so many people who know their purposes
Wanting to contribute positively but not knowing how
Questioning their profession
Feeling dissatisfied, even after successes or accomplishments
Comparing themselves to others and being disappointed
Envying people who have found their purpose
Focusing on what's missing rather than what the character has
Feeling worthless, like they have nothing to contribute and no one would miss them if they were gone

HINDRANCES AND DISRUPTIONS TO THE CHARACTER'S LIFE

Changing jobs frequently
Difficulty recognizing their own achievements
Starting new ventures but not following through (always moving to the next big thing)

Needing praise and approval to counter their doubt
Missing opportunities to align with people who are doing meaningful things because the character is searching for their own sense of purpose
Filling their time but still feeling empty

EMOTIONAL WOUNDS IT COULD STEM FROM: A Terminal Illness Diagnosis, A Toxic Relationship, Being Fired or Laid Off, Being Legitimately Incarcerated for a Crime, Failing at School, Growing up in the Shadow of a Successful Sibling, Living with a Critical Medical Diagnosis, Living with Chronic Pain or Illness, Prejudice or Discrimination, Wrongful Imprisonment

SCENARIOS THAT MIGHT TRIGGER THIS FEAR

Pouring themselves into an outlet that turns out to be unfulfilling or not what they thought it would be
Seeing close friends or relatives succeed in meaningful areas of life
Being left behind by a colleague who moves up the ranks quickly
Being accused by a loved one of not having enough drive, vision, or passion
Hitting an important milestone and feeling dissatisfied with life
A friend or relative dying, leading to an epiphany about how fleeting life is
The character being rejected in their efforts to create meaning (not being selected for a promotion, being replaced on a volunteer board, etc.)
A crisis that awakens the character's desire to be a champion for the greater good
Receiving a critical diagnosis that will shorten the character's life, leaving less time to find their purpose

HUMAN NEEDS THAT COULD BE IMPACTED

Self-Actualization: A character with this fear may believe that only audacious goals will provide true purpose. This can result in them missing out on less high-minded pursuits that could provide great satisfaction and fulfillment (such as raising a child or serving the people within their circle).

Esteem and Recognition: A character with no purpose may spiral into self-doubt, insecurity, or even self-loathing when they're unable to find meaning.

Love and Belonging: The character's zealous pursuit of purpose may sideline important relationships, creating distance with loved ones.

HOW THE CHARACTER CAN MINIMIZE OR OVERCOME IT

Exploring a variety of passions until they find the one that "clicks"
Redefining purpose so it's attainable: being the type of person who consistently shows up, acts selflessly, and adds to the lives of others
Remembering the reason behind a goal and focusing on that (e.g., seeking to lift their family out of poverty by becoming a concert pianist)
Finding a sense of purpose in daily, small acts, such as cleaning the house, replacing bad habits with good ones, or trying something new each day

LEAVING NO LEGACY

NOTES: A character can leave different kinds of legacies. Sometimes, it's the accumulation of substantial assets, such as money or land, for their children. A legacy could also be the furthering of their lineage or doing something worthwhile that will be remembered after their death. Legacy is often tied to purpose, so a character with this fear will go to great lengths to leave their mark and prove that their life had meaning and substance.

WHAT IT LOOKS LIKE

Being ambitious
Accumulating wealth or status (degrees, membership in exclusive clubs, etc.)
Having high expectations for themselves and/or others
The character focusing intensely on the path that will make their legacy a reality
Passionately pursuing acclaim and creative endeavors
Having strong self-control and self-discipline
Believing in the value of sacrificing for something greater
Focusing on health and wellness so they'll have plenty of time to establish their legacy
Donating significant amounts of money to charities, hospitals, or the arts
Having biological children to carry forward the family name
Pushing their children toward financial or creative success
Volunteering
Keeping meticulous records and photos for posterity
Seeking to be viewed as special, a cut above the rest
Overspending to impress the right people and win recognition
Making decisions based on how they'll impact the character's legacy
Being fixated on the future and not paying much attention to right now
Never having enough; always wanting the legacy to be more
Protecting the legacy above all else

COMMON INTERNAL STRUGGLES

Feeling guilty for missing family milestones in pursuit of the legacy
Wanting to leave a legacy despite knowing it won't last forever
Fearing they'll die without having left a mark
Feeling like they're at the mercy of fate while trying to build their legacy
Fearing they'll never do enough to establish their legacy, no matter how hard they work
Wanting to build some kind of legacy but not knowing what it should be
Worrying about who will continue the legacy when the character is gone
Seeing an opportunity to build the legacy but knowing others will be harmed by it
Being tempted to use unethical means to reach the goal

HINDRANCES AND DISRUPTIONS TO THE CHARACTER'S LIFE

Difficulty balancing the legacy with other areas of life
Missing family events and having to deal with the fallout
Competing with friends and siblings (to earn more money, be more successful, etc.)

Living with regret as time goes on over sacrifices made in pursuit of the legacy
Working tirelessly to build a legacy only to have their children say they don't want it

EMOTIONAL WOUNDS IT COULD STEM FROM: A Nomadic Childhood, Becoming Homeless for Reasons Out of One's Control, Being Disowned or Shunned, Being Forced to Leave One's Homeland, Declaring Bankruptcy, Experiencing Poverty, Having One's Ideas or Work Stolen

SCENARIOS THAT MIGHT TRIGGER THIS FEAR

Seeing someone fade into obscurity after their death
A parent dying without assets, leaving nothing behind for the character and their siblings
Struggling with infertility
A long-standing record being broken
The character being unable to overcome an obstacle threatening their legacy
Having to declare bankruptcy
The character falling dangerously ill while in debt
An advancement (AI, a medical cure, an invention, etc.) threatening the character's built-from-scratch business
The character being told that nothing they do matters

HUMAN NEEDS THAT COULD BE IMPACTED

Self-Actualization: If the character's legacy is part of a higher calling or purpose—especially one that will allow others to become fully actualized—being unable to provide that could keep the character from fulfillment.

Esteem and Recognition: For some, legacy is more about making a mark and gaining recognition than providing something for others. A character with this mindset will be dissatisfied until they achieve that legacy milestone and the acclaim that comes with it.

Love and Belonging: A character obsessed with leaving a legacy will make that their top priority, sacrificing other people and relationships in their pursuit of the goal.

HOW THE CHARACTER CAN MINIMIZE OR OVERCOME IT

Gaining perspective on what's important, such as being available for people now
Recognizing that legacies can be forgotten or removed but kindness, compassion, and empowerment live on
Focusing on serving others now, not amassing accolades or awards
Being honest about whether stuff has made anyone happy
Recognizing the internal hole they're trying to fill by providing the legacy, and reevaluating if their goal will really satisfy them
Examining different kinds of legacies (such as Mother Theresa's life's work of serving others) and the character reevaluating their own goals
Recognizing that the people they remember the most fondly are those who left behind memories of love and support, not money or things
Pursuing a legacy of investing in people rather than stockpiling material goods

MISSING OUT

NOTES: This fear arises when a character sees what other people are experiencing and believes they're missing out on something rewarding. At its core, it's the perception that others are living fuller lives. Rather than simple disappointment, this fear induces anxiety, envy, and a deep sense of dissatisfaction.

WHAT IT LOOKS LIKE

Scouring social media to see what others are doing
Checking their phone frequently for missed calls or texts
Eavesdropping on the conversations others are having
Hesitating to commit in case something better comes along
Saying yes to every invitation
Strategically choosing friends based on who's at the center of the fun things happening
Gossiping (to prove the character is in the know)
Fixating on insignificant decisions
Making choices based on how the outcome will look to others or contribute to the character's image
Spending more than is wise to keep up with other people
Lingering at social gatherings
Taking a lot of photos
Only posting or sharing pictures that make the character look good
Needing to be on all social networks
Sacrificing sleep, nutrition, or other healthy behaviors
Taking unnecessary risks to fit in or be included
Difficulty being present with others
The character's school or work performance suffering as it takes a backseat to social activities
The character engaging in activities they aren't really interested in so they can be part of what's happening
Prioritizing good photo ops instead of enjoying the moment
Failing to respect others' boundaries—e.g., showing up to events uninvited
Not showing gratitude for what they have
Losing track of time while scrolling
Social climbing; pursuing relationships because of the opportunities they could bring
Quickly moving on when something is no longer popular
Avoiding commitments that could tie them down
Fantasizing about the perfect life

COMMON INTERNAL STRUGGLES

Worrying they're being deliberately excluded
Being exhausted from going nonstop
Fixating on what they could miss instead of what they have
Struggling with discontentment and envy
Feeling trapped in the comparison game
Having moments of uncertainty about who they are

Their self-esteem plummeting because they think there's a reason they aren't included
Feeling like a loser
Their obsession with appearances making them feel fake, like an impostor

HINDRANCES AND DISRUPTIONS TO THE CHARACTER'S LIFE
Missing out on a good opportunity because they didn't want to commit
Procrastinating on a decision and having a situation go from bad to worse
Being ruled by a device and the need to constantly keep posting
Appearing wishy-washy, unreliable, or superficial
Important relationships being sacrificed for ones that provide the right opportunities
Never being content; always having to keep up with someone
Developing an anxiety disorder
Being focused on short-term rather than long-term goals
Running short on funds due to overspending

EMOTIONAL WOUNDS IT COULD STEM FROM: Being Raised by Parents Who Loved Conditionally, Being Rejected by One's Peers, Experiencing Poverty, Falling Short of Society's Physical Standards, Social Difficulties

SCENARIOS THAT MIGHT TRIGGER THIS FEAR
Not being invited to an important social event
Being the last to know
A friend hitting a milestone the character hasn't yet reached (getting into a prestigious college, announcing a pregnancy, etc.)
Seeing pictures of a coworker on a dream vacation
A setback that makes it harder to keep up with everyone else (losing a job, getting divorced, etc.)

HUMAN NEEDS THAT COULD BE IMPACTED

Self-Actualization: A character with this fear may become so focused on keeping up with other people that they fail to identify or pursue their own dreams.

Esteem and Recognition: Comparison is a key component of this fear, and confidence is hard to come by for a character who is always comparing themselves to others. This can also lead to identity issues as they chase an ideal life instead of pursuing self-discovery and figuring out who they are.

Love and Belonging: A character who chooses relationships strategically will miss out on the deeper connections that come with being authentic, accepting others as they are, and being accepted in return.

HOW THE CHARACTER CAN MINIMIZE OR OVERCOME IT
Seeking validation from within, not externally
Finding joy in the act of working for something over instant gratification
Place limits on social networking and texting
Building habits of seeing something through rather than leaving things unfinished
Putting the phone away and enjoying the moment without needing to record it

NEVER FINDING HAPPINESS

NOTES: A character may fear they'll never be happy if they've experienced many of life's disappointments or secretly believe they're unworthy or undeserving of happiness. This fear creates a dichotomy of emotions, with the character either spending their time chasing happiness or running from it.

WHAT IT LOOKS LIKE

Searching for the one thing that will light the fire within them
Trying many different hobbies and pastimes
Viewing the next opportunity as the one that will finally satisfy them
Researching philosophies, religions, and other ideologies
Spending a lot of time alone, soul-searching
Never being content or truly grateful for what they have
Hopping from job to job to find the perfect one
Retreating or hiding from the world
Engaging in negative self-talk
Pessimism; expecting the worst
Struggling with making decisions
Feeling different from others, like an outsider
Good moods being short-lived because the character expects something bad to ruin the moment
Being unable to make a move toward something they desire
Being unable to find things that excite them
Having a *Why me?* attitude
Abusing drugs or alcohol to find peace or numb the pain
Trying to be perfect
Hating life and everything in it
Lashing out at others in frustration

COMMON INTERNAL STRUGGLES

Struggling constantly with painful longing; wanting what others have
Wondering what's wrong with them and why they can't be happy like everyone else
Feeling numb even when something wonderful has happened
Focusing on past hurts, even when things have gotten better
Worrying about the future instead of being grateful for the good things in the present
Being unable to see their own value
Experiencing guilt or shame though they have done nothing wrong
Wanting close relationships but being too afraid they'll end in heartache

HINDRANCES AND DISRUPTIONS TO THE CHARACTER'S LIFE

Having a difficult time making friends
Not going after what they want in life
Self-sabotage; derailing something positive out of a fear it will be taken from them

Foregoing promising opportunities; settling for the status quo
Chronic substance abuse
Being stymied by depression, social anxiety, etc.
Believing that fate/God/the universe is working against them
Being driven by negative thoughts and emotions

EMOTIONAL WOUNDS IT COULD STEM FROM: A Miscarriage or Stillbirth, A Nomadic Childhood, A Terminal Illness Diagnosis, A Traumatic Brain Injury, Battling a Mental Condition, Being Bullied, Being Forced to Keep a Dark Secret, Living with a Critical Medical Diagnosis, Living with an Abusive Caregiver, Living with Chronic Pain or Illness, Social Difficulties, The Death of One's Child, Unrequited Love

SCENARIOS THAT MIGHT TRIGGER THIS FEAR

Being victimized
Losing something that makes it seemingly impossible for the character to follow their passion (a musician going deaf, an athlete losing a limb, etc.)
The character being laid off from their perfect job
Experiencing a series of losses in a short span of time
A large-scale disaster (a weather event, economic depression, pandemic, etc.) negatively impacting the character
A health crisis that takes away something the character enjoyed, such as diabetes or Celiac's disease requiring them to give up certain foods
A sibling announcing they're engaged or expecting a baby
A promising opportunity falling through at the last minute

HUMAN NEEDS THAT COULD BE IMPACTED

Self-Actualization: A character with this fear may avoid opportunities that would bring happiness and fulfillment because they're too afraid of being disappointed.

Esteem and Recognition: A character may have developed this fear because they believe they're unworthy of happiness and suffer from low self-esteem.

Love and Belonging: Loving friends and family members may become weary of a character who complains of unhappiness that's perpetuated by their own bad habits or reluctance to make necessary changes.

HOW THE CHARACTER CAN MINIMIZE OR OVERCOME IT

Recognizing how social media and television distort reality
Realizing happiness isn't a destination but comes from the day-to-day journey
A willingness to try new things and be open-minded
Embracing the good with the bad because they both give life meaning
Living in the present rather than yearning for a specific future
Setting meaningful, achievable goals that the character must stretch themselves to fulfill, making success that much sweeter
Being open to all sorts of healthy relationships and growing through them
Seeking guidance from people who were once in a dark place and were able to escape it

REGRET

NOTES: A character who fears regret typically has experienced this deeply unsettling emotion in the wake of some past decision, words, action, or inaction. As a result, they'll strive to always do the right thing as they move forward and make choices that will keep this feeling at bay.

WHAT IT LOOKS LIKE

Being highly neurotic
Risk-aversion
Indecisiveness
Needing a lot of time to consider options before making a decision
Using flowcharts, lists, and other tools to help with decision-making
Over-researching
Seeking the advice of others to counter their own doubts and assuage their fears about an important decision
Only moving forward when they're certain it's the right thing to do
Reversing decisions that have been made—even the thoroughly thought-out ones
Worrying over even the most trivial of decisions: *Should I dress up or down?* or *Should I run errands today or tomorrow?*
Self-correcting to avoid regretful situations from the past (always locking the door to the house, being cautious before beginning new relationships, etc.)
Over-correcting for past regrets (obsessively checking door locks, avoiding strangers, etc.)
Sticking with the status quo, even in a bad situation
Making choices based on what will bring the least regret rather than what's best for the character
Delaying gratification—for instance, saving to buy a car rather than going into debt to buy one now and regretting it later
Becoming controlling (believing that control will keep regretful things from happening)
Needing to do things perfectly so mistakes aren't made
Taking advantage of every opportunity so they don't regret missing out on something good

COMMON INTERNAL STRUGGLES

Being paralyzed with indecision
Believing they're emotionally unequipped to deal with regret in any form
Seeing only the risky or uncertain outcomes for possible choices
Second-guessing decisions that have already been made
Constantly reliving past regrets
Struggling with feelings of inadequacy and incompetence
Regret leading to self-blame and self-loathing

HINDRANCES AND DISRUPTIONS TO THE CHARACTER'S LIFE

Being unable to enjoy life because they're constantly obsessing over a choice to be made
Waffling over decisions that have already been made
Being seen by others as flaky, wishy-washy, or weak-minded

Choosing not to choose, and becoming professionally, relationally, spiritually, or emotionally stagnant
Staying in a bad situation because they believe it's less risky than making a change
Living a life well below their full potential
Being caught in an ongoing cycle of regret and fear of regret

EMOTIONAL WOUNDS IT COULD STEM FROM: A Child Dying on One's Watch, A House Fire, Accidentally Killing Someone, Being Legitimately Incarcerated for a Crime, Being Sent Away as a Child, Caving to Peer Pressure, Choosing to Not Be Involved in a Child's Life, Making a Very Public Mistake, Misplaced Loyalty

SCENARIOS THAT MIGHT TRIGGER THIS FEAR
Facing a decision that doesn't have an obvious solution
Facing a decision that has no good outcomes
Being offered an opportunity that comes with downsides—e.g., a great promotion that requires a cross-country move
A sizable investment opportunity that comes with risks attached
Witnessing someone's fall from grace due to a bad decision
Facing a choice that could have negative ramifications for others
A loved one approaching the end of their life and being consumed with regret

HUMAN NEEDS THAT COULD BE IMPACTED

Self-Actualization: A character who is paralyzed by decision-making will often opt to maintain the status quo, resulting in them advancing their career, improving their relationships, and growing personally.

Esteem and Recognition: A character with this fear will often think poorly of themselves due to past mistakes and choices. Their difficulty knowing their own mind and easily making decisions can lead them to believe unkind things about themselves.

Love and Belonging: Friends may become annoyed with a character who is always reluctant to take action. On the flip side, a character who embraces every opportunity because they're afraid to miss out can be equally frustrating to the loved ones being dragged along.

HOW THE CHARACTER CAN MINIMIZE OR OVERCOME IT
Determining to gain stability by making decisions according to their core values rather than in-the-moment criteria that may fluctuate
Learning to give themselves grace (and accept it) for past mistakes
Learning from painful past events so they gain purpose, diminishing regret
Setting deadlines for researching decisions and taking action within those timeframes
Visualizing the future and making choices that further those goals

APPENDIX A: SURVIVAL RESPONSES WHEN FEAR IS ACTIVATED

What's your character's go-to response when fear arises? Kickstart the brainstorming process with these body cue examples so you can accurately convey their emotion in the moment.

FIGHT

Confront to Regain Control

INTERNAL

Rising temperature and increased adrenaline
Agitation, anger, or contempt
Rigid thinking and a need to be right

EXTERNAL

Making the body appear bigger
Eye contact and unflinching focus
Stepping closer; invading another's space
Challenging authority
Taking charge or dominating others
Casting blame and making accusations
Pushiness, arguing, or yelling
Intimidation and threats
Physical aggression (grabbing, shoving, etc.)
Violence (hitting, throwing things)

FLIGHT

Escape the Threat

INTERNAL

Heightened anxiety and stress
Feeling restless or trapped
Overthinking
A rising sense of panic and need to escape

EXTERNAL

Taking a slow step back
Jerking away from a perceived threat
Raising hands to ward off or shield themselves
Backpedaling; making excuses
Procrastinating and avoidance
Canceling plans; avoiding people
Glancing around for an escape
Moving toward the exit
Withdrawing, hiding, or fleeing

FREEZE

Shut Down and Be Still

INTERNAL

Mental fog
A feeling that time has slowed
Decision paralysis
Experiencing dread
Tunnel vision
Shutting down
Disassociating

EXTERNAL

Stumbling to a halt
Holding in breath
Becoming non-responsive
Going still; being unable to move
An unblinking gaze
Squeezing the eyes shut

FAWN*

Appease to Deescalate

*Learned Response

INTERNAL

Heightened anxiety
Feeling trapped
Overthinking

EXTERNAL

Adopting a soft, reasonable tone
Being agreeable and accommodating
Apologizing profusely
Offering compliments and flattery
Taking responsibility or accountability
Prioritizing the other's needs
Reinforcing that the threat is in control
Using distraction so emotions can be regulated
Smiling and adopting care-taking gestures
Moving slowly and carefully

Download your own copy of this resource from our Free Writing Tools page (https://writershelpingwriters.net/writing-tools/).

APPENDIX B: CHANGE ARC TURNING POINT MAP

Map major turning points as the character becomes aware of their greatest fear, acknowledges its role in keeping them from achieving their goal, and strives to overcome it. These moments typically occur at specific times (see the associated percentages below) and act as mile markers to keep your story on track as you record the character's journey to fulfillment and happiness.

For more information about each turning point (and a sample map for a well-known character), see the chapter on **The Role of Fear in Fiction**.

My Character's Greatest Fear: ______________________________

Turning Point 1 (12%): What crisis, opportunity, or challenge disrupts the character's world and reveals a new path forward? *At this point, they are in denial or unaware of their greatest fear, yet it still subconsciously influences them, generating reluctance, uncertainty, or mixed feelings about the new journey.*

____

____

____

____

Turning Point 2 (24%): What new complication, development, or problem clarifies the character's approach to reaching their goal? *This moment should provide a glimpse of who they could be and what they could do if they abandoned fear and embraced their true self.*

____

____

____

____

____

Turning Point 3 (50%): What new development or revelation signals victory or defeat, causing the character to reevaluate their methods? *This assessment—resulting in them doubling down on their current approach or shifting away from what isn't working to a new practice, mindset, or perspective—should lead to some measure of success.*

____

____

____

____

Turning Point 4 (68%): What devastating setback—a brush with some form of death—tells the character that all is lost and they simply can't win? *In this moment, their fear will challenge their determination to obtain the goal and satisfy their unmet need.*

____

____

____

____

Turning Point 5 (85%): What ultimate battle must the character fight and win to achieve the goal? *To succeed, they'll have to renounce their fear, discard misbeliefs, and trade faulty coping behaviors for new knowledge, skills, and resolve. Often a sacrifice is required for them to prevail.*

____

____

____

____

APPENDIX B: FAILED ARC TURNING POINT MAP

Map major turning points as your character becomes aware of their greatest fear and attempts to overcome it but ultimately fails to do so. These moments typically occur at specific times (see the percentages below) to keep the story on track as you record the character's journey toward tragedy and continued brokenness. Note that while fear plays a part in their failure, these characters may never truly acknowledge it or view it realistically. Even so, readers need to see the fear at play in each turning point decision.

For more information about the turning points (and a sample map for a famous character), see the chapter on **The Role of Fear in Fiction**.

My Character's Greatest Fear: ______________________________

Turning Point 1 (12%): What opportunity arises that feels like an escape, allowing the character to exit an undesirable situation or achieve a long-desired goal? *This will start them on the path to fulfilling the unmet need that plagues them. At this point, the character may be aware of their fear, ignorant about it, or have a skewed perception of it.*

____

____

____

____

Turning Point 2 (24%): What new complication, development, or event shakes the character, triggering their fear? *This moment will often make them doubt the goal as a worthy objective or the methods they've been using to achieve it. If they do decide to keep moving forward, they'll do so with less confidence.*

____

____

____

____

Turning Point 3 (50%): What new incident or revelation signals either defeat (tempting them to give up on the goal) or a false victory (because the character was moving further from the goal or using questionable means to reach it, and is now encouraged to continue)? *Their fear will influence their response to this event and may drive them to a compromise that will eventually result in them failing to obtain their objective or resolve their unmet need.*

____

____

____

____

Turning Point 4 (68%): What brush-with-death event triggers a belief that all is lost and they can't win? *In this moment, the character's fear will push them to reject the goal or whatever they hoped to change at the start of the story.*

____

____

____

____

Turning Point 5 (85%): What climactic battle must they fight and win to achieve the goal? *The character, still in denial of or unable to fully master their fear, responds to this confrontation with avoidance, half-measures, or old methods that ultimately work against them. With unresolved fear still ruling them, they fail to reach their objective and find fulfilment.*

____

____

____

____

Download additional copies of these templates from our Free Writing Tools page (https://writershelpingwriters.net/writing-tools/).

UNEARTH YOUR CHARACTER'S BACKSTORY WITH *THE EMOTIONAL WOUND THESAURUS*

If you've found *The Fear Thesaurus* helpful, you might also be interested in *The Emotional Wound Thesaurus: A Writer's Guide to Psychological Trauma.* This guide spotlights 118 traumatic events and the fears, lies, personality shifts and dysfunctional behaviors that can arise from them. It contains a masterclass of information on character arc that shows how painful experiences shape who a character is on page one, but also how they must change—and face internal battles along the way—to achieve the story goal.

For your convenience, here's the list of wounding events covered in this book, broken down by category:

CRIME AND VICTIMIZATION
A Carjacking
A Home Invasion
A Physical Assault
Being Held Captive
Being Sexually Violated
Being Stalked
Being Treated as Property
Being Victimized by a Perpetrator Who Was Never Caught
Identity Theft
Witnessing a Murder

DISABILITIES AND DISFIGUREMENTS
A Learning Disability
A Physical Disfigurement
A Speech Impediment
A Traumatic Brain Injury
Battling a Mental Disorder
Being So Beautiful It's All People See
Falling Short of Society's Physical Standards
Infertility
Living with Chronic Pain or Illness
Losing a Limb
Losing One of the Five Senses
Sexual Dysfunction
Social Difficulties

FAILURES AND MISTAKES
Accidentally Killing Someone
Bearing the Responsibility for Many Deaths
Being Legitimately Incarcerated for a Crime
Caving to Peer Pressure
Choosing Not to Be Involved in a Child's Life
Cracking Under Pressure
Declaring Bankruptcy
Failing at School
Failing to Do the Right Thing
Failing to Save Someone's Life
Making a Very Public Mistake
Poor Judgment Leading to Unintended Consequences

INJUSTICE AND HARDSHIP
An Abuse of Power
Becoming Homeless for Reasons Beyond One's Control
Being Bullied
Being Falsely Accused of a Crime
Being Fired or Laid Off
Being Forced to Keep a Dark Secret
Being Forced to Leave One's Homeland
Being the Victim of a Vicious Rumor
Being Unfairly Blamed for Someone's Death
Experiencing Poverty
Living Through Civil Unrest
Living Through Famine or Drought
Prejudice or Discrimination
Unrequited Love
Wrongful Imprisonment

MISPLACED TRUST AND BETRAYALS
A Sibling's Betrayal
A Toxic Relationship
Abandonment over an Unexpected Pregnancy
Being Disappointed by a Role Model
Being Disowned or Shunned
Being Let Down by a Trusted Organization or Social System
Being Rejected by One's Peers
Childhood Sexual Abuse by a Known Person
Discovering a Partner's Sexual Orientation Secret
Discovering a Sibling's Abuse
Domestic Abuse
Financial Ruin Due to a Spouse's Irresponsibility
Finding Out One Was Adopted
Finding Out One's Child Was Abused
Getting Dumped
Having One's Ideas or Work Stolen
Incest
Infidelity
Learning That One's Parent Had a Second Family
Learning That One's Parent Was a Monster
Losing a Loved One Due to a Professional's Negligence
Misplaced Loyalty
Telling the Truth but Not Being Believed

SPECIFIC CHILDHOOD WOUNDS
A Nomadic Childhood
A Parent's Abandonment or Rejection
Becoming a Caregiver at an Early Age
Being Raised by a Narcissist
Being Raised by an Addict
Being Raised by Neglectful Parents
Being Raised by Overprotective Parents
Being Raised by Parents Who Loved Conditionally
Being Sent Away as a Child
Being the Product of Rape
Experiencing the Death of a Parent as a Child or Youth
Growing up in a Cult
Growing up in Foster Care
Growing up in the Public Eye
Growing up in the Shadow of a Successful Sibling
Growing up with a Sibling's Disability or Chronic Illness
Having a Controlling or Overly Strict Parent
Having Parents Who Favored One Child over Another
Living in a Dangerous Neighborhood
Living in an Emotionally Repressed Household
Living with an Abusive Caregiver
Not Being a Priority Growing Up
Witnessing Violence at a Young Age

TRAUMATIC EVENTS
A Child Dying on One's Watch
A House Fire
A Life-Threatening Accident
A Loved One's Suicide
A Miscarriage or Stillbirth
A Natural or Man-Made Disaster
A Parent's Divorce
A School Shooting
A Terminal Illness Diagnosis
A Terrorist Attack

Being Humiliated by Others
Being Tortured
Being Trapped in a Collapsed Building
Being Trapped with a Dead Body
Divorcing One's Spouse
Getting Lost in a Natural Environment
Giving up a Child for Adoption
Having an Abortion
Having to Kill to Survive
Losing a Loved One to a Random Act of Violence
The Death of One's Child
Watching Someone Die

Read on to see a sample entry or visit our store (https://shopwritershelpingwriters.net/collections/emotional-wound-thesaurus) to dive deeper into this writing guide and learn how it will help you write more human stories.

EMOTIONAL WOUND SAMPLE ENTRY: ACCIDENTALLY KILLING SOMEONE

EXAMPLES

Driving a car in which a passenger, pedestrian, or cyclist is killed
Unknowingly serving food to someone who's highly allergic to it
A child consuming a fatal dose of medication while in the character's care
A child drowning in the character's pool or tub
Killing someone while impaired
Instigating a prank or dare that goes wrong
Campfire carelessness that leads to fatalities
A boating or jet ski accident
Peer pressure that ends in an unintentional death (e.g., pushing drinks on a friend who later dies of alcohol poisoning)
The mishandling or misfire of a weapon or firearm
Home protection incidents, such as shooting at an intruder and hitting a family member
Poor home maintenance (stairs collapsing, someone falling through a rotten floor, etc.)
Hitting someone too hard in a fight
Selling or giving a friend a bad batch of drugs
A sport-related accident
Malfunctioning equipment, such as a tanning booth electrocuting a client
Horseplay between kids that turns deadly
A police officer killing a bystander in the line of duty
Bumping a friend who falls from a high balcony or ledge

BASIC NEEDS OFTEN COMPROMISED BY THIS WOUND: Safety and security, love and belonging, esteem and recognition, self-actualization

FALSE BELIEFS THAT COULD BE EMBRACED

It should have been me.
I'm a terrible and worthless person.
I don't deserve to be happy or safe.
I'm only capable of hurting people.
I cannot be trusted with responsibility of any kind.
People will hate me if they know what I did.
I should suffer for the pain I caused.
I can never fix what I did, no matter how hard I try.
It would be better for everyone if I was dead too.

THE CHARACTER MAY FEAR...

Making another mistake that takes someone's life
Responsibility; making decisions that impact others
Losing control (if irresponsible behavior led to the death)
Things not being safe enough (if disrepair or a lack of safety protocol was involved)

POSSIBLE RESPONSES AND RESULTS

Paranoia or obsession regarding circumstances that led to the death (installing safety railings everywhere to avoid someone falling, not allowing children near water, etc.)
Over-preparing—e.g., researching dangers tied to a location and packing for a trip accordingly
PTSD symptoms (flashbacks, anxiety, depression, etc.)
Avoiding friends, family, or the public at large
Not chasing personal dreams because the character feels unworthy
Punishing themselves by giving up the things they love
Taking risks due to the belief that the character has no value
Taking risks in hopes death will occur so they can atone for the mistake
Drinking or using drugs to cope
Blaming others for what happened rather than accepting their role
Avoiding situations and people tied to the event
Being hyper-aware of potential danger and safety issues
Choosing to stay close to home most of the time
Becoming a helicopter parent or being overprotective of loved ones
Hiring professionals rather than attempting do-it-yourself repairs
Keeping their vehicle, home, etc. in top shape
Having well-stocked medical supplies and working fire extinguishers
Taking safety training, CPR, or other life skill courses to be prepared in the case of an accident

PERSONALITY TRAITS THAT MAY FORM

Attributes: Alert, appreciative, cautious, cooperative, disciplined, empathetic, focused, generous, gentle, honest, honorable, humble, independent, inspirational, kind, loyal, mature, merciful

Flaws: Addictive, apathetic, cowardly, defensive, disorganized, fanatical, humorless, impulsive, indecisive, inhibited, insecure, irresponsible, martyr, morbid, obsessive, oversensitive, reckless

TRIGGERS THAT MIGHT AGGRAVATE THIS WOUND

Hearing about a similar accidental death on the news or in the community
Important life milestones for the victim (the anniversary of their death, their birthday, the day they would have graduated from high school, etc.)
Running into a family member of the victim
Experiencing a near-miss similar to the accident
A loved one being involved in an incident that could have turned deadly
Someone being injured on the character's property

OPPORTUNITIES TO FACE OR OVERCOME THIS WOUND

Wanting to support a close friend who accidentally hurt or killed someone
A close friend or family member being accidentally killed
The family of the victim filing a wrongful death lawsuit
Being placed in a situation where the character has to kill to protect themselves
A situation where the character must keep another person alive

FEAR THESAURUS BONUS RESOURCES

Take what you've learned in *The Fear Thesaurus* even further with exclusive bonus resources designed to help you apply these concepts directly to your characters and stories.

Use this link or scan the QR code to visit our Fear Thesaurus Companion Hub (https://writershelpingwriters.net/fear-thesaurus-resource-companion-hub/) and access the resources that follow.

Fear By Genre Overview: A printable handout that outlines how fear is used in some of the biggest genres and provides quick tips for giving readers exactly what they want.

Your Character's Greatest Fear Worksheet
A printable sheet to help you identify which fear holds your character back so you can use it to shape their behavior, relationships, and character arc.

The Fear Factor Workshop (Recorded)
A free companion workshop that will strengthen your understanding of how fear alters perception, logic, and behavior—and how to show it on the page. Watch at your convenience.

A Surprise or Two
Not only can you explore the wealth of knowledge housed at our award-winning Writers Helping Writers® site, but you may find a few additional bonuses or discounts too.

When you're ready to dig deeper, these companion resources can help.

VISIT OUR WRITERS HELPING WRITERS® WEBSITE

We hope this thesaurus helps you with your current story and all those to come. Exploring someone's inner self and understanding what makes them tick is deep work that leads to authentic, unforgettable characters that readers will love to read about.

If you'd like to continue learning to write breakout fiction and further your author career, please join us at Writers Helping Writers (https://writershelpingwriters.net/). This hub was made for you—a place to grow your skills, find valuable resources and support, and connect with story experts who have knowledge to share. There, you'll find…

Practical Articles for Writers at All Levels
For 20 years, we've covered the craft of writing, helping writers understand the basics and go deeper into all story elements—plot, characters, arc, voice, subtext, and show-don't-tell, just to name a few. Our clear, actionable articles will help you write and improve scenes, humanize characters, and craft worlds readers won't want to leave.

The Complete Thesaurus Collection
If you love The Fear Thesaurus, you'll find even more support in the rest of our descriptive guides, including The Emotion Thesaurus, The Conflict Thesaurus, The Emotional Wound Thesaurus, and many more. Each one gives you brainstorm-friendly lists to help you show, not tell, and offers practical teaching you can apply immediately to your manuscript.

Writer-Focused Tools and Worksheets
We offer free downloadable tools and story-building aids that help you dig deeper into character motivation, structure your novel, and tackle revision with confidence.

Expert Guidance from Our Resident Writing Coaches
Every week, our team of seasoned writing coaches and editors share fresh craft insight to help you get unstuck, see your story more clearly, and build your skills. These practical posts demystify key concepts, support your creativity, and keep you motivated.

Stay Connected and Keep Growing
Sign up for our blog updates (https://writershelpingwriters.net/newsletters/subscribe-to-our-blog/) to get weekly writing advice delivered to your inbox. You can also subscribe to our Master Storytelling Newsletter (https://writershelpingwriters.net/newsletters/join-our-master-storytelling-newsletter/) for deeper insight, special resources, and behind-the-scenes updates about new books and tools designed to strengthen your craft.

We look forward to helping you further at Writers Helping Writers!

PRAISE FOR THE WRITERS HELPING WRITERS® SERIES

THE EMOTION THESAURUS

"One of the challenges a fiction writer faces, especially when prolific, is coming up with fresh ways to describe emotions. This handy compendium fills that need. It is both a reference and a brainstorming tool, and one of the resources I'll be turning to most often as I write my own books."

~ James Scott Bell, best-selling author of Deceived and Plot & Structure

THE POSITIVE AND NEGATIVE TRAIT THESAURUSES

"In these brilliantly conceived, superbly organized and astonishingly thorough volumes, Angela Ackerman and Becca Puglisi have created an invaluable resource for writers and storytellers. Whether you are searching for new and unique ways to add and define characters, or brainstorming methods for revealing those characters without resorting to clichés, it is hard to imagine two more powerful tools for adding depth and dimension to your screenplays, novels or plays."

~ Michael Hauge, Hollywood script consultant and author of Writing Screenplays That Sell

THE URBAN AND RURAL SETTING THESAURUSES

"The one thing I always appreciate about Ackerman and Puglisi's Thesauri series is how comprehensive they are. They never stop at the obvious, and they always over-deliver. Their Setting Thesauri are no different, offering not just the obvious notes of the various settings but going into easy-to-miss details like smells and tastes. They even offer to jumpstart the brainstorming with categories on potential sources of conflict."

~ K.M. Weiland, best-selling author of Structuring Your Novel

THE EMOTIONAL WOUND THESAURUS

"This is far more than a brilliant, thorough, insightful, and unique thesaurus. This is the best primer on story—and what really hooks and holds readers—that I have ever read."

~ Lisa Cron, TEDx Speaker and best-selling author of Wired for Story and Story Genius

THE OCCUPATION THESAURUS

"Each and every thesaurus these authors produce is spectacular. The Occupation Thesaurus is no different. Full of inspiration, teachings, and knowledge that are guaranteed to take your writing to the next level, it's a must. You need this book on your craft shelf."

~Sacha Black, best-selling author of fantasy and the Better Writing series

THE CONFLICT THESAURUS, VOLUMES 1 & 2

"If characters drive the story, then conflict operates as the engine to every tale. Writing experts Angela Ackerman and Becca Puglisi return with their most ambitious, hefty thesaurus yet, examining conflict in multiple dimensions and on multiple levels. Every writer should keep this volume handy as they work."

~ Ekta R. Garg, editor and author of The Truth About Elves

THE EMOTION AMPLIFIER THESAURUS

"Whether you're a seasoned storyteller or just starting to explore the writing realm, this guide amps up your emotional arsenal. Let's get those characters feeling, reeling, and revealing their inner chaos for all to see."

~ Stuart Wakefield, Author Accelerator Certified Book Coach

Curious about our books? Download our Show-Don't-Tell Pro Pack (https://shopwritershelpingwriters.net/pages/show-dont-tell-pro-pack), which contains samples from all the volumes in our thesaurus series.

A POWERFUL STORY SUPPORT PLATFORM: ONE STOP FOR WRITERS®

Ready for a game-changer?

In today's crowded market, only exceptional fiction gets noticed. So the authors of this book created One Stop for Writers® (https://onestopforwriters.com/)—a go-to web app that will activate your imagination while providing the tools and resources you need to create stronger, fresher stories. It contains:

- The largest show-don't-tell "Thesaurus" descriptive database available anywhere
- A powerful character builder
- Custom character arc blueprints
- Story maps, scene maps, and timeline tools
- Idea generators
- Templates, worksheets, tip sheets, and checklists that simplify fiction elements and refine prose
- Craft tutorials and terminology glossaries
- The Storyteller's Roadmap, a step-by-step system for planning, writing, and revising a novel

If you've been searching for a way to shorten the learning curve and help you create authentic characters who are part of well-structured, engaging plots ... well, One Stop for Writers will change the way you create fiction. No more staring at the screen, wondering what to write. No more wishing you had an expert to help you navigate story craft. Get ready to write stronger fiction faster.

Visit One Stop for Writers and test-drive our two-week free trial. If you choose to subscribe, use the **ONESTOPFORWRITERS** code for a one-time discount of 25% off any plan.

See you at One Stop!

ABOUT THE AUTHORS

Angela Ackerman and **Becca Puglisi** are story coaches, international speakers, and co-authors of *The Emotion Thesaurus: A Writer's Guide to Character Expression* and its many sequels. Commonly called "the Gold Standard of writing guides," these best-selling books are sourced by universities, recommended by agents and editors, and are used by novelists, screenwriters, and psychologists around the world. To date, their series has sold over 1.4 million copies and is available in ten languages.

Long-time writing partners, Angela (a Canadian) and Becca (an American) first met in an online critique group, and after reading a few of each other's stories, quickly became each other's biggest fan. They began collaborating in 2012 and, through a mutual passion for helping writers, co-founded Writers Helping Writers, a popular description and how-to hub, and One Stop for Writers, an innovative creativity portal for one-of-a-kind tools that give writers exactly what they need to craft unbelievably rich stories and characters.

www.ingramcontent.com/pod-product-compliance
Lightning Source LLC
LaVergne TN
LVHW081258100826
845148LV00005B/909

* 9 7 8 1 7 3 6 1 5 2 3 5 5 *